Rain
Dodging

Rain Dodging

A Scholar's Romp
through Britain in Search
of a Stuart Queen

Susan J Godwin

She Writes Press

Published 2023
Printed in the United States of America
Print ISBN: 978-1-64742-569-2
E-ISBN: 978-1-64742-570-8
Library of Congress Control Number: 2023909760

For information, address:
She Writes Press
1569 Solano Ave #546
Berkeley, CA 94707

Interior Design by Tabitha Lahr

She Writes Press is a division of SparkPoint Studio, LLC.

Observe how system into system runs . . .
May tell why heav'n has made us as we are.
—ALEXANDER POPE, An Essay on Man,
Epistle I: Of the Nature and State of Man,
with Respect to the Universe

She fit right into crazy.
—SUSAN J. GODWIN

Contents

To my darling Tony

Mary of Modena by Simon Verelst, c 1680

Chapter One:

Getting There

———— ⚜ ————

*Take the Adventure, heed the call, now ere the irrevocable
moment passes! 'Tis but a banging of the door behind you,
a blithesome step forward, and you are out of the old life
and into the new! Then some day, some day long hence,
. . . sit down by your quiet river with a store of goodly
memories for company.*
—KENNETH GRAHAME, *The Wind in the Willows*

EVEN THROUGH THE GROGGY FOG OF FATIGUE, the
splendor and senses of the city of dreaming spires inspired
me. Recognizing Oxford's honey-colored sandstone, I felt
the comfort of returning to a place I belonged. Did it erase
the taste of a seventeen-hour travel nightmare originating at
Newark International? Taste, maybe. Smell? Not so much. I
was covered in airport and coated in airplane.

Finally. Midnight, London time, the jet landed at
Heathrow. Yes!

Not so fast. My suitcases were still in Newark, which
meant queuing up in the stuffy, cramped baggage-claim office.

I am resilient. But now and then I crumble.

Outside the claim office, exhausted and disoriented, I melted into tears. How cruel. Thwarted only ninety minutes away from my destination.

At the thought of another night in an airport polyurethane chair, I whimpered.

A Heathrow official—tall, slender, Indian, and elegantly dressed in a tailored pin-striped suit—noticed my obvious distress and approached. Sympathetic eyes were all I needed to revive my meltdown.

Embarrassed, I blubbered out my predicament. "I'm . . . just . . . so . . . tired," I mustered between barely suppressed sobs.

He guided me to an elevator. Art deco cufflinks caught harsh fluorescent light—a gold geometric design centered with cabochon-cut sapphires.

I breathed in. *Hmmm, Armani.* Delicious.

I must be feeling better.

He accompanied me to an express tram, where he caught the eye of another passenger, an unassuming man-child, not more than twenty years old, fair and slight.

"Young man, would you kindly help this woman get to the airport bus station? She needs the coach to Oxford, and she's found herself a bit turned around."

I began to calm down, my agitation settling. Man-child Tobey and I small-talked in the tram and during our ten-minute walk, through dreary tunnels and up a decrepit elevator I recognized from my previous trip.

What a relief! Bus bays emanated from a curved curb, even if only a few were occupied. The brightly colored coaches were encouraging. I'd make it to Oxford yet.

Tobey and I sat on a worn bench next to a burping vending machine.

"So, Susan, what brings you to England?"

He walked over to the vending machine and gave it a kick. No luck.

Feeling positively gregarious by this time, I explained, "A fellowship. I have the summer to research. It's the chance of a lifetime to return to the Bodleian."[1]

"Lucky lady. Working at the Bod. What's your research?"

"Ever hear of James II's queen, Mary of Modena?" (pronounced mō‘ di nə)

"No, love, never."

"Well, beginning when she was Duchess of York, in the late seventeenth century and throughout her regency, she had several women in her court who were writers, *exceptional* for the time."

I had Tobey's attention.

"It resonated within me. How did this come to be? It clicked, striking a chord . . . a chord I knew to recognize whenever a seed of an idea started to germinate."

Needing to stretch, I got up and tried the vending machine myself. No luck either. Looking over at Tobey, I continued. "You may find this interesting. Back in the States, English majors are expected to come up with their own paper topics. Intimidating at first, but I grew to love it. Speaks to my creativity."[2]

"Aah, a kindred spirit."

Tobey had just finished a gap year watercolor-painting his way through Thailand.

"So when I find the seed, I grab it. I feel like a detective in the stacks." I laughed.

Tobey reached in his backpack and pulled out a watercolor journal.

"I get it."

I always knew when I found an idea to pursue. My heart would race. And then, not a click but more like a stab. I knew I wanted to pursue this unusual court of women writers. There was something about Mary of Modena's story that intrigued me.

While I glanced through Tobey's journal, he got up and kicked the vending machine again. No dice.

I decided I would take a chance.

"You know, there *is* one more reason I love coming to England."

"What's that?"

Man, I love a British accent.

I laughed. "This is going to sound crazy to you, but we'll never see each other again, so what the hell."

"You sure now?" He laughed too.

"I have an overpowering sense that here in Britain, I lived a previous life. Think I'm crazy?" I winked at Tobey.[3]

A royal blue coach heading for Oxford rolled into its bay. We wished each other the best of luck. I was certain young Tobey would be the first of many strangers I would meet over the next five weeks. Not even a bus driver's scowl—I didn't have the proper change—could put a damper on my elevated mood. Climbing the two coach steps, I sighed with relief. The last leg of the journey.

Finally, after six years, I was on the coach that would whisk me back to Oxford. I sat in the comfy front seat behind the driver and nodded off.

Chapter Two:

Meet Mary

———— ·❦· ————

SOMETHING ABOUT THE RESILIENCE OF WOMEN who wrote and published in an age that did not support them brought forth an emotional reaction, one I did not yet fully understand.

After I had returned home to Tennessee from my first Oxford summer, I was reading books related to my research, but I suffered disruptions of focus and rhythm in study while I waited for books to arrive through interlibrary loan. This was compounded by a heavy, demanding teaching schedule. As a result, I often felt disoriented and subsequently overwhelmed. I realized that without the ability to visit settings, my writing would lack sense of place, an essential ingredient I stressed to my students. At times, it was hard to keep motivated. Thanks to the fellowship, I was attending a summer tutorial at Lincoln College, Oxford.[1] I had completed the required reading at home and was ready for the course.

Just past a slight bend on narrow, quaint Turl Street, the college was designed in irregular quadrangles of honey limestone draped in ivy. From my room atop The Grove, one of the quads, while mulling over word choices and citing sources, I could gaze past the trimmed lawn of the Rector's Garden to Lincoln's famed All Saints library spire—one of the city's "dreaming spires."

The freshman handbook stated, "Unlike most colleges, we have no grotty sixties annexe to spoil all the pretty bits."

I was fortunate to conduct literary research with Dr. Peter McCullough, esteemed Oxford professor and Fellow of Renaissance Literature. Also, a sweetheart. For five invigorating weeks, I studied eighteenth-century literature and the arts with the brilliant and delightful Peter and four others in the graduate tutorial. We met three times a week in his spacious study in Lincoln's six hundred-year-old Front Quad. We gathered opposite the fireplace, three of us in armchairs and two on the soft, upholstered couch. Peter always sat in his well-worn chair to the left of the fireplace. He would jump out of his armchair, a curly dark-brown lock falling over his eyeglasses, à la Elvis Costello, to look up a word at his desk computer in the online *Oxford English Dictionary* or check a citation in a passage of *Paradise Lost*.[2] Peter's course energized, making constant connections between history, literature, and artistic movements. Even years later, Peter claimed, "You were the most engaged, curious learners I have had the opportunity to teach."

I'm honored.

While researching my final paper for Peter about poet Anne Finch, Countess of Winchilsea (the "a" is silent), and her poem "Nocturnal Reverie," I stumbled onto the late-seventeenth-century Stuart court of Queen Mary of Modena, consort to James II.[3]

The click. The heartbeat. The seed. The stab.

Before heading back to the States, I met with Peter to discuss my book idea stemming from that research. Peter, having stunned me with his compliment of my paper, saying, "One of the most beautiful [graduate] papers I've read . . .

The work of an artist by an artist," was encouraging about my book idea. True to his MO, he dashed to his computer and gathered up a beginning bibliography for me to pursue.

A court of women writers would be *extraordinary* in this time. How did this come to be? What exactly *was* court culture? How might these women have interacted and inspired one another? What was Mary of Modena's role in this? In seventeenth-century Christian tradition, women were seen as temptresses who personified original sin and lured men to evil. French writer François Rabelais (1494–1553) declared women were not fully human beings, not endowed with a soul, and not created in the image of God, who, after all, was male.[4] I had questions I felt compelled to answer regarding Mary's captivating story.

Part of the joy of research—and for me, it is joyful—is the ability to explore freely. I wanted to sense their spaces, to breathe the same air, to imagine their lives.

I couldn't wait to get started.

Chapter Three:

She Was a Bitch but the Room Was Lovely

———·⟡·———

WHEN I AWOKE ON THE RIDE FROM Heathrow, the bus was just outside Oxford. From the east, approaching Oxford, the oldest university in the English-speaking world, the coach passed beloved landmarks: the stone walls of legendary Magdalen Bridge; High Street's quaint shops; and St. Aldate's Street with famed architect Christopher Wren's glorious Christ Church gate tower, Great Tom. In centuries past, the multiton tower bell would chime 101 times each night, for the original 101 students to return for nightly curfew, which had been 9:05 p.m.

I missed curfew tonight. Big time.

The coach from Heathrow pulled into Gloucester Green, a traditional British square surrounded by shops and restaurants, now closed. We sleepy passengers exited. Memory aiding me this time, I walked down a cobblestone alley, St. George's Place, to its end, where the familiar taxi queue on George Street was located.

After an eight-pounds-and-a-handful-of-pence taxi ride, my bed-and-breakfast hostess, Emma, waited for me at the door of Painter's Cottage, her narrow brownstone off Cowley Road. I had expected a warm welcome, despite the time, since it was a five-week reservation.

Not to be.

Weary-looking, the graying-blonde Polish émigré was cross with my tardiness, though I had called her around 1:00 a.m. from Heathrow, apologizing. She couldn't dampen my mood any more than the low-spirited coach driver.

Up narrow stairs, I lugged my heavy carry-on, which she criticized.

"Books," I said over my shoulder, "for my research."

No answer.

She may have been a bitch, but my room was as lovely as advertised online. Pale green walls, dark hardwood floors, slightly threadbare antique Oriental rugs, an ample pine writing desk, a red-lacquered wardrobe with art deco brass knobs, and a fireplace. The Georgian mantel provided the perfect place to set a *few* sentimental trinkets I'd brought for ambiance and a connection to home.

When would I learn to travel lightly?

I opened the street-facing front windows wide, which would become my routine every evening upon entering. I breathed in intermittent rain. Cool, windy breezes were heaven sent, clearing my brain of stale concourses and airplane claustrophobia.

Breathe.

I enjoyed a luxurious shower, washed my panties and hung them to dry, then sat stark naked atop a luxurious garnet satin duvet on the double bed. I rested against cushy pillows, not Diego Velázquez's *Venus at Her Mirror*[1] but *Susan at Her Laptop.*

Not *Venus at Her Mirror* but *Susan at Her Laptop*.
CREDIT: Diego Velázquez, public domain, via Wikimedia Commons

All I had was filthy, overnight airport clothing. I pledged to wear none of it again.

I never did.

I journaled briefly and soon slept soundly.

I spent the next day in a clean white T-shirt I found in my backpack and in dry, *clean* panties. My darling daughter's came from Victoria's Secret, mine from Walmart. Nothing wrong with Fruit of the Loom. Gotta love grapes.

After organizing some of my research, I tried tracking down my luggage. One bag arrived around 6:00 p.m. that evening, thankfully the one with most of my clothing. Now I had pants!

After changing, I went for a walk in a slight summer rain, relishing the diverse Cowley Road neighborhood. Bustling traffic—cars, buses, and bicycles—coexisted in peace. Small ethnic markets thrived. A Turkish restaurant here, a computer shop and stationery store there. Passing up the

Tesco Metro supermarket, I purchased cheese and almonds for dinner from the small Middle Eastern market at Divinity Road, close to my B and B.

The rain quickened. I returned home. *Hmm.* I called Painter's Cottage "home." I was already easing into the calm of solitude.

Long after the house went to sleep, I sank into the pillows of an inviting old love seat at the downstairs front window. Phone in hand, I waited to hear news about my missing second piece of luggage. I didn't dare wake Emma up with a ring of the phone or door. She might have killed me.

I watched recurrent downpours, hypnotized. Streetlights illuminated rain through the bay window. Growing up, I had spent countless melancholy night hours, winter-dreaming at the window of an empty upstairs front bedroom, sometimes the wind so fierce that flakes blew sideways. Fallen snow, revealed by a nearby streetlight, would shimmer like white diamonds. Memories flooded back. I used to ponder, *Will there ever be happiness in my life?*

I thought back to the Yom Kippur when I had been fifteen.

AN UGLY OUTLINE HAD REMAINED WHERE the pocket on my dress had been. Determined, I stepped into the dress anyway. I loved the texture of the cornflower-blue fabric. Besides, my mother would notice. Sitting next to me in the synagogue would force her to remember.

My father's voice called up from the front hallway. "Kids, it's time to leave."

I joined my two brothers and baby sister, already marching down the stairs. On to worship.

From a high-backed chair on the bima, the rabbi approached the lectern. A dignified man, even more so in his long black robe. Eyeglasses perched, he peered out and read, "Our God and God of our fathers, pardon our transgressions, remove our guilt, and blot out our iniquities on this Day of Atonement."

I looked down at my dress and remembered what had happened in March, five months earlier.

Perpetual winter gray had owned the early spring sky, as usual. My mother's face disappeared behind the heavy sage-velvet window drapes. How late had I been? Not over fifteen or twenty minutes, but she had seen Charlie walking me home. I grabbed my geometry books from his arms, not daring a touch let alone a kiss. I ran up the driveway before he could respond.

Out of the corner of my eye, I saw Charlie remained on the sidewalk, watching, worried. Stopping only for a deep breath, I turned the knob. Abruptly, the door opened. Mother yanked me by the arm until we were both in the dark hallway.

My books crashed to the floor.

"When will you get it through your thick skull? You are to be home on time!"

I froze, knowing what would come next. Shouts turned into screams, screams into hysteria, hysteria into rage. The familiar pattern. I escaped into the weary tunnel of my thoughts. I startled when hands grabbed for the gold chain around my neck.

"Please. Don't," I begged. But I knew it was no use.

Mother looked down. She saw the small St. Christopher's medal hanging at the end of the chain. She went crazy.

"Charlie gave this to you?"

I was too frightened to reply.

"Answer me!"

"Yes," I mumbled.

She easily ripped the delicate chain from my neck and threw it on the floor. The St. Christopher's medal rolled like a dime until it hit one of the geometry books and stopped.

"What's next? A crucifix? Mass?"

I bit my lip. I wouldn't give her the satisfaction of seeing me cry. Silence was my only weapon.

The rabbi's commanding baritone penetrated the sanctuary, breaking through my recollection. He continued reading from the *Union Prayer Book*.[2]

"Thus hast Thou placed a particular task upon us, as mothers, wives, and daughters. We are proud to be privileged to radiate Thy love wherever we may dwell."

Love. Proud. Daughters. Mothers.

My mind wandered back to my mother's meltdown.

She tore off my cornflower-blue dress with one giant slash, catching my twisted right arm in the brass purse chain hanging from my right shoulder.

Five-year-old Kathy ran into our shared bedroom closet, whimpering. Even normally stoic Matthew cried, begging our mother to stop. I noticed his two front teeth were finally coming in. They looked like upside-down tulips. Embarrassed that my kid brother could see me half undressed, I tried to cover the torn fabric over my exposed breast. *Where is Mike?* I wondered. Probably at wrestling practice. At least he had an outlet.

Her mouth contorted, front teeth growing bigger and bigger.

The rabbi continued. "Praised be Thou, O Lord our God, who freest the captive. Amen. Praised be Thou, O Lord our God, who liftest up those who are bowed down. Amen. Praised be Thou, O Lord our God, who givest strength to the weary. Amen."

My silence had driven her crazy. It was the only power I had. She interpreted the silence as indifference, further fueling her rage. She was too incoherent to notice my eyes, trapped in the numbness of anger and frustration. I wanted to scream, explode, release my own emotions, but I was stuck within myself, pinned to the mat before having the chance to fight.

The rabbi prayed, "Keep her tongue from evil and her lips from speaking guile. Be her support when grief silences her voice, and her comfort when woe bends her spirit."

She was out of control, whipping my side with the brass chain. Welts formed. Her tirade with the purse chain continued. I could barely stand it.

She finally tired herself out. She dropped the chain and left me alone in the hallway.

The rest of my purse had flown open during the outburst. Contents were strewn around me.

At first, I couldn't move, unable to break ripples of shame and despair in my chest. Eventually, I picked up the books and the St. Christopher's medal. I scooped up my purse and its scattered contents. But I left the chain where it lay. She needed to see it again.

I walked to my bedroom, not wanting my feet to touch the floor. Touching the floor made me feel more shame for some reason.

My eyes panned the bedroom. I knew where little Kathy would be. I set down my things and carried her from our closet, held her to me, and rocked her until she fell asleep. Pain and silent anger filled my eyes. I took off the tattered cornflower-blue dress.

The rabbi was nearing the end of the Yom Kippur service. "Remove from her heart all rancor and hardness, that I may forgive freely even as I hope to be forgiven."

A finger grazed my dress where the pocket had been. I glanced at my mother's beautifully manicured fingernails.

"May our worship in this Day of Atonement direct the hearts of parents to their children and the hearts of children to their parents."

The rabbi closed his prayer book and looked out over the congregation. He walked away from the lectern.

I glanced down. I saw not a sea of cornflower blue but a shimmer of white diamonds.

"Thus hast Thou placed a particular task upon us, as mothers, wives, and daughters."

Conflicted feelings started early, even before I was consciously aware.

Tragically, my brothers and I modeled the only approach to anger we knew.

This is what I would say to them—if I could: "The violence between us shames me now."

Both left home at different points, one never to return or communicate with any of us again.

Chapter Four:

The Bod

BACK AT PAINTER'S COTTAGE, THE PHONE CALL about my luggage never came. I surrendered around 2:00 a.m., put Emma's phone back into its cradle underneath the stairs, and trudged up to my room.

I woke up about nine thirty the same morning to an empty house. Unwilling to wait around another day, I left a note on the front door for the delivery service. Walking to the bus stop, a sense of freedom overcame me. Number one on my list? No question. The Bodleian—my magnet pull—to register for my reader card so I could resume my research. How delicious to be back to the "mother church" of libraries.

It is a sacred space for me and for anyone passionate about books and learning.

My daughter Jesse and I can laugh now about how she lost her patience with me when college hunting years before. In NYC, walking the Columbia campus, I had pointed out its famed library, its facade well-photographed during the controversial 1968 Vietnam protest.

"Mom!" she had snapped sharply enough to make me jump. "Would you stop pointing out every library we see?

Fuck!" She sighed in disgust and walked away toward other university buildings.

I followed. I knew "normal" mothers got chastised by fed-up teenage daughters.

Jesse and I joke about it now. When I visit her in a new town, she makes a point of showing me the library on my first visit. Smart-ass!

The neoclassical Radcliffe Camera rotunda where I conducted my research is a legendary part of the Bodleian Library system, an exquisite beacon. International tourists linger in the quad, longing to go inside the famous library. They settle for snapping photos outside the wrought iron fence.

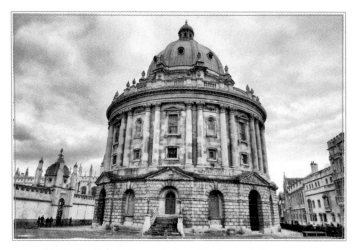

The Radcliffe Camera, from Latin, meaning *room*
CREDIT: Becks, 2012, CC BY 2.0 (https://creativecommons.org/licenses/by/2.0), via Wikimedia Commons

I felt the privilege extended to me. I felt it every time I climbed the twelve wide stone stairs to enter, opened my bag for inspection, and found my spot for the day, hoping for a window seat. Having stopped at the admissions office, my library reader card was proudly in hand. I flashed my new

ID to the guard with just a shameful smidge of arrogance. I accessed the Lower Reading Room by descending a short set of stairs. Double doors opened to the reading room.

Ahhhhhhhh.

The Lower Reading Room was circular, below the spectacular light-filled dome, the third largest in Britain. Eight arched study bays radiated like glorious bicycle spokes from a center workstation. One bay served as the entrance. Clockwise, the next bay contained the iron-grilled stairway down to the Gladstone Link open shelves, a maze of white metal one floor below, new since my last visit.

I had to investigate. I descended the narrow steps and entered an underground cavern of books, white walls, white metal, and white light. Quite a stark contrast to the old bindings upstairs and their smell of antiquity. Here, the only break in white were the large gray cranks at the end of each row of shelving. To be time efficient, some scholars chose to remain in this enclave, researching at white-Formica-topped carrels.

I would suffocate. I returned upstairs, relieved to be back. *Breathe.*

In the reading room, elegant oak tables ran the lengths of the remaining six bays, separated by mahogany-trimmed bookcases. Shelf upon shelf was stuffed with theological and literary volumes. Each pediment dead-ended with seventeenth-century arched casement windows, under which double oak reading tables seated four. Heaven was finding an available window seat, the casement open just enough to allow the breezes in. Heaven, for me, was spending the day reading and writing there. Library exploration was part of the process. Mystery was ever-present and sat on my shoulder like a Philip Pullman daemon. *Will I find what I am looking for?*

The thrill of the search. I let the quest take me where I needed to go. It was part of the intellectual energy.

Having bid hello to the Radcliffe Camera's cherished reading room, I crossed the Bodleian's early-seventeenth-century Old Schools quad to Broad Street and the iconic Blackwell's Books. After a joyful browse, I found a sturdy, laminated folding map of Oxford. Walking back out to Broad Street, high winds embarrassed any attempt to keep my umbrella from turning inside out.

At this point, Broad Street was unusually wide. It narrowed again within eyesight. Long rows of bicycle racks lined both sides of the street—the circular Christopher Wren–designed famed Sheldonian Theatre[1] on one side, rows of colorful shops on the other.

Because of the wind, I postponed the plan to pick up my bicycle rental. Instead, on Cornmarket Street, I stopped for a pita wrap at Pret A Manger and sat on one of the many benches along the cobbled pedestrian-only boulevard. Munching on my avocado-and-cucumber wrap, I people-watched, listening to Celtic street musicians on flute and guitar. The breezes embraced, and I breathed in. Reluctantly, I returned to the house to check on the missing bag.

Emma was driving up in her yellow VW Beetle. "Your delivery is coming," she said.

She had a mild Polish accent, reminding me of my beloved Russian *bubbe* (pronounced *bu'bee*), gone at age seventy, senile and alone.

Emma continued. "They said baggage would be here between five and eight o'clock."

At the curb, she disappeared into the back seat of her car to retrieve packages.

Would waiting to hold the brownstone's front door open be too suck-ass? I asked myself.

Yes. I went on inside. *Do I give Emma a pass because she is an artist?*

"I MUST CREATE WHAT I THINK, NOT WHAT people want," she declared the next morning, my third.

She was in her backyard, in the wildflower garden that separated the cottage from her airy, wood-framed studio at the back of the property. She smoked her cigarettes out there among the foxglove, bluebells, and yarrow, while contemplating her next brushstrokes. Her oil paintings were disturbing, she admitted.

Sometimes, while fixing my morning coffee with the smaller of her two French presses, I would see her through the kitchen window, lost in thought, exhaled smoke floating out the open studio door.

It reminded me of finding my mother in her garden, after our Shaker Heights home flooded when I was a young teenager. The interior had been destroyed after the main water pipe had burst on the third floor, pouring through the house while we had been in upstate New York for three weeks. I had been nervous, worrying about how far back this blow would set her. My family was surveying the damage for the first time when I looked out an upstairs window and saw her appear in the back garden. Gardening was my mother's escape, as drawing was my own.

She had looked wistfully at the trumpet flowers in full blossom and then stooped to her knees, face-to-face with a cupid statue amid the primrose. She lit a cigarette, took a deep inhale and exhale, and started sobbing. Next, my mother pulled out dazzling roses, bush by bush. Poppy red, salmon, crimson, and garnet. Without gloves to protect her beautifully manicured hands, they grew bloody from thorns. Once tired out, she lit another cigarette, leaving only a fragile trail of smoke hanging in the garden air. She had never noticed me.

Many mornings I pondered my mother's trail of smoke, speculating on her demons. But she always remained a mystery.

Despite Emma's off-putting behavior, the house was picture-perfect—Asian design meets homey and eclectic. I was happy. Aloof was far more preferable than nosy and chatty. She had two other rooms for hire on the second floor, though I had yet to meet another guest. The three guest rooms shared a modern glass-and-ceramic-tiled bathroom. Emma's suite was on the third floor. I was more than curious about it.

I went up to my room, the largest, and checked email.

Hurray! Ben Arnold, head of Special Collections at the Bodleian—I'd been corresponding with him for months—had returned my request. Tomorrow, I would start my search of seventeenth-century manuscripts in my quest to learn more about Mary of Modena and her court of female writers.

Amen.

Chapter Five:

All in the Family

————··✦··————

THE DUCHY OF MODENA, MARY'S HOME, WAS A small
but powerful Italian state that existed from the mid-fifteenth
to the mid-nineteenth century in northwest Italy. It was close
to Bologna, home to the oldest university in the world, the
University of Bologna. The noble House of Este ruled the
state of Modena.

Descended from the Bourbon royal family of France
and the Medici family of Italy, Maria Beatrice Eleonora
Anna Margherita Isabella d'Este, or Maria di Modena, born
in 1658, was an educated, artistic princess growing up in a
matriarchy of strong, prominent women. Her father, Alfonso
IV d'Este, Duke of Modena, had died young, at age twenty-
seven, from tuberculosis. Maria's widowed mother, Laura
Martinozzi, ruled her estates and her family with wisdom and
intelligence. She was one of the famed seven Mazarinettes,[1]
the nieces of the very influential Cardinal Jules Mazarin. The
d'Este family had produced four cardinals.

Uncle Jules, the reputed lover of Louis XIV's mother,
was powerful. He served as chief minister of France for both
Louis XIII and XIV. Cardinal Mazarin was also an important

patron of the arts, introducing Italian opera on a grand scale to Paris and assembling a famed art collection, much of which is in the Louvre today. Mazarin also founded the first true public library in France, the Bibliothèque Mazarine. The cardinal brought his seven nieces from Italy to France with huge dowries for them to find marriageable, wealthy French and Italian princes.

They all did.

Mary of Modena's mother, Laura Martinozzi, was one of the seven nieces.

As a daughter of a Mazarinette, Mary of Modena was exposed to powerful, independent women all of her young life. But in 1673, she was powerless, an unwilling fourteen-year-old political pawn instructed to marry James II, then still the Duke of York, by proxy. She refused more than once, insisting she needed to live a life of study in religious seclusion in the convent her mother had founded, the Order of the Visitation, next to their palazzo.

Maria Beatrice was no bashful maiden with sentimental leanings toward the religious life but a strong and stormy Italian personality with regal pride inherited from an imposing line of ancestors. To strengthen the alliance with France, Maria Beatrice's mother, Laura, had also married by proxy, at sixteen. Laura's cousins, the famed Mancini sisters, Hortense and Maria, mentioned in their memoirs that it was not unusual for girls to marry this young, even younger, in the seventeenth century.[2] Eventually, d'Este family pressure intervened and in a handwritten note, heavily leaning on Maria's devotion to church, Pope Clement himself convinced the young princess of her duty to spread Catholicism across the channel.

Guilt by religion.

Married by proxy—the Earl of Peterborough was the representative for James, the Duke of York—Maria left home on her fifteenth birthday, after two days and nights of tears and anguish. The treacherous journey took Maria over the Alps,[3] up the Loire, and on to the dreary French port of Calais to begin a stormy, perilous English Channel crossing to Dover.[4]

Imagine saying goodbye to family, possibly forever, then departing to a foreign country. Imagine trading a dazzling sun-draped palace for, as famed English writer Daniel Defoe put it, "one of the largest and dirtiest houses in the world,"[5] in an assuredly bleak, damp climate.

Mary of Modena landed in Dover, greeted for the first time by her husband, the Duke of York. (Remember she was married by proxy.) Witnesses noted, "Mary of Modena was seized by him." She could "hardly bear to let [him] touch her." Yet in the duke's notebook, he noted on November 21, 1673, the "Princess of Modena had arrived at Dover and had been wedded and bedded that same night."[6]

One month after her fifteenth birthday.

My stomach churns.

Tears.

Sigh.

Breathe.

To add insult, the British Parliament criticized the fifteen-year-old princess, now Duchess of York, because of her beloved Catholic religion. Once infamous (Catholic) Henry VIII originated the Church of England in the 1500s so he could divorce and remarry. The British lived in a schizophrenic political climate, where royal religion violently volleyed from Protestant to Catholic like a Ping-Pong game.[7] Catholic Charles I had been executed in 1649. Restoration, in 1660, quietly brought his son, Charles II, and James, Duke of York, back from exile in France, after the Protestant-sympathetic–Parliamentarian-ruled Protectorate collapsed.[8] When Charles II died in 1685, he had no legitimate children, although he had plenty of "natural" illegitimate offspring.[9] James II, Maria of Modena's devoutly Catholic husband, became king.

Don't underestimate the religious divide.

The prejudice against popery in England at the time was fanatical.

The sons brought French culture to Britain upon their return, in 1660. When Mary of Modena arrived in England in 1673, she entered into the licentious Restoration culture created by her brother-in-law, King Charles II, the Merry Monarch, who could have been the twin of Disney's Captain Hook. According to Charles II's ministers, his good humor and relatability preserved his popularity. He had good taste in art and literature and loved science, particularly chemistry. The Royal Society, United Kingdom's National Academy of Sciences, was founded in his reign. However, his affability covered a multitude of sins. His likeability couldn't mask that the corruption of private morals of the Restoration period correlated directly to Charles's example of "uncontrolled and flagrant debauchery." One of his own Privy Councilors, George Saville, Marquis of Halifax, wrote further, "I am apt to think his thinking was as much as any man's ever did in the lower region."[10]

Not so delicately translated, *He thought with his dick.*[11]

Testament to Charles's charms, even devout Mary of Modena was quite fond of him. Besides, Charles II's belief in progressive learning paved the way for her to proceed with her own agenda.

Mary of Modena's court was as close as England ever came to the world of the *précieuses*, the intellectual and literary circles that formed around French women a few generations earlier, in the first half of the seventeenth century. The label "précieuses" was coined in the early 1650s. By the next decade, the term commonly applied to all women from polite society who frequented Parisian salons.

Were the *précieuses* my kernel?

Mary provided a model of female patronage for women artists. She offered a world where women exchanged various genres of writing. She created a place where women's education and imagination were taken seriously. Moreover, she was a descendant of women who began this tradition.

Finding this connection was crucial to my continued research.

Chapter Six:

Special Collections and
a Bearded Maître d'

THE MORE I DELVED INTO MARY'S BACKGROUND, the more I learned of her family's influence in moving women's rights in academia and the arts. I got excited. Being back at the Bod helped me revert to research mode. It had taken a bit of time to readjust—to cars, bicycles, and buses on the other side of the road, but—

The black van drove up. Hallelujah! The bag with all my toiletries, shoes, tour guidebooks, and alarm clock had arrived. Now I could really get settled and focused. I unpacked these last belongings and ventured out to celebrate.

In Oxford, summer skies stayed light until after 10:00 p.m., so in broad daylight, I window-shopped for a dinner restaurant. After a few blocks, Le Kesh, a Lebanese fusion bistro, beckoned me in. A salt-and-pepper-bearded maître d' guided me through a dark, narrow back hallway.

Where was he taking me?

What a lovely surprise awaited in their back garden. An intimate seating area of sumptuous, cream-colored lounge chairs on a stone floor. A billowing, cream-tented partition blew in strong breezes. Large potted plants, albeit droopy, scattered through the patio. Ceramic covered ashtrays dotted Moroccan-tiled tables. An oversize oil painting of a French café on a fountained wall. Decorative hookahs along a long, rustic shelf, the length of the patio. Aged straw fencing enclosed the enchanting space.

The restaurant owner, a dashing young Mediterranean, was watching the Euro-football championship on a mounted corner television. The soccer match against Sweden was just beginning. While "God Save the Queen" played stirringly. (How strange that Her Majesty is gone now.) He kindly explained a bit of the championship to me. However, eventually his attention turned to the arrival of two dazzling Brazilian women, so I returned to admiring my space. I understood his shifting focus. I had been young once.

Swinging an incense pot, the bearded maître d', who resembled a Turkish priest complete with kufi cap, reentered the patio. A group of young Eastern Europeans followed him. They settled into a grouping of cream-cushioned chairs next to my small tiled table. Soon, they began smoking hookahs. After two glasses of zinfandel, I felt emboldened enough to ask about the hookahs.

No buzz? Why bother?

I enjoyed a delicious dinner of mussels smothered in wine, accompanied by fried toast. Returning to my enchanting room, front windows wide open, I deduced England had won the game when cheers reverberated from the pubs down on Cowley Road.

A new adventure begins.

THE ALARM RANG AT 7:00 A.M. I TOOK MY TIME getting ready for my first trek to Oxford's Special Collections, feeling an edge of anxiety, not knowing Collections' procedure. I prepped for the day mindfully, and I purposefully walked past the five houses to the bus stop. Once more burdened by a heavy backpack, I boarded a red double-decker with my newly purchased bus pass, pretending I was a native Brit. Beyond the Plain roundabout and its octagonal late-nineteenth-century Victoria Fountain, we crossed over the Magdalen Bridge arching over the River Cherwell. Sublime. I exited on High Street, in the city center.

First, I bought another avocado-and-cucumber pita sandwich for later. (I'm a diabetic; I need to make sure I eat regularly.) Next, I walked down Catte Street—more like a seventeenth-century alley—which turned into Parks Street and six picturesque blocks to the Radcliffe Science Library. Special Collections was temporarily located there due to major Bodleian Library renovation. Passing All Souls College, I giggled, visualizing the scene in Deborah Harkness's *A Discovery of Witches* where Professor Diana Bishop, a beautiful blond witch, first dines with Matthew Clairmont, a handsome vampire geneticist, in his All Souls apartment. "Vampires are breathtaking but nothing prepares you to see one," she observes.

I also stopped in front of Hertford College's landmark, Bridge of Sighs and watched giggling Japanese tourists pose for photos. When they finished, we bowed, and I took some bridge photos, too, for a possible later painting.

I was in a new part of Oxford for me. Next to the science library, completing the neo-Gothic Museum of Natural History's expansive front lawn, was a gigantic dinosaur skeleton. The two buildings shared a small parking lot including a maze of bicycle racks.

Good to know. I'll get on that bicycle yet.

The wind was still up. *Ahhhhhh*. Freedom. Happiness.

Gardens were everywhere. Since it had rained the night before, trees emptied raindrops to the footpath—sidewalk—below, making them slippery. I breathed in the scent of light rain in the trees. I marveled at moments leading to this moment. I'd always credited an American Library Association annual conference in downtown Nashville years before for redirecting my career path.

THE DAY OF THE LIBRARY CONFERENCE HAD started well enough. One of those rare mornings when everything played out as planned—good hair, skirt swishing stylishly, daughter not dawdling. A minor miracle. I treated myself to a cup of lukewarm coffee for the road.

But before even reaching the first four-way stop, I hit a pothole that I'd avoided for years, spilling coffee all over my skirt. Instead of being on time for the keynote speaker, after dropping my daughter, Jesse, off at school, I was in the Nashville Renaissance Hotel lobby restroom, my not-so-stylish-now skirt hiked up over my hips, drying my coffee-scented crotch with a hair blower, borrowed from a smirking, pimple-faced front-desk clerk.

It was a Melissa McCarthy moment. Countless frumpy, gray-haired librarians, complete with eyeglasses hanging from neck chains, came in and out of toilet stalls while pretending not to notice me blow-drying between my legs.

Wouldn't that make a great cartoon?

I missed the ALA keynote speech, but a presentation later in the day was my landmark moment. Why it took me twenty years to figure it out, I chalk up to the cosmos. I could blend my love of teaching with my passion for books.

Duh.

In a medium-size convention center room, the late, great Rebecca Bain, host of NPR's *The Fine Print*, was talking about one of her author interviews. I started getting goosebumps. Teaching *and* books. What a concept. Epiphany.

At the time, I was library director of a county branch, close to the quaint hundred-year-old farmhouse that I shared with Jesse, fifty miles south of Nashville. I was feeling restless again. Not long after listening to Rebecca Bain, I decided to return to school, where I finally found my niche. Back in school, I acknowledged and embraced my intellect. If Ms. Bain were still alive, I would send her dozens of roses.

Six years after the American Library Association conference, while still a full-time librarian, I earned my add-on certificate in English literature, but I yearned for more school. I knew I needed to make more literary connections to feel legitimate.

Jesse was then fifteen, a gifted and passionate dancer attending a two-week summer workshop at Bates College in Maine. Upon her workshop's end, I flew into Manchester, New Hampshire, checked out the lovely University of New Hampshire in picturesque Durham, and drove my rental north to Lewiston, Maine, where I watched Jesse's performance. Afterward, I whisked her away to the next destination: debate camp at the University of Vermont in Burlington, four hours west. My little go-getter! Following her drop-off in Burlington, I had two weeks to scout out New England graduate programs in English for me.

On the night drive to Burlington, Jesse read her summer reading choice by flashlight. I delighted that *Wuthering Heights* delighted her.

Damn, I love my girlie.

As she raved about Emily Brontë's genius, I chugged lousy convenience store coffee and watched for deer, known for darting across Vermont's low-lying I-89.

Next morning, after a Staples pit stop, I delivered Jesse to the university. My five-part plan was as follows:

1. Travel from Burlington through Vermont and New Hampshire's Green and White Mountains.
2. Take picturesque Route 2 through the Maine woods to check out the University of Maine.
3. Proceed to its coast and explore! Eat lobster.
4. Ferry to Nova Scotia, then Prince Edward Island just for adventure.
5. Head back to Burlington.

An hour after leaving Jesse, I found the magical road up to Middlebury College's Bread Loaf School of English in Vermont's Green Mountains. I had learned about the graduate school consulting a *Princeton Review*. Bread Loaf was so named for the gently arresting mountain over the next ridge north from the mountaintop campus, the same campus where Robert Frost held court for years before his death in 1963.

After my first day on the road, I journaled:

Today was thrilling, although I tired late-afternoon. The drive from Middlebury up to Bread Loaf brought tears to my eyes, with the smell of fresh pine and log fires and the rush of water over the rocky Middlebury River, which followed the winding road up the mountain.

At Ripton's Country Store, I told the clerk I would be back. The Robert Frost Interpretive Forest was a spiritual experience. I walked across a grove of pine needles to the commemorative plaque. Complete calm. Serenity. Contemplation. Standing, I had a moment of mindfulness before reluctantly returning to my car.

One more mile up the road, past a scattering of forest, farmhouses, and grassy fields, I finally arrived at Bread Loaf:

I pulled into the large grass-and-gravel lot beyond a pon-derosa pine grove. I faintly heard students conversing, the air thick with learning vibes. Adults of varied ages studied at wooden tables or rustic Adirondack chairs, set between ochre-colored cottages with forest green trim. Very tempted to return. Strong sense I will. I want to be part of this.

I continued my jaunt. Walking back to my rental car after lobster stew at Tall Barney's in Jonesport, Maine, I fought back the melancholy of long ago, which creeps into my psyche when I am not vigilant. However, waiting for the ferry to depart for Nova Scotia, I was the only one out on the wind-swept bow . . . a magic moment after a flute of champagne. I gave thanks for this blessing and promised myself I would conjure it back whenever things got too crazy, especially at work. It worked for a bit.

Along Nova Scotia's Acadian shore, I listened to French radio stations, car windows down, and breathed salt air and the scent of fish. At Mahone Bay, I sipped German champagne on the patio at Mimi's Ocean Grill as the sky darkened and the stars came out, matching the restaurant's twinkling lights.

The next morning, I was off to Pictou, on Nova Sco-tia's north shore, where I would board another, smaller ferry over the Northumberland Straight to Prince Edward Island. I missed the first ferry by eight cars but didn't care. I read, lying on my car's hood. I soaked in the sun, my back against the windshield. *Ahhh, crisp air in the sunshine.*

A rustic room with light sky-blue walls, casement win-dows, and simple, natural pine crown molding awaited me

at the Bayberry Cliff Inn, more like a Scandinavian tree-
house on the cliffs of the Northumberland Sea. Charming.
Wandering by sunset to Brehaut's Restaurant, I was an out-
sider, not lonely but a little restless. I think I had pancakes.
Comfort food.

As I drove over the fertile hills of Prince Edward Island, I
listened to CBC Radio's *Hitchhiking Stories*. Back in Maine, I
picked up Route 2 again and relished the ride through glades
of silver birches—my favorite tree—a sign to me that Robert
Frost's school beckoned me someday.

> I'd like to go by climbing a birch tree,
> And climb black branches up a snow-white trunk
> Toward heaven . . .[1]

I followed the Kennebec River to scenic Rangeley Lake.
There, strolling along Main Street, I found Books, Lines &
Thinkers, which had rows and rows of packed oak bookcases,
an inviting story-hour cubby, and a vibrant coffee scene in
the back.

They're still there. I Googled.

Back at the inn, dinner for one on the patio. Perfection.

Next morning, I took Route 16, heading for New Hampshire, but first stopped for coffee and biscotti. Near the
Maine–New Hampshire border at Wilsons Mills, I curved by
the long-since-closed Bennett-Bean Covered Bridge. Bliss.

Back in Burlington, I sat in a sumptuous four-poster bed
at the Old Stagecoach Inn. The room was welcoming. It
smelled like baby powder. I took inventory: two wing chairs;
two old trunks, one a leather camelback; a mirrored armoire;
an antique sewing machine; a mahogany chest of drawers; a
cherry chifforobe; and two rocking chairs, one with forest
green leather upholstery, the other a string back. Leaded glass
bay windows, lace covered, opened to sixty-degree breezes,

adding up to a room that elicited a deep sigh of pleasure. I felt a slight nag of regret that I was surrendering splendid solitude and visions beyond the turns of the road.

Had I soaked in enough of the calm to last through any future rough times?

Chapter Seven:

Commencements

———— ·⟨⟐⟩· ————

I MATRICULATED AT BREAD LOAF. SCHOOL OF English. Over a handful of unforgettable summers, I earned my second master's, this one a complete labor of love. The first had been twenty-five years before, in educational planning and design at Case Western Reserve University, while I was teaching second grade at a Shaker Heights elementary school. However, that was more of a "might as well finish what I started to get tenure." In addition to a perfect summer at Bread Loaf's campus at Oxford's Lincoln College, I experienced three idyllic summers on the Vermont mountaintop. I received one of only a few named Bread Loaf scholarship awards. I could hear my dear husband Tony whistling from the audience as I received my degree from Middlebury University's president. And my cane![1] Prominent literary scholars left their universities to come teach at Bread Loaf every summer. Jenny Green-Lewis, a professor at George Washington University during the regular academic year, had nominated me for the writing award:

Susan has turned out to be one of those rare and unexpected gifts to the seminar—an amused and amusing student who has been completely absorbed in the work and whose writing has moved from strength to strength. She was always prepared and read widely, with avid interest. She wrote lucidly and with sophistication. Her final paper on *Marriage as Dance* in Virginia Woolf's writing was lively and original, occasionally threatening chaos, and yet finally righting itself. It was ambitious (she drew on a wide range of critics and theorists) and yet thoroughly down-to-earth. These words also describe her.

This was so different from another graduation, decades before.

Commencement Day. I awoke, excited. As vice president of my junior high school class, I would be onstage reading the names of graduates as they received their diplomas. I put the last coat of mascara on my lashes, a few hues darker than the chocolate-brown suede I was wearing. It had taken a long time to save up for it with my babysitting money. The dress fit closely with a matching bolero jacket. I clasped an antique cameo choker at my throat. Bubbe had given it to me for graduation.

"Darlink, you're a classic beooty," she had said. "So olt-fashiont lookink and petite. Your profile belonks on a cameo brooch."

Maybe my Russian grandmother thought I was pretty, but I was invisible to boys my age, except for Kenny North. But his voice hadn't even changed yet, and he ironed his coarse bright-red hair. I wasn't comfortable with boys, at least not the popular ones. The only place I felt comfortable was in art class where varnishes and oil paints greeted me like a favorite perfume.

I smiled softly, slipped on suede Pappagallos, and dodged old sneakers, baseball mitts, and a pile of library books to eat breakfast.

Right away, I knew my mother was in a dangerous mood. A cigarette dangled from her lips. Silence hung over the kitchen like the stagnant smoke. I played with a strand of hair already escaping its butterfly comb.

She prowled around the kitchen. Every corner of her face sucked into its center, forming one giant scowl. I prayed to get through breakfast without being a target of anger. No such luck.

"You forgot to turn on the dishwasher last night. I came down here this morning ready to fix your father's eggs, and the pan is rotting in there."

She stared at me, exhaling cigarette smoke. "How many times do I have to remind you to finish what you begin? How would you like eating on a crusty plate? Answer me."

I had learned arguing only made things worse. Besides, she terrified me.

"I wouldn't like that."

"Well, let's see you eat your breakfast off one of the filthy dinner plates you didn't clean."

She shoved the plate in front of me. Eggs and toast topped last night's dried-up pot roast and green beans.

"That should teach you to be more thoughtful of the other people in this house. What, might I ask, is your excuse this time?"

"I guess I was busy thinking about the posters I had to finish for the graduation ceremony today. I guess I forgot."

"'I guess I forgot,'" she mimicked. "Well, I guess you can forget about us being at your graduation today. Now finish every bite on that plate."

She stalked out of the room, slamming the door behind her. The trail of cigarette smoke slowly faded.

On the way to school, I struggled to keep back sobs. My mother's smile could be so beautiful, but it could also contort into a frightening hole. Her teeth would grow bigger until she resembled a snarling, fang-baring wolf.

I shouted into the muggy morning mist, "It's not fair. It's not fair!"

It was a horrible morning. I couldn't believe my parents really wouldn't show up. But after the ceremony, with the junior high school hall thick with parents and students talking about high school next year, I wandered anxiously, searching for them. I finally gave up.

MY PURSUIT OF A GRADUATE DEGREE IN literature had given my life new direction and was finally an acknowledgment of my intellect. I had come from a family of scholars. My father was nationally known for his brilliant legal mind and writing. His second cousin, Emmanuil Kazakevich, won the Stalin Prize for literature (state prize of the USSR) post-WWII. My father's brother, David, was chair of English at Tufts and an accomplished author. Even his son, Max, my first cousin, followed in his father's footsteps as a published professor of English at the University of Pennsylvania.

Growing up, my brothers outshined me in school. My younger brother was H²—Harvard undergrad, Harvard law.

He now writes the quarterly law supplements for my father's books.

My older brother, Michael, was the brightest light of all four of us. As a photojournalist, Mike's writing was magnificent—his words were like shooting stars, stunning readers with their brilliance. Tragically, his long-standing bipolar symptoms eventually accelerated into schizophrenia, in part due to a frontal lobe injury from a truck accident while working for a Colorado copper mine.

His receptive and expressive processing is painfully slow. It's hard to know how much he absorbs, though he still asks for books—from Edmund Burke's *Philosophical Inquiry* to Elmore Leonard suspense novels. The adventurer who bicycled over northern Europe, worked in a coal mine in Colorado, and toiled in a salmon cannery in Alaska now walks with a limp and doesn't venture outside. He writes voraciously, though, regularly requesting paper and blue Bic pens.

I never considered myself on even keel with either brother's intelligence. I went off to university when most coeds went to college to find a husband. By the time I graduated, I was supposed to burn my bra. It was confusing. My generation of women came from behind in our awakening. But now *I* was winning various writing awards for my literary research papers, including one from the University of Michigan for my research on a paper concerning female patronage and John Donne. (I bought an $800 pallet of rocks for my garden with the prize money.) I realize now that a pattern was evolving in my research without my being aware—a feminist bent.

AFTER ALL OF MY GRADUATIONS, HERE I WAS, walking to Oxford's temporary Special Collections. I walked up the footpath next to the Museum of Natural History. Though I tried not to look like I was a Special Collections virgin, I failed to figure out how to scan my reader card . . . outed before even getting through the digital turnstile.

In a clipped but friendly British accent, the librarian said, "Go downstairs to the lockers, empty your belongings, and store them in a locker for the day, £1 deposit. You may only take your laptop, notebook, and pencil—no pens."

Mission accomplished. I walked out of the locker room.

Across from an antiquated elevator, I ascended three short stone stairs to double doors. I checked in at the circulation desk, where a wall of shelves filled with books awaited other researchers, spines of all ages, colors, and sizes.

Definitely a basement. No windows here. A librarian explained the online catalog and where to sit. She pointed me to the indexes. Another librarian gave me a brief tutorial on how to use the indexes for the Rawlinson Manuscripts, a collection containing letters, papers, and records from 1253 to 1753. He also gently admonished me for the chewing gum he apparently smelled on my breath. Yikes, this was the real deal.

The library closed early on Saturday in the summer, and six hours passed quickly. I went through almost all the Rawlinson indexes and still had the seven-volume F. Madan indexes to go, a summary catalog of Western manuscripts. I ordered the maximum number of five books and five manuscripts for Monday. The notes from my vast reading at home had helped pinpoint my search.

Backtracking down ancient Catte Street, I window-shopped on High, making my way to the Queen's Lane bus stop. Again, I had planned to pick up my bicycle rental, but it was still exceedingly windy and I didn't feel confident yet about cycling in bustling Oxford traffic. Would I ever? I returned to Painter's Cottage, dropped off my heavy backpack, and went out searching for a place to eat. I walked all the way back over the Magdalen Bridge, stopping to watch a punt boat driver push easily against the riverbed with his pole. His passengers, a young couple, cozied up to each other.

Onto glorious Magdalen College and High Street's east end. When I turned left onto Merton Street, I was in front of the Examination Schools, Oxford's largest city-center event venue. The architecture elicited an "Oh my God," even partially blocked by a white commencement tent.

Designed by Sir Thomas Jackson, one of the most distinguished British architects of his generation, it was constructed in the late 1880s to house the Oxford examinations. It boasted three acres of floor space, sweeping marble staircases, prism window glass, sumptuously carved ceilings, wood-paneled walls, and an ornate clock tower. No need to conjure up England's architectural splendor while reading a Jane Austen novel or vicariously watching *The Crown*. It was right in front of me.

I marveled again how little I had explored during my first visit to Oxford . . . typical "freshman" behavior. Only a half block off High Street, this had been where Queen Henrietta lived when her husband, Charles I, was forced from London for a few years. He conducted business from what is now the old Bodleian Library chapel.

Bread Loaf students at Lincoln College take the reader-card oath in that room.[2]

I was still jet-lagged when I took the oath six years before, and my memory was fuzzy. But I was aware of the history of the room, though not yet connected to it.

I walked back to Cowley Road and found a restaurant, Door 74, small but airy. Being early, I was the only one there until shortly before I left. I had aubergine—eggplant—over couscous with a fabulous chutney and parmesan sauce and a grilled hot zucchini salad.

How satisfying to feel settled and know my way around.

Since all the Oxford libraries would be closed the next day—Sunday—I seriously toyed with taking the train to Bath to visit the ancient Roman Baths, where my heroine, Mary of Modena, had bathed at the medicinal Cross Bath after suffering several miscarriages. Afterward, she finally gave birth to a son that lived. Unfortunately, his birth also began the motions for Mary and James II's flight into French exile only three years after ascending to the throne. The British thought it was all right to have a Catholic queen but not a Catholic heir.

I'll go if the weather isn't too rainy, I told myself. Bath was an easy day trip, seventy minutes by train, only one change in Salisbury.

Back in my room at Painter's Cottage, I searched online for the train schedule to Bath. Next, I looked at the Oxford map spread out on my bed, to find a back way to the Special Collections library without having to cycle in the crazy Oxford traffic. *I am accident prone*, I rationalized.

Night descended. My bedroom windows were open, and I heard a torrent of fireworks. I went to the window, but all I could see were the smoke remnants in the darkness. It must have been another commencement celebration. Earlier in the day, Balliol College graduates walked around town with their robes unzipped and shirts untucked. They wore leis and party hats, young and joyous, different from the tone of the Joan Didion book I had begun the night before, *Blue Nights*. The small memoir was a loose sequel to the *Year of Magical Thinking*, Didion's classic book about mourning. *Oh, shit, a death story*, I had first thought when I picked it up and read the back cover. But Didion was a gifted, lyrical writer, so I stayed with it.

Five years earlier, when my Jesse was an undergrad at NYU—yay, she chose New York City—we saw Dame Vanessa Redgrave perform her poignant one-woman show, *The Year of Magical Thinking*, on Broadway. It centered around the death of Didion's own daughter and husband, who died only a few weeks apart. Redgrave and Didion were close family friends. Who knew that three years after seeing her on Broadway, we'd learn that Ms. Redgrave's own daughter, Natasha Richardson, would also die young, due to a tragic skiing accident. She died from the same traumatic brain injury that my husband had suffered a mere month before she'd sustained hers.

Tony's accident changed our lives forever.

Chapter Eight:

Ochre and Burnt Orange

———— ·⟨◦⟩· ————

"DAMN, IT'S FROM WORK. I'D BETTER ANSWER."

I apologized to Heather-Red, my longtime hair-color guru, as redheaded as a crested cardinal.

I had trouble maneuvering my cell phone to my ear because foil-wrapped hair was spiking out from my scalp. Heather-Red laughed.

"H-h-hello," I stuttered, still trying to find my ear.

"Susan, is that you?"

I recognized the voice of our dear middle school secretary.

"I think so," I laughed, looking in the mirror.

I looked more like a space alien, especially with eyebrow dye bleeding out, which made my brows look more like those of a clown than an English teacher with graying temples. Unbeknown to me, it would be the last laugh for a good long while.

"I am so sorry to bother you, but I got a call from Tony. He couldn't reach you. He's okay, but he's been in an accident."

Oh, no. Tony already lived with chronic, intense back pain because of a truck accident ten years before.

"He's okay, though?"

"Yes. But he wants you to call. Right away."

"Of course. Right away, Nance. Thank you."

Inwardly I marveled at the coincidental prescience of leaving my temporary cell number with Nancy on my way out the school door. Higher power?

I called Tony immediately. He sounded normal and assured me he was fine, so Heather-Red finished with my highlights quickly. I drove to the accident scene less than two miles away, assuming AAA would tow the car and I would take Tony home.

What I found was alarming. Tony was not "okay."

Caked blood had hardened from ear to chin, stemming from somewhere on his right temple. His head was wrapped in make-do gauze bandaging. His voice was reedy, sounding like it hurt to think. A heavyset policewoman was in her patrol car, writing on a clipboard.

Tony had accelerated while checking a yield lane over his left shoulder. An elderly man had stopped his aging Cadillac, cold, in front of Tony's car on the I-440 entrance ramp. The man had been ambulanced to a local hospital already, although he was seemingly uninjured. Tony had denied transport, thinking he was all right. I listened to Tony explain the accident while we emptied contents from the trunk of his new Toyota into my car. His Camry's front end was so accordioned, clearly he would never return to it.

February wind was strong and cumbersome along the bleak ramp. It was probably rush hour. Vehicles dashed by, incessantly. Tony's voice sounded more and more tinny, and I became more and more alarmed. Internally I had debated whether to take him to an ER. Now I was very anxious to do so. He was wandering along the side of the interstate ramp, repeating questions . . . all signs of concussion.

"Just take me to Aunt Mary's and let me sleep for a while. Just take me to Aunt Mary's and let me sleep for a while," he recited like a mantra.

Tony was also becoming atypically argumentative, but I listened to my inner voice. I coerced him into the car and merged from I-440 onto I-40, away from Aunt Mary's and toward Vanderbilt or Baptist Hospital. I wasn't sure which, yet. Even before we got off the interstate, I had to pull over so Tony could throw up. Pain that had begun on the ramp was accelerating to unbearable proportions.

The six hours in ER's triage were intolerable. He was in terrifying pain and furious that they wouldn't give him any meds until X-rays were read. Still, I assumed a doctor would come in and say, "Tony has suffered a concussion. Go home. Keep him awake for the night." He would give us antibiotics and send us on our way.

It was not the way it played out.

The doctor came in. "Tony has suffered internal bleeding in his brain. He has a depressed skull fracture. We must remove debris to avoid infection. He needs an emergency craniotomy. We'll be taking him up now."

The grizzled, gray-haired surgeon mentioned possible effects of the surgery. I didn't listen closely, my thoughts focused on dear Tony. Besides, we had no choice. We signed the papers.

I waited alone in the surgical waiting room, numb, while they cut into his brain in the middle of the night.

I sat beside ochre lamplight, on an ochre and burnt-orange love seat, amid ochre and burnt-orange waiting-room furniture. I gazed at a black sky through ochre and burnt-orange curtains.

I should call Tony's mother, I thought fleetingly.

I clutched an ochre-and-burnt-orange pillow.

IT HAS BEEN A HANDFUL OF YEARS NOW. WE ARE blessed Tony's accident did not end fatally, as Vanessa Redgrave's daughter's had. For a long time, I felt guilty about not rushing to the scene, staying put because of hair coloring. Now I realize that if I had gotten there sooner, before his symptoms worsened, we might have been fifty miles away at our farm, instead of close to Nashville hospitals. My Tony suffered brain damage, severely compromising his short-term memory. As well, he has OCD tendencies and suffers heightened impulsivity. He qualified for disability the first time we applied, which is very unusual. It filled me with unease. *This must be bad.*

In the weeks and months that followed, I ascended Kübler-Ross's levels of mourning—denial, anger, bargaining, depression, acceptance.[1] I vacillated between depression and acceptance.

But ours is a love story.

If Tony and I hadn't already shared over twenty years together and such a loving history, would I have had the strength? I confess, there were moments of inner fantasy—*Just pack up, purchase a recession-priced condo on Demonbreun Hill close to school. Breathe.*

Now Tony is more temperamental. He hyperfocuses on American politics, shouting at commentators on cable. He has memory issues, so he can't find glasses, keys, phone, or wallet. In the beginning, Tony forgot a high percentage of everything I said. A movie we watched one day, he'd watch the next day, never realizing he had just seen it—though that has improved quite a bit. More problematic, though, was his difficulty with receptive and expressive language. We didn't have a complete conversation for the first three years. Afraid of forgetting, it compelled him to interrupt constantly, to be disputatious, and to walk out of a room in mid-conversation. That is also much better, however.

Tony is still the essence of who he was—kind, giving, hardworking, funny—but our life has changed.

In the beginning, I felt more caregiver than wife. I tried two different caregiver groups, but they were during the workday, which didn't fit my teaching schedule. I thought of starting one myself, but that was too much to even think about. Feeling overwhelmed, I returned to therapy. I will never forget receiving the first callback from Gary. The counselor at school, a dear friend, had referred him. I was in an aisle in Lowe's, living-dead walking. In between paint thinners and wood stain, I couldn't stop tears and intermittent sobbing as I gave him some background. Over time, Gary helped me adjust to my new life. He also helped me unfold more of my twisted past.

Tony has improved so much, but sometimes, I become frightened or overwhelmed. I don't know which of the two I am more ashamed of. I have learned, though, that grief is cyclical. I return to different stages over time, which I now know is normal. But I do live more and more in the present.

Tony has handled all this with characteristic inner grace and elegance—the traits that made it so easy to fall in love with him, way back when. Mourning a life that is no more has grown into acceptance. But sometimes I feel so alone.

One spring Saturday morning, early in his recovery, I was crying, feeling miserable and guilty, filled with self-disgust.

Tony said, "I love you, Susan. I will love you forever. But this is who I am now. You have to decide whether you can handle it."

My instantaneous reaction was, *I love you too, and I will love you forever, and no I don't want to leave.* But I remained silent. Maybe my father had been right. Maybe I was a quitter.

I was hoping my summer in England would be a respite to recharge my weary psyche. I loved this man without hesitation—and I was moving forward—but I confess, not proudly, that I practically leapt from the car when he dropped me off at the airport for the trip. Just like seventeenth-century-poet Anne Finch, one of the writers in Mary of Modena's court, I needed a bit of calm and solitude.

Chapter Nine:

LA or Bust

My first Oxford Sunday was a travel day. I'd decided to train to the ancient Roman Baths and maybe squeeze nearby Stonehenge into the mix, less than an hour from Bath by rail and coach.

Call me "Sheldon Cooper," but trains are a rush.

I almost moved to Boston decades before rather than buy another car after my beloved pure white MG died a dastardly death in Palo Alto during my Stanford summer. First, on the way west from Cleveland, it wouldn't climb beyond Denver, and I was a week late waiting for repairs. Not pretty when one of your classes is Theory of Statistics. I never did catch up. But I did sneak to Disneyland. Gotta love teacups.

And what about my real entrée into the LA scene a few years later?

You wouldn't see that on the streets of Cleveland, I thought, peeking to my right at an LA traffic stop on Sunset at La Brea. One lane over, also waiting for the light to turn green, a bikini-clad woman was sitting on top of a chestnut quarter horse. Bikini-clad was eating a taco. Salsa dribbled down her chest.

I watched it head for her left breast and laughed, thinking of Candye's letter daring me to show up for her wedding:

Suze! You've been buried in that damn free clinic too long. Screw the therapy, too. Heard you're thinking of heading this way for good. High time. I'm getting married at The Palomino between sets, Saturday night, April 10, so take off your reading glasses, come enjoy yourself in the City of Angels, and leave behind that pompous bald-headed lawyer you call a lover. Kisses, Candye

She was right. My life was as exciting as the monthly government report forms I filled out at the free clinic. Garrison, an attorney and my latest beau, was as warm as his legal pad. Work seemed stale and meaningless. Again. I was stranded again at the intersection of Thinking and Doing. I needed a drastic change. Again. Who better than Candye to provide it?

Candye Kane, an ex-stripper/part-time phone-sex operator turned country music and blues queen, had a fifty-four-inch bustline, a heart as big and warm as the San Fernando Valley, and a smile as sweet as the two put together. Unlikely soul mates, we'd met at a free-clinic benefit and clicked. I loved Candye's honesty and the way she bucked society. I envied her extensive vocabulary of four-letter words. And I secretly admired the tattoo above her right breast that spelled "Marty Forever" in hearts and coiled snakes. Too bad the groom's name was Thomas.

What do you choose to take on your grand adventure if you can only take what fits in the back seat and trunk?

One thing for sure: Hanging from my car ceiling was a laminated dartboard lovingly handcrafted by my free-clinic family. Each slice had a different photograph of the therapists I had nagged for chart comments every day for two wonderful years. In the bull's-eye was the photo of none other than

Dr. Adhasva, the shrink who stopped in daily at the clinic to medicate our more seriously ill clients. The only time he ever spoke to me in my two years there was on afternoons he would hurry in, late, and demand that I run to the clinic's pharmacy and get him two Tranxene, 7.5 milligrams.

"Susan, just one thing," he would say, in his clipped Hindi accent.

On my car's glove box, I taped a sign—"BREATHE"—in case I forgot. That was from my therapist.

"I think you are leaving before our work is done," Parker, my therapist, maintained.

"So be it."

It was time to stop thinking about life and start living it again. Put some hard-fought lessons to the test.

Breathe.

I loved living in the Coventry neighborhood of Cleveland Heights, but it was time to leave its leafy, eclectic charm. I packed up my enchanting apartment on Overlook, stored belongings in my younger brother's Hudson, Ohio, basement, and moved into my folks' Shaker Heights home for the winter—they were at their Florida place—to save up money before taking off for California. April 3 was D-Day. I had made my packing decisions. How could I part with my Neil Young albums or my worn Monopoly game? My car was ready and waiting in the terracotta-tiled attached garage. *I won't miss scrubbing its floor*, I laughed to myself, remembering the monotonous chore we children hated.

April 3. I pushed the button to open the garage doors and—typically Cleveland—two feet of snow had fallen silently throughout the early April night, blocking my departure. It had never even occurred to me to peek outside a window, like I used to do as a kid deciding what to wear to school. My balloon burst. Deflated but still determined to leave, I grabbed a snow shovel and began digging. *Nothing* was going to stop me, not even the winter-snow-removal contract that had expired at the end of March, three days before. Eventually, a man in a freelance plow, seeing an excellent opportunity to make a few bucks, shoveled me out, for free no less. Sometimes looks were power in the most unexpected ways.

The author at thirty, Laguna Beach, early 1980s.
CREDIT: photo from author's collection

I would have paid any amount of money.
I was off.
It took six hours to drive what should have been a two-and-a-half-hour drive to my first stop, Columbus, Ohio, home of my old college roommate, the lovely Lady Jane. We had met on a memorable elevator ride in Read Hall.

"EXCUSE ME, DEARY, COULD YOU GIVE THIS old woman a hand?"

I looked closer at the Indiana University coed playacting an old woman.

"Hurry up, deary, I don't have all day."

I didn't know whether to laugh or help "Old Woman."

Though still confused, I went along with it. I set my boxes down in front of the dorm's elevator and helped the old woman over the elevator-shaft crack.

"I just hate these newfangled contraptions, don't you?" she asked, with a crochety rasp.

"Oh. Well. I guess I'm pretty used to them by now."

What in hell is going on?

"Speak up, girl!" the old woman scolded.

I actually thought Old Woman was going to hit me with her cane.

"What floor?" I shouted.

"That's better," harped the old woman. "Three."

I pressed three, which was my floor, too, this year. I loved Read Hall. For my sophomore year, I was trying a different wing, though. My freshman year had proven that I was the type who believed in changes.

When the elevator stopped, I helped Old Woman hobble across the crack again.

"Goodbye, deary. You're a good girl."

She winked at me through fawn-like eyes made up to look old and tired, and she walked down the corridor with the help of her cane.

I giggled and picked up my boxes, almost getting stuck between the doors of the "newfangled contraption."

I limped down the hallway, trying to carry my heavy load, barely able to see over the top box. Stonewall, my gray stuffed bulldog, the one Charlie had given me in ninth grade, peeked out of the top, my stuffed companion through many nights of high school tears. Charlie and I had broken up senior year.

No need to cry here.

I made my way down the dormitory hallway checking room numbers, looking for mine. By the time I made it into my new room and unloaded my boxes, I was dripping wet from the southern Indiana humidity. *Damn Bloomington summers*, I thought, wiping unruly curly hair away from my damp forehead. But I'd take this barren single room in Indiana to my bedroom in Ohio any day. Besides, I'd make the dorm room cozy in no time.

I put my ear to the door that separated me from my new suitemates, hearing rowdy laughter coming from the adjacent room. I was nervous and excited, and I shivered in spite of the heat. A new year.

Here goes. Let's get this over with. It's what you wanted, I reminded myself as I knocked.

"Come on in," lilted a female voice through the wooden door.

I opened it. A tall, slender girl, with pin-straight blond hair cut in a short pixie looked up from her suitcase. She had a beautiful smile in an open, friendly face.

"Hi. I'm Taz!

Another girl, with long wavy brown hair, halfway through a Virginia Slim, sat in an old leather chair.

"I'm Meg, your other suitemate. And this"—she halted for a moment, as though searching for words—"is Lady Jane."

I glanced over at the worn armchair near the opposite wall.

"Pleased to meet you, deary."

Old Woman slowly rose from the chair and winked.

I shrieked in laughter. Then I curtsied.

"The pleasure is all mine, Lady Jane. I'm sure!"

PLEASURE INDEED! THANKS TO THESE WILD and crazy Michigan City girls, I learned how to have fun. Clear and simple.

Even after Meg and I killed Goldie.

Taz didn't just talk the talk. That October, a presidential year, she hopped on a Greyhound bus to Detroit, where she helped with voter registration in its Black community. Before she left, she asked Meg and me to care for her goldfish, Goldie. So what did we do? We had a wild party in our adjoining rooms. Apparently, someone poured beer into Goldie's bowl, because next morning, she was floating on top of the water. Uh-oh.

When Taz returned from Detroit, Meg and I shamefully confessed.

But I had one more confession to make. For weeks, Taz had been raving about a guy named Ron Faley and what a great kisser he had been. She had dated him briefly over the summer.

When he showed up at our party, well, I just had to find out.

Yep. I almost came. From a kiss. *Is this what it's like to kiss a girl?* His lips were like velvet. Yikes.

I knew Taz wouldn't mind. By then, she was in a hot and heavy romance. I went out with Ron Faley a few more times, once for a juicy homemade cheeseburger in his shabby house on Grant Street. Mm-hmm good—the couch kisses, not the cheeseburger!

Another time he and I ended up skinny dipping in Lost Lake in Brown County. Ironically, I lost the custom-made aquamarine ring my parents had purchased for me on one of their visits to the Caribbean. The ring caught on a rock and slipped into the depths. We dove under time and time again to no avail. *Damn, I loved that ring.*

One summer later, I remained in Bloomington to work instead of going back to Cleveland. All through undergrad,

Taz and I worked at the main library on Tenth Street, in Course Reserves. To afford my apartment on Hunter Avenue without "Lady Jane," who had decided not to stay for the summer, I sublet her half of our second-floor apartment to an exceedingly serious Armenian grad student, Sue Fargsyan. Taz and Meg lived in an apartment downstairs, just at the bottom of the outside stairway. We wore that stairway out.

Sue was heavy into anthropological research and kept to herself pretty much, but one hot and humid late afternoon, Taz and I were smoking a doober in the living room. When it began to storm, Sue came out of Lady Jane's bedroom and joined us. Somehow the topic of "best kisser ever" came up. Taz and I exalted the skills of Ron Faley, without mentioning his name. Sue's serious brown eyes grew big and round.

"Are you talking about Ron Faley?" she asked.

We looked at her incredulously.

"He was *superior*!" Sue avowed.

"I know!" I blurted. "I came when he kissed me!"

She and I high-fived.

Taz chimed in, mimicking Rose Nylund from *The Golden Girls*, "I don't know how he did it, but he'd make a helluva yodeler!"

Thus the Ron Faley Fan Club was born. I had buttons made. Anthropology indeed.

I FINALLY REACHED LADY JANE IN COLUMBUS, and I'd clutched the steering wheel so hard on my six-hour drive from Cleveland that I had difficulty unlocking my fingers. Jane came out to the car and helped me. We had a terrific stay, catching up over a bottle of Prosecco. Lovely Jane.

Next stop: My folks' place on the sugar-white sands of Longboat Key. Three weeks soaking up strength with sunshine on the Gulf of Mexico, walking the miles to the end of the key and back. Journaling by the pool. Flinging mildly with the lifeguard. Then, off around the Florida panhandle and through the mysterious Louisiana bayou to New Orleans for a few days in the French Quarter with Taz. She was joining me on the first leg of my grand adventure. Driving over bayou bridges under ominous skies gave us the Louisiana voodoo willies.

We journeyed on to sweltering Houston, staying with Meg and her husband, Rob, a wild night drinking ouzo (not Taz—she was pregnant with her first) and dancing at a Greek restaurant somewhere near the port. Did I really get on the tabletop? I think so! It was my last hurrah with college friends who had taught me how to shed my uptight skin and enjoy partying and carrying-on, away from the repression of my childhood. I breathed in their love and friendship and packed it along with my other car choices.

It was time to go it alone. My stomach was tight, and it wasn't from my seatbelt.

Driving north to Amarillo then west to New Mexico was greener and more rolling than I had imagined. But I was just as alone as I had imagined. The creepiest moment was looking for a motel on the Texas–New Mexico border, late into the night. Tacky neon, tacky billboards, tacky sinister. The place I landed was like a motel you see on investigation shows, where perverts conceal hidden cameras. The next morning, eating breakfast alone in the adjacent motel diner felt foreign and uncomfortable. I would grow to enjoy those solitary meals.

At an elevation of 7,200 feet, Santa Fe, New Mexico, was my favorite of all the overnight stops. A wood-burning fire in the kiva greeted me in a double adobe home on Acequia Madre Street, as a guest of gracious friends of friends.

Early next morning, I walked into town, the Sangre de Cristo Mountains at my back. A drizzle left from overnight rain comforted. Rainwater dripped on the pinon pines, releasing their spicy scent. I meandered by galleries on Canyon Road, on my way to The Plaza, a mix of Spanish and Pueblo architecture. Underneath the Palace of the Governors overhang, I browsed authentic silver and turquoise jewelry of Native American artists from nearby pueblos.

Would I want to stay here in Santa Fe? I was in an eclectic coffee shop, enjoying a strong brew. *Tempting but no, keep going. Not quite yet.*

Out of Santa Fe, I wound up the mountain to Taos. Everyone had said, "You must go to Taos."

So I did.

I had a picnic lunch and took a "sitting-up nap," leaning against Kit Carson's headstone! Surrounded by orange and azure, I basked in the high-desert sun, breathing in the crisp air.

On to Arizona.

Breathe.

At Barstow, California, two hours northeast of LA, I-40 melts into I-10. I started to get nervous. After Candye's wedding, I planned to stay in LA for the summer at Jimmy's —my recent ex, a musician—maybe earn a bit of money, and then move north up the coast until I found that place that "felt like home because home never had." Would I know home when I saw it?

Hopefully, I'd be emotionally ready to leave LA by the end of summer.

A few hours later, I checked into a white stucco art deco Santa Monica hotel. The woman registering in front of me was talking to an enormous cockatoo perched on her shoulder. When I called Candye and relayed the incident, she didn't seem surprised.

"Welcome to LA, honey. Now get your ass over to the club tonight. I'm playing my last gig as a free woman. You can't miss the place," Candye said. "It's right next to Queenie's Weenies."

Sure enough, next to the club, on the east end of Sunset, approaching Silver Lake, was a hot dog vendor in drag.

I walked into the dimly lit bar.

"Suze-a-belle!" Candye's voice rang out. "You made it! Glory frickin' Hallelujah!"

She reached out her arms and gave me a big squeeze, burying my head in her grand bosoms.

"Candye," I laughed, "I knew I was right to start this adventure with a dose of you."

"Damn straight, girl. I have to get up on that stage and belt a few numbers, but get yourself a drink. Put it on my tab."

I settled in at a corner high table, wiped off the sticky, and watched Candye approach the stage. She looked good, though perhaps a bit larger than the last time she played Cleveland, in the Flats. She fiddled with the microphone, then tossed her wavy dark hair back and spoke.

"Good evenin', everyone. I want to thank y'all for coming out to hear me sing. It's the night before I get hitched to my true love!"

The LA crowd roared.

"Someone came up to me earlier and asked me was I pregnant or did I just love to drink beer?" She patted her belly with her hands. "I am pregnant. And I do love to drink beer. And I'll be damn thirsty for one by the time this here bambino is born!"

Amid cheers and applause, Candye broke into her first set. I had forgotten how spectacular her rich contralto voice was and what control she had over an audience. Two fans in particular were under a spell. They could have been ex-strippers themselves or casualties from a bad 1960s acid trip. I asked Candye about them when she came to sit with me during her first break.

"Oh, they're my Candye Canes. They come to every LA gig." She took a deep sip of bottled water. "The redhead is my maid of honor."

I gulped my Dos Equis. Candye went back up onstage.

The Candye Canes belly danced in front of the stage all evening. Every few minutes, Redhead would shimmy over to my high table, readjusting her black pipe-stem bustier and rewinding her Isadora Duncan neck scarf. Before prancing off to resume her drunken gyrations, she'd hang on me like yellow burr weed and exclaim how pretty I was.

I didn't know what to do.

I asked Candye about that during her next break.

"Susie-Q, honey. Red is a horny little shit. You're gonna have to pretend you're shooing chickens or she'll keep right on peckin'."

I took a bigger gulp. I was a little miffed. Surely Red knew how exasperating ignoring "no" could feel.

While she hovered, the phone on the wall right next to me kept ringing. Curiosity piqued, I answered it twice. Each time, a voice like a cement mixer repeated, "Annie's ambitious and deserves to do well." A drug deal gone haywire? A gangster teasing out a job prospect? Either way, I was realizing anything was possible in this town of eccentrics. I was loving every minute. What wonderful offbeat surprises were in store for me at Candye's wedding?

Plenty. Entering the legendary Palomino Club on the fringe of North Hollywood was like stumbling onto a B-grade spaghetti western set. Walking past the bouncer, "Tiny," a 300-pound Hoss Cartwright doppelganger, into the dark, musty club was like time-traveling back to an era when men were men and women were unimportant. It seemed it had been that long since the floors had been swept. Dusty signed photographs of every country-western star imaginable crowded worn imitation wood-paneled walls. Above a long banquette of red Naugahyde booths, hand-painted Day-Glo posters illuminated by black light advertised coming attractions: Dwight Yoakam, Jerry Lee Lewis, Asleep at the Wheel,

John Anderson. There were so many leftover staples in the wall from removed posters, I couldn't lean back. Linda Ronstadt had performed at The Palomino on amateur nights when she was still a hippy with hairy armpits. It was the perfect hole-in-the-wall for a rowdy evening of great music. But it was the kind of place where you peed before you went and prayed you didn't have to again until you got home.

Every guest was attired in their most splendid garb, be it funk, folk, or fairy. The Candye Canes were in their Saturday Night Specials. Red was draped in gold lamé. The other, I never caught her name, brought to mind a Greek fertility goddess. Ruddy-faced cowboys mingled with leather-wrapped punkers and rockers. Even hats took on life-forms. Forget spaghetti westerns; I was lost in a spectacular Salvador Dali canvas, country-western style. The only thing missing was Joni Mitchell.

I would love *to fulfill my cocktail-waitress fantasy here.*

As Chicanos from Candye's old neighborhood guzzled Coronas with the hip Hollywood crowd, voices rose to a fevered pitch. The air thickened. If there had been windows, they would have been steaming.

Guests buzzed around asking, "Have you seen her? What's her wedding dress like? Is she showing yet? Have you seen the groom? He looks like he's about to walk the plank."

I thought the room was going to explode. Just when anticipation reached its climax, Candye strutted onto the stage. Her smile reached from one end of the large, darkened room to the back patio. Everyone cheered. She twirled to model her wedding gown. The crowd stood and roared approval.

Candye never dreamed she'd own anything so magnificent. The designer, Manuel, had created the gown as a wedding gift. Made of imported antique black lace, it was delicately hand painted with red roses by the French artist Marousha and studded throughout with black rhinestones.

The low-cut bodice was laced up the front with black satin. Victorian sleeves were fitted at the bottom with ruffled detail. At the top of the black chiffon-and-silk wedding train, red and black ribbons cascaded from hand-sewn silk roses. Haute couture meets Wild West.

Candye performed a hot set. Her groom, Thomas, bass player for an up-and-coming rockabilly band, intense and sexy, stood at the foot of the stage while their throng of friends danced around him. While the Canes carried on and people partied, Thomas stood motionless, his eyes glued to the vision of his bordello bride. She threw a red rose from her long black hair into the hands of her groom. Candye left the stage. It would be a quick break. She was dripping with impatience.

Sure enough. The piano player approached the bench. He began a boogie-woogie wedding march. Candye's father, a slight, unassuming gentleman bewildered by the chaos, walked his daughter up to the stage.

Reminding me of Lauren Bacall straight out of *To Have and Have Not*, Candye sauntered. The crowd was on its feet, whistling and howling. Her father retreated, timidly.

The reverend looked like a cross between Frank Zappa and Captain Hook.

I laughed in the semidarkness. "If he's clergy, my roommate's the Singing Nun."

Damn. What if I had just offended a friend of the minister?

I apologized sheepishly. Yikes, I was begging pardon to the Marlboro Man.

His turn to laugh. He leaned back. "No offense taken. You were right on the mark. That's Marty."

"I don't follow."

"You know, Candye's tattoo," he qualified. "Marty's a hairdresser and part-time porno actor. Ordination courtesy of the United States Postal Service."

He tapped my forearm lightly and then teased me, "I'm J. D. Don't wander away. I want to hear more about that roommate of yours."

Reverend Marty stuttered through the ceremony. Candye's voice was uncharacteristically soft as she recited her vows to Thomas. His voice was strong and sure. The "ring-bear" was a Teddy bear belonging to Candye's little boy, Cale. He joyously tossed Teddy up in the air when Candye and Thomas were pronounced husband and wife.

The reverend let out a wild western "yeehaw!"

I was exhausted. It had taken all my restraint to keep from looking at Mr. Marlboro during the ceremony. The only men I knew with initials for first names wore three-piece pinstripe suits and tasteful ties.

Just at the instant I started to wonder what to do next, J. D. handed me a champagne flute, filled.

"This is The Palomino, so not the best label . . . but to good intentions."

I tapped his flute with mine. "To good intentions."

It was the groom's turn to perform. Feedback from an amplifier startled me, and I spilled champagne on J. D.'s sleeve.

"Oh, yikes. I am so sorry."

I reached for a cocktail napkin.

"Are you kidding? If you leave The Palomino without whiskey stains, it means you didn't have a good time."

So I dribbled a smidge of champagne on my jacket. We both laughed.

Still laughing, J. D. said, "Listen. You've already apologized to me twice. I don't even know your name."

Shaking his hand, I introduced myself, "Susan. From Cleveland. Cleveland, Ohio."

"Ah! The lawyer's daughter!"

I blushed. I hated when I blushed.

"Candye was giddy when she heard that you were coming."

"And you? What's your connection to Candye?"

"Mostly session work. Piano."

Kindly, J. D. signaled for a Palomino waitress to refill our flutes.

I'm leaving her a nice tip.

When she was gone, he asked, "So what do you think of LA?"

"A breath a fresh air."

"You must be from out of town," J. D. teased.

"Here now, though. I'd promised myself that I wouldn't still be living in Cleveland when I hit thirty. Two years to spare." I sipped from my flute. "I plan on taking off north, driving until I find a place that feels like home. But I'm not quite ready yet," I added.

Damn his eyes are blue.

"Good for you. I vote for change."

"Maybe we should take a poll."

He glanced around.

"Any doubt what the outcome would be?"

Chuckling, we clinked our flutes again and talked until closing time. He was a good listener with a killer sense of humor. It felt good to admit to someone that maybe, just maybe, I was escaping "the pressure to succeed."

Tempting as it was, I didn't accept his invitation to go home with him. Too complicated. And not healthy.

He walked me to the parking lot. He opened my car door and kissed me on the cheek.

"I have to skip the reception tomorrow, getting ready to tour. I'll be gone for a while. Sure you wouldn't—"

"No."

I laughed, started my car, and drove off to my Santa Monica hotel.

Back in my oceanfront room, I sat amid cushy pillows and let my senses take over, listening to the sounds of the ocean waves—the breezes drifting filmy window curtains back and forth—acoustic guitar music from the café patio below. Sounds cliché, but it was true. I drifted off to sleep, proud of remaining true to myself, despite the allure of J. D. and his turquoise '59 Thunderbird convertible—top down.

In the morning, I sipped on coffee and took a long bath. I had plenty to think about before putting on my party hat.

THE WEDDING RECEPTION WAS HOSTED by the groom's record producer at his estate, nestled in the Hollywood Hills. I splurged on a taxi, which meandered up and around narrow cobblestone streets. Breathtaking.

I gave the taxi driver a nice tip.

Descending rustic wooden stairs, winding through lush foliage and landscaped rock gardens, I found a party in full swing. Most people had not been home to sleep or to change clothes.

Candye was wearing her cherished wedding gown as though she'd turn into a cinder girl if she took it off. She and Thomas were sitting on the edge of a large stage platform in front of a midnight-blue swimming pool. While the couples' musician friends performed, the newlyweds held hands, dangling their bare feet like Tom Sawyer and Becky Thatcher. Candye's stage makeup had long since rubbed off. She had freckles! Lipstick was gone from her lips. Thomas had it smeared all over his.

Glorious hills crowned the estate. The LA sky was clear and blue. There is a hue to LA air that I have never seen elsewhere. It's practically tactile. Children were weaving around, through laughing guests. A beautiful West German woman breastfed her infant daughter. I was in a relaxed state of mind.

A rough-looking woman approached center stage. She started belting out a gutsy rhythm and blues number.

Something was wrong. Her words slurred. She started writh-
ing on the platform floor, masturbating with the microphone.
She unzipped her motorcycle jacket, revealing bare breasts,
and she began fondling them. As she stumbled about, her
beer spilled all over Thomas's stand-up bass. Reverend Marty
tried to coax the woman off the stage. No one knew quite
where to look or what to do.

Candye took care of that dilemma. She came bounding
up the stage, cursing and gesturing.

"You bitch. Where do you think you are? My grandmother is here. My aunts are in the audience, you cunt."

And she pushed the woman into the swimming pool below.

"There. Cool it off, bitch," Candye shouted after her.

Candye had hardly finished her tirade when the drummer
pushed her into the water. My heart stopped. Before Candye
came to the surface, all you could see was black lace floating
at the top of the water, wet and mottled.

Like a chivalrous knight, Thomas, still in his rented
tuxedo, jumped in to save his soggy bride. She came up
ranting and raving, shaking her fists at the drummer as she
treaded water. The Marty tattoo glistened like a beacon light
to lost sailors.

"You cocksucking dick. My gown. My beautiful gown.
It's ruined. I hate you, you motherfucking asshole. Get out.
Get out. Get out of here."

Thomas steered her toward the pool's edge, trying to
console her. Manuel, who had designed the gown, was at the
reception and was standing there when the incident occurred.
He helped Candye out of the water and cradled her.

Manuel, like a courtly Italian count, spoke to her softly
until Thomas could climb out of the pool.

"My dear, the gown will be all right. We can fix any last-
ing problems."

Thomas cradled his bride's arm as they wound up the garden steps to dry off at the main house.

It was an abrupt end to a lively party. Musicians packed up their equipment.

Guests shared reluctant goodbyes.

I called for another taxi.

Two hours later, I was walking through the hotel lobby after checking out.

I passed a group of house phones when one of them rang. I stopped in my tracks. I looked around. No one seemed to notice. I couldn't resist.

After picking up the receiver, I answered, "Hello?"

"Good evening. Are you the lady of the house?"

Again, I couldn't resist.

"Yes," I lied.

"I'd like to take a moment of your time. I'm calling from the LA chapter of the Jews for Jesus Burial Referral Service."

I hung up. And giggled.

That had made about as much sense as my bewitching weekend. Time to jump in my car: a summer with musician Jimmy, then off to northern California or beyond, until I found a place that felt like home because home never had.

Chapter Ten:

Never Anger a
Stalwart Stallion

WEEKS LATER, I REENTERED THE LEGENDARY Palomino to see the Everly Brothers on their long-awaited reunion tour. I was with Jimmy. He had misinterpreted my move west as a commitment to him, which made me uncomfortable. But I wasn't confident enough to move on yet, so we shared a grubby efficiency apartment off the Hollywood strip.

Immediately I thought, *Yes, I really could work here at The Palomino. It would be fun. Yes, grungy, raucous fun!* The San Bernardino mountains seemingly within arm's touch, there should have been a marquee flashing: "Lousy food, expensive drinks, great music." Indeed, I *could* indulge my closet fantasy here to be a cocktail waitress. A few years before, in Cleveland, I was sitting in a back tier at a Friday happy hour with teaching colleagues, in front of a trio playing good jazz. My dear old friend, Joanne Lockley, was serving a tray of cocktails. I hadn't seen her in a few years. She was smiling and partying along with her tables—at least that's what it looked like to me. How fun to help people have a good time. No responsibility, no teacher anxiety following you home each night.

Summer turned into autumn in the City of Angels and a nearly depleted savings account. For weeks while sipping morning coffee and perusing through the Sunday *LA Times*, I had noticed regular ads for help wanted at The Palomino. So three days after the Everly Brother's rousing performance, I returned for their weekly Monday-morning cattle call.

The first impression that comes to me in looking back on my waitressing days at The World-Famous Palomino Club is to compare its long tables extending lengthwise from the stage to the dining hall at Oxford at High Table.[1] Think Hogwarts's Great Hall, but substitute the master paintings of John Wesley, Cardinal Wolsey, and Henry VII with dusty eight-by-ten-inch autographed glossies of the likes of George Jones, Dottie West, and Conway Twitty.

High Table at Lincoln College, Oxford
CREDIT: painting by author

Hired to serve cocktails and overpriced, undercooked dinners by maniacal owner Tommy Thomas, I chose my requisite two free Palomino T-shirts, one pink, one powder blue, both V-neck. Jenette, a tattoo-covered waitress before tattoos were the cultural norm, had walked me to the T-shirt closet in Tommy's cramped office behind the front bar.

In the weeks that followed, I regularly picked up Jenette on the way to work. The first time, she was still getting ready in her squalid one-room studio. As she changed into her tight-fitting Palomino T-shirt and jeans, I discovered that Jenette, quiet and statuesque, was covered with tattoos from her collarbone to her toes. There were psychedelic swirls, skulls and crossbones, tigers, a veritable plethora of tattoo regalia. The first time I saw them, my eyes grew as big as Candye's bosom. Another "What's a nice Jewish girl" moment.

I'd bet all my Saturday-night tip money that I am the only server in Palomino history who went to the public library to research names of cocktails before showing up for work my first night. I had lied—and expected my mother to swoop down from the heavens and strike me—when writing on my application that I had cocktail-waitress experience, not that it ended up mattering. Of course, I was outed the first night by Frank, The Palomino head bartender, who was as misplaced as I. He should have been lecturing in front of a college classroom, not behind the bar where they had filmed the Clint Eastwood–orangutan bar scenes in the Philo Beddoe *Every Which Way* and *Any Which Way* films.

Frank disdainfully corrected me when I, trying to act experienced, called a chimney a brand of scotch when giving him my order.

"A chimney . . . is a glass," he sneered, under his elegant mustache, as he set the tall glass on the pouring tray.

Busted.

Picking up his cigarette from a black polyurethane ashtray, he took a dramatic drag and exhale. Pulling at his fourteen-carat gold cuff-linked sleeves, he waited for me to slink away, shamed. We ended up being solid friends once he realized I had an ounce of intelligence and could stick it out at the tawdry Pal. I made it through the first few months despite Retta, the head waitress, a diminutive, very-bleached-blond Broad with a capital "B." She gave me poor stations, I found out later, because I wasn't a "coke whore" like many of the other waitresses. I never bought from her. With my genomic history, I figured cocaine would push me right over the edge. Ping.

But I had so much fun. First, the music. Stars in the making like The Mavericks, Lucinda Williams, Jimmy Lauderdale. Stars from the past like Doug Kershaw, Ray Price, Jerry Lee Lewis. It was my introduction to Emmylou Harris, who caused a sensation. She was revered, with people lining up on Lankershim Boulevard for hours. On New Year's Eve, I waited on Rita Coolidge and her backup singers, such strong vocalists in their own right. In their bus, back behind the outdoor seating, it was like a loving, spirited women's group. Yes, so much fun.

And who could forget the waitresses? Besides Retta and Jenette there was willowy, ethereal Pam, quiet but strong. And Meg, a low-to-the-ground bundle of sass from Brooklyn. Patsy, a Scottish former hairdresser, was the life of the party. And my closest friend, wanderlust Australian Gail—pronounced *Gile*, rhymes with *bile*—was my freckled, fellow adventurer, full of spunk. How I wish I knew what happened to her.

In four brief months, I was one of the three senior waitresses. Turnover was endemic. I had a blast despite Tommy Thomas's mood swings and despite returning nightly to a shabby efficiency on Cherokee Avenue behind the Hollywood strip where Jimmy jealously waited, imagining in his paranoid mind I was screwing every customer between tray runs.

Yikes. How fucked-up am I when it comes to men? Ahh, let's consider: When I was in third grade, John Wagner tied me to his swing set and ran over me with his silver-blue junior half-scale Austin Healey. I went running home, crying.

My mother responded by saying, "It just means he likes you."

And what about the summer after I met Lady Jane? I was waitressing on Mackinac Island, Michigan. After the day tourists had sailed away on the last ferry, I met other young island workers partying on the north side of the island. But I wanted to call my boyfriend, so Herv, a swarthy, wiry, indigenous Chippewa, offered to give me a ride back.

"I can cut right through the island and have you home in a few minutes," he said.

I lit my cigarette, holding on to it *and* my drink with one hand and Herv's waist with the other. Dusty, Herv's stallion, was angered at our slow pace. So he reared. High. I felt myself falling backward, unable to hold on. How could I, holding on to a vodka and tonic? Idiot. My head hit the rocks. I saw stars. Dusty fell back on me, then stepped on my crotch trying to get up. Excruciating pain.

Spooked, Dusty ran off despite Herv's commands. We were stranded far away from anywhere by foot.

My jeans were soaked in sticky, iron-smelling blood. I could barely walk. It took over an hour from where we fell to stumble to the poverty-stricken Chippewa village in the middle of the island, a side of Mackinac tourists and summer help never saw.

Abject deprivation. Shacks formed an uneven square around a common area where horse blankets and bed sheets were hanging on lines, seen by the light of a half-moon. Herv grabbed another horse, threw a soiled blanket over its saddle, and cautiously hoisted me over it, like an injured cowboy on a *Lone Ranger* episode. I made it back to my dorm room by early dawn. I soaked in the claw-foot tub and cried, afraid, as caked blood turned the bathwater pink.

A few days later, I left Mackinac Island abruptly and painfully, hitchhiking to Saginaw's Tri City Airport with an antiquing hippie couple in a beat-up pickup.

Back home, attending a summer Shakespeare class at John Carroll University, I was reading *Measure for Measure* at the pool, falling in love with the Bard. My father had told his plaid-panted golf buddies about my accident. Back behind the swimming pool, between the ninth and tenth hole, he strolled up with his cronies on their way to the drink house.

Laughing, he said, "Unsnap your cutoffs and show them your bruises."

Though embarrassed, I unzipped my pants and pulled them far enough down so they could see my heavily bruised inner thighs below my bikini bottom.

And why didn't I protest when my college allergy doctor would hear a rasp through his stethoscope and say, "Better take a look at it," having me disrobe from the waist up. Once, he even asked, "Has anyone ever told you that you have beautiful breasts?"

It just means he likes you.

And Jimmy? I knew the time would come, hair dryer in hand, when I would leave him. Early one spring Sunday morning when I woke up because he was pouring ice water in my ear from a large yellow Italian ceramic soup tureen I had purchased at a yard sale for fifty cents. He started beating my head before I could react.

"That'll teach you!" he raged, standing over me.

We slept on a mattress on the living room floor, so I strained to sit up and maintain balance. It took considerable cajoling to calm down his raving. Repeatedly I reassured him that I was not screwing any of the customers or bartenders.

While I mentally plotted my escape, I talked him into walking around the corner toward Las Palmas Avenue to pick up a quart of orange juice and the Sunday *Times*. Once I heard the two hallway fire doors slam, I grabbed that hair dryer, a handful of Palomino T-shirts, and a few pairs of jeans and panties. I stuffed them into a plastic Ralph's grocery bag and ran out of the apartment building, berating my poor judgment once again. My heart was pounding, fearful he would catch me. Ah, *The Perils of Pauline*.[2]

Running across the meager front grass, diagonally, to my car, I turned my ankle but continued my beeline. Fortunately, the car was parked away from the direction Jimmy had sauntered. Heading hurriedly toward Franklin Avenue, I drove in circles for quite a while, until the shaking stopped— I can't remember if I cried—eventually ending up at fellow Pal gal Patsy's airy apartment on Highland, just north of Santa Monica Boulevard.

Patsy, my hairdresser friend from Scotland, had recently pronounced she was gay. It relieved me to be enveloped by her gaggle of lesbian friends. The thought of looking at a man that morning was nauseating.

My eyes were blackening from Jimmy's pounding. In her lilting brogue, Patsy invited me to stay on her couch as long as I needed. Retta, possibly the victim of a domestic dispute or two, found room in her hardened heart for pity on me that evening. Despite my swollen ankle and her initial antipathy, she gave me a great station for once. I made the best tips ever that night.

While carrying a full tray of Coronas and Dos Equis, while the trumpet section of Jack Mack and the Heart Attack kept a steady beat, I thought fleetingly of my old friend Joanne, the elegant arm of her dancer's body raised, tray extended, winding her way through the hip Cleveland crowd. No responsibility. I thought about how in a few hours, I, along with all of the other Palomino girls on duty, would be cleaning all of the dirty glasses in the two squalid sinks behind the bar at 1:00 a.m., while the male bartenders counted their tips and drank beer—courtesy of owner Tommy Thomas—at one of the dilapidated red Naugahyde booths.

Then and there, I resolved that the next fantasy I would play out would not involve a musician or a serving tray.

Chapter Eleven:

Wasn't Much fer Stickin' Around but He Sure Could Make Me Laugh

———⁘———

J. D. HAD BEEN RIGHT: LA IS A SMALL TOWN IF you're in the music business. I didn't know that night at The Pal that the designer of Candye's wedding dress, Manuel, was sitting at my station. When he saw my bruised face, he automatically shifted into caretaking mode.

"Who did this to you?" Manuel asked in his thick Spanish accent.

Hardly the reaction I got from his girlfriend the first time I had waited on them. A few months before, Tommy had sent me over, frantically, during a sold-out Jerry Lee Lewis show when they hadn't been served. Later I discovered that Tommy and Manuel were best friends.

"Go wait on Manwell. Go wait on Manwell. Run a tab for Manwell."

I hurriedly wrote M-a-n-w-e-l-l at the top of a new bar receipt.

"Where, Tommy?"

"Over there in the Chimayó coat, the man with the long silver braid."

He pointed over to the designer, sitting with a leggy redhead.

"Oh . . . Manuel," I replied, remembering him from Candye's wedding reception.

We meet again.

I went over to the couple. I was stunned by his unbelievable Chimayó blanket coat with suede hand-tooled sleeves. I had passed Chimayó, famous for its weavings, on my way from Santa Fe to Taos. I had never seen anything like his coat, and I told him so.

"Thank you, my dear."

"He made it," his leggy girlfriend quipped in a part-British, part–Valley Girl inflection.

"Bring me a Tanqueray and tonic. Manuel will have a double shot of 1800 with a Corona back," she snapped, turning her back on me.

Ouch. What is a lovely man like this doing with a bitch like that?

After the show, Manuel's lady, Vic-*tor*-ia, lost a one-carat diamond stud earring and was in a panic. I got down on my hands and knees on the disgusting Palomino floor to search, finding it up against the table leg. Returning it to her, she grabbed it from my hand and brushed me away, as if I were a scullery maid.

Wow, what a piece of work.

Manuel looked miserable, and I could see why. I chalked up the "Victoria floor crawl" to another "What's a nice Jewish girl doing in a place like this" moment. I wiped my sticky hands with the rag I had been using to clean my station and dipped it back in the soapy bucket before going behind the bar to clean up with the other Palomino girls.

Since that night, Manuel and Victoria had broken up. He often came in after work to sit at the bar and eat a cheeseburger and drink Coronas, buying drinks for the regulars, bartenders, and waitresses. He certainly looked happier. Once in a while, he would join us waitresses and bartenders at Denny's for breakfast after closing. Bartender Frank never came. He probably went home to a smoking jacket and brandy.

It was great fun to show up at the Pal for a drink on nights off, knowing my dear friends—Frank included—would protect me from drunken cowboys, drug dealers, or Hollywood stuntmen. *If* I wanted them to. Over twenty years later, when one of my student's dads turned out to have been a bouncer at the Pal years after my stint, we had quite a laugh when we realized that the same regulars had still been sitting at the bar. My closest Palomino buddies were Hal, a mysterious Henry VIII look-alike who was my antique-browsing friend, and Uncle Richard, a diminutive hunchback big-rig driver who once showed up at our rural Tennessee home, big rig and all.

Manuel, a legend in country music, was outraged at my bruised state and took it upon himself from then on to take care of me. The last thing I wanted at that point was a relationship of any kind. But frankly, I was tired, weary to the emotional bone. I had spent my life taking care of myself, not always very well. Although the timing sucked since I had no intention of staying in LA, I needed some care just then, some time to shed my resilient coat. Manuel was different from anyone I had ever met, courtly, European, but fun-loving. Besides, hadn't I always been a sucker for a foreign accent? I sensed that I needed to get to know this unusual man who mingled with music legends but loved eating a burger at a dive-bar stool.

When Manuel said, "I want to make a puppy with you," little did I realize that conceiving a baby was just what we would do. He courted me persistently. Finally, months later, I acquiesced. The first time we made love in the back of his LA boutique, on a couch in the spacious western-chic VIP dressing room, he kept his socks on. Later I learned it was because many of his toes were deformed because of a botched surgery. I looked down in the twilight and laughed: *Hmm, I am screwing the Pillsbury dough boy in custom crocodile cowboy boots.*

What's a nice Jewish girl doing in a place like this?

I was forever bucking my rigid upbringing. Manuel's fun-loving nature—"Tequila was my mother's milk," and "I never miss a party"—was just what I needed. One morning he rolled over in bed and teased in his Spanish accent, thick even after two or three decades in America, "So, my dear, what are you going to worry about today?"

Well, I just had to laugh.

No one knows for sure how old he is; even he has probably forgotten, although where he fits in the sequence of eleven siblings narrows his choice for fudging with his age. Three years after meeting, we married at our favorite French restaurant, Le Petit Chateau, on Lankershim Boulevard,[1] the same place he proposed and the same place I told him I was pregnant after three years of trying for that "puppy," having been told by doctors that it was virtually impossible.

Six years later, we divorced. I had thought I was being healthy when we married. In fact, Manuel is a remarkable man; he just doesn't have a "family gene." We weren't a couple in the truest sense. To him, I was a young woman who needed protection. To be a protector was his need with people. I outgrew my need for protection. Many times, I told him I was drifting away, but it never caused him to come home, ever, until the early morning hours. I grew more and more detached after each conflict he wouldn't (or couldn't) partner to resolve. Finally, after a huge financial lie, it felt like he had slapped me in the face. He tried to scare me about leaving.

"It will be too hard for you. You won't make it."

But I *am* resilient. I made the ultimate drift away.

The marriage may not have lasted, but Manuel changed my life in so many ways. He taught me how to *l-i-g-h-t-e-n up*. He helped me enjoy life again. He gave me our daughter.

Motherhood gave me a landing place. The fears of repeating my mother's physical and emotional abuse never surfaced. For the first time I was grounded. Jesse continues to be the joy of my life. I suffered postpartum *elation* for years. Manuel's inability to deal with our issues doesn't negate the intangible gifts he gave me. Above all, Manuel has zest for life and that changed me. It was just like Luke's mother, Arletta, said in *Cool Hand Luke*: "Oh, I had me, I had me some high old times. Your old man, Luke. He wasn't much good fer stickin' around, but dammit, he sure could make me laugh."

Our daughter will forever bring me supreme delight, the best of both parents. Who knew that over a quarter of a century later, she would be a law student, turquoise-haired and as tattooed as any Palomino girl!

"Mom, don't worry, I have to wear a suit in court anyway. The tats won't show," my darling daughter insists.

It's a new generation. She is a successful litigation attorney now in Los Angeles, after three years of clerking for two federal judges. My pride and joy.

Chapter Twelve:

Training

————·❦·————

I WAS OFF TO BATH AND STONEHENGE FROM Painter's
Cottage to the Oxford railway station. The Sunday morning
number-five bus was chill compared to the weekday bustle,
when a mix of ages, cultures, and strata vied for seats. Younger
riders always made for the steep stairway up to the top of the
red double-decker. Whenever I rode, I heard a party going on
above. However, this particular Sunday, I was the only rider
along with a young, trimly bearded father in the back, who
read *The Wombles* to his daughter.

"You had three helpings of mussels over fried toast for
supper. How can you be hungry in the least tiny bit?" he read.

I delighted in hearing my La Kesh meal from the evening before mentioned in a classic children's story. Even a
phone book sounded enchanting when read by an English-
man. I remembered Sunday mornings reading Dr. Seuss
books to Jesse.

LA memories?

Memories of joking around with Waylon Jennings back-
stage at the Greek. Apologizing to Larry Gatlin for nursing
Jesse in front of him. He had said it was one of God's great

miracles. Memories of sharing a drink and a giggle with Tammy Wynette at a pool party. She was just as short as I was.

Once, at the CMAs, an appreciative K. D. Lang welcomed me into her dressing room when no one else was interested.

I comfortably chatted with Robert Duvall before his Oscar win for *Tender Mercies*, and I thrilled when attending an invitation-only Emmylou Harris recording session at the legendary Ryman Auditorium. It didn't escape me that only a few years before, I had been waiting tables at The Palomino while she had performed.

Dwight Yoakam loved Manuel. When Dwight wasn't touring, he would come into the store at night several times a week to talk into the morning. We all occasionally antiqued together, but I never felt comfortable in his presence. He sent a magnum of Dom Pérignon after Jesse was born, which my sister and I downed mischievously. I nursed Jesse, put her in the stroller, and off went Manuel for a long, long walk!

A few years later, Linda Ronstadt teased that she was paying for Jesse's college tuition—I wish—by ordering so many designs from Manuel. Jesse won a total scholarship to NYU's Gallatin School of Individualized Study, but man, that NYC rent.

Every day was different. Yet it was lonely in many ways. Excluding the Nitty Gritty Dirt Band members Jeff Hanna and Jimmie Fadden, who came often to many of our spur-of-the-moment Sunday get-togethers—and Jeff Goldblum, he was a *hoot* when he came in for a fitting—for most of the famous folks I met I was more of a hand-mirror. It was an empty feeling. With the exception of Johnny Cash and Neil Young, for whom I was awestruck, tongue-tied, and absolutely dumb-fucked, fame—in the words of Shania Twain about celebrities—*don't impress me much*. Intelligence and power, now that was fascinating.

I had the good fortune to design a logo for Neil Young's *Hot Pink* tour. He came in for a fitting and was very shy. Which made me shy. But, boy, was it a thrill to meet one of my musical heroes. Attending his show at the Pal later that night, at a front table—close to where I had done the "Victoria floor crawl"—Manuel teased that he'd never seen a smile that actually went from earlobe to earlobe before.

Johnny Cash walked into the boutique one day dressed in a khaki windbreaker and khaki pants. Even through beige drabness, he exuded charisma. Standing next to the jewelry case that showcased magnificent silver pieces, he outshone in khaki. It was as if all of the energy in the room sucked into him. At the same time, he was humble, unassuming. I was reminded of Kris Kristofferson retelling how when Bob Dylan met Johnny Cash, he just walked around him like he was a huge tree and nodded, "Hmmm."[1]

I couldn't speak either.

I had a few chances to meet Bob Dylan at fittings, but I turned them down. I didn't want to be disappointed by another poet/musician hero. Now, whenever I listen to his music while walking my hilly country road, I do have a tinge of regret. We are all getting older.

EARLY ON THIS OXFORD SUNDAY, ARRIVING AT the rail station on Park End Street, I had such a silly sense of satisfaction in knowing how to purchase a ticket, go through the turnstile, retrieve my ticket, and wait on the platform for the train. Simple pleasures. A Japanese woman actually asked *me* for help as I waited at Didcot Parkway for the second train that would take me to Bath, via Salisbury. I felt as if I belonged here in Britain.

Indeed, in England, sheep do graze on gentle sloping fields, patchwork quilts of green. Smatterings of thatched-roof cottages and old burnt-sienna brick houses stand alone but not lonely. Trees serve as hedgerows, their forests having been cleared for grazing. Cumulous clouds share their own shadow designs.

On the train, as the town of Swindon approached, I admired wildflowers and grass growing up around abandoned rails. When we stopped, mothers accustomed to train travel seemed to assume their children would follow—and they did, in shiny silver gladiator sandals or pink skirts with fleece tops. I could determine who the passenger was by their shoes.

The train lurched forward. Swindon dropped away. There was no suburban sprawl. Vistas returned to sheep and barns, thatch on a not-so-distant hillside, a quaint walking bridge to nowhere. Meandering streams—why don't they meander in the states?

We passed Chippingham, pronounced "Chipnum." Bath was "Both," and I laughed at myself remembering how the day before, in Oxford, I was stupefied when directed to "Dum'inums" to purchase my city bus pass. I had absolutely no idea what the woman was saying. It turned out to be the department chain, Debenhams. I never did understand what the waiter called the grilled zucchini at Door 74.

At first, Bath seemed too touristy—several million people visited annually. Daniel Defoe, eighteenth-century author of *Robinson Crusoe*, called it "a place of raffling, gaming and levity."[2] I walked through a trendy glass-and-chrome shopping area, toyed with stopping to try on better walking shoes, but after considering the inflated pound—everything was almost double the American dollar at the time—I showed financial self-restraint for a change. I found my way to the Bath Abbey's churchyard, history in the cobblestones of the grand piazza. Being a Sunday after Mass, people were subdued as the priest led his subjugates out the vast abbey doors. The congregants encircled him.

I still felt like a herded tourist after standing in line to pay for my Roman Baths ticket, thrust into a mob of people selecting headsets and proceeding forward. Farther into the bathhouse, the crowd thinned out. No American accents, only foreign. Thus, I was never drawn into overhearing conversations, so it was easy to lull back into my favorite hypnotic state.

The Baths proved *spectacular.*

I listened attentively to the audio plugged into my ear. Legend had it that in 863 BC, a Celtic prince, who suffered from incurable leprosy, was banished from the land. His only recourse was to be a swineherd, a pig minder. Among his herd, he discovered that sores on his pigs miraculously disappeared after the pigs splashed in mineral water from a hot spring. After bathing in the water, the prince was cured. He reclaimed his kingdom and founded the city of Bath, later described as "The Florence of England." The Romans overtook the valley in 43 AD and remained for almost four hundred years. They believed they were enchanted by the waters. The Roman Baths were rediscovered and restored again in the late nineteenth century.

I stayed for a long, long time, sometimes retracing steps, imagining the past. But the humidity inside the Baths was very *now.* Off-putting smells of the past mixed with the closeness of the present, nudging me back in time. It was easy to confuse which time was which.

Once back outside, I referred to my map and wandered until I found the road that led to Cross Bath. When I got closer to the surprisingly modest structure, at the road's dead end, I listened to a walking guide with his group as he explained how the medieval bathhouse above the spring-well was constructed in the twelfth century. It took its name from the cross that stood in the center. At one point, virulently anti-Roman Catholic Henry VIII halted restoration. I'm surprised he didn't have it destroyed.

Cross Bath was Mary of Modena's bath. In 1687, grieving after her mother's death in Italy from pneumonia, Mary journeyed to Bath, desperately longing to conceive a male heir for her king. In ten years, Mary had suffered through two miscarriages, three stillborn births, and five infant deaths. Her health was weak, her sorrow unimaginable. Mary had begun to lose hope.

But ten months later, a son was born.

After Mary's visit, the existing cross, centered in the bath itself, was enlarged and embellished in her honor, but all that remains of the original bath interior is an elegant relief carving of a vase and one *paterae*, a broad, shallow dish. The name Cross Bath survived, though, as did its reputation as effective for barren women. I listened to the walking guide and imagined Mary of Modena's desperation, her ten losses, taking the baths for a last-ditch miracle. She was almost thirty and running out of seventeenth-century time. I could relate, given the miracle of Jesse's birth, after being told conception was virtually impossible.

Leaving Bath Street, I walked until the Parade Gardens loomed ahead. I looked down from a stone bridge and reflected on Mary of Modena's trip here. Below me, garden after lush garden of glorious color fanned out, but it was too neat and tidy for my taste. I could have explored Bath longer, but I focused on my mission. Just enough time for an afternoon journey to Stonehenge. Would this adventure, too, prove to be a game changer?

During Mary's time, roads in all parts of Britain were challenging. Many of them dated back to Roman times. Seventeenth-century *solo female* traveler, Celia Fiennes, wrote, "Respectable ladies are sometimes taken to church in ox-drawn wagons and Sussex men and animals have grown long-legged from pulling their feet out of clay."[3]

Before 1690, there were few signposts in Britain. A fledgling stagecoach service was established in 1660, but they were slow, averaging thirty miles a day and expensive. Attacks from robbers were common. Naturally, private coaches were faster, but even royal coaches weren't exempt from accidents. Once, the royal coach hit a rut and fell over, with James and King Charles II inside.

I imagined Mary and her entourage bumping along in slow-moving black and crested royal coaches through the English wilderness—too early to call it countryside. Travel for pleasure was still very unusual. This made Celia Fiennes more remarkable. She was born four years after Mary of Modena, in Salisbury, a fifteen-minute modern-day drive to Stonehenge and a one-hour drive from Bath. Her family wealth—and her single status—likely explained the freedom and opportunity Celia had for such adventurous travel. She rode sidesaddle through every county in England, and she traveled alone except for two servants. The journal she kept, later published as *Celia Fiennes, Through England on a Side Saddle in the Time of William and Mary*, was first publicly published in 1888. The title contains "in the time of William and Mary" and not "in the time of" any of the Stuart kings. There was no mention of Stuart kings in any part of her journal, either, though much of her travel would have been done during that time, including during the short reign of James II. If Mary of Modena had stopped at Stonehenge and lunched with her court, Celia would not have been welcome for a goblet of wine with Mary, nor would Celia have been enticed. What a topic of gossip she might have been. A true free female spirit. Were they jealous?

"I was trapped, but I didn't know I was trapped," Prince Harry had insisted to Oprah Winfrey during the infamous 2021 interview. "My father and my brother, they are trapped. They don't get to leave."[4]

The Bath Spa train station platform had a perfect view of where Mary, at that moment still the Duchess of York, might have lodged on the picturesque hillside overlooking the town, not knowing how soon she would be queen. Now, 350 years later, a couple affectionately waited for the train. I pondered their story. The man, in chinos, expensive loafers, and crisp white shirt, did not get on the train. They were parting. Across the train platform, I sensed their melancholy.

In complete contrast, once sitting on the train, I felt revitalized, musing out the window while passengers continued to board . . . mothers with children, businesspeople heading back for weekdays in London, older women returning from visits with sons and daughters. I found an unreserved seat in a facing-table grouping of four. No one occupied the other seats in the cluster yet, but the seats had stubs on the tops of their backrests that claimed they were reserved, listing in small print both the originating and the destination stations.

The carriage doors opened and two flustered women burst in, finding their reserved seats across from me. Boisterously, they told a hilarious tale of a very confused taxi driver. They were jolly, fun-loving English gals—best buds, Val and Julia, from Bradford-on-Avon, southeast of Bath, returning home from a "hen's weekend."

Julia was round and blond and hungover from Sambuca, an Italian anise-flavored liqueur. She mostly talked to her dad on her cell but she piped in occasionally. Scottish, dark-haired Val was married and the mother of two young girls. She and I chatted about the British education system and about finding our niches later in life. She was a hairdresser and dreamed of returning to school. I encouraged her. I asked her about British schools and the pros and cons of the National Health System.

"I know it sounds good," Julia said, "and yes, it is free. But the waiting time to be seen is often eighteen months or more and two years for elective surgery."

Outside, the landscape was hilly and close, breaking out to level pastureland, the Salisbury Plain. Julia pointed to a large white horse painted or carved on the hillside. The horse looked like it was made of chalk.

"What on earth?" I asked.

Julie explained. "There are at least twenty-four hill figures in Britain, over a dozen here in Wiltshire. Most of the white horses are chalk hill carvings. They'd cut away the top layer of soil on hillsides and expose the white chalk beneath. It's common in these parts. Seventy million years ago, these hillsides projected from a seabed."

"You're an ocean of information, pun intended," I teased.

"We had the history pounded into us in primary school."

I laughed back, thinking of my forced knowledge of the sedimentary rock formation that bordered the winding road from the heights to Cleveland's University Circle area and downtown. Every teacher on every field trip downtown mentioned it as every school bus descended.

"Come to think of it, love, there is actually a village—Uffington—yes, that's it, in Oxfordshire. They have a Chalking Day, you see. A cleaning ritual. Gone on for three thousand years, the teachers drilled into us." Julie continued. "Hammers, buckets of chalk, kneepads—they're all handed out and everyone is assigned an area. The chalkers kneel and smash the chalk to a paste, whitening the stony pathways in the grass inch by inch. Goodness."

I grabbed my camera. The stark contrast of the white shapes against green, grassy hills was stunning. Julie smiled and returned to her cell phone.

After we passed the towns of Ditton Marsh and Warminster, I said my goodbyes to the duo and exited the train at Salisbury. I bought a vending machine coach ticket in the station and then walked outside. To my left, the double-decker coach for Stonehenge was just pulling up. What terrific timing. Tourists returning from Stonehenge exited the bus.

A chubby, balding driver poked his head out. "Hallo. I'm Milton. I'll be right back, need a bathroom break."

Upon his return, he opened the door of the bus. One of the first in line, I snatched a prime front seat on the second level, like a second grader vying for first place in the recess line. Nothing but spacious plate glass in front of me. An international group of college students loaded, and I said a silent prayer of thanks for getting there early. I shared my seat row with a solemn young coed from China, Chen Li, I'm sure with her own story to tell. We politely introduced ourselves, but clearly we both preferred to think in solitude. I wasn't looking forward to more crowds, but I couldn't rationalize being so close to Stonehenge and not stopping. Besides, in 1684, Mary, as Duchess of York, had stopped there with James, on a trip to Salisbury, three years before her trip to Bath.

By the time the coach passed Aynsebury, clouds were forming in puffy layers, white to dark gray. They were low and ominous, somehow fitting. They lulled me into a hypnotic state. Passengers were subdued. We wound through the Wiltshire countryside, a spellbinding view through the expansive upper-deck windshield. Because I suffered from a chronic angry left-leg nerve, long-lasting vestiges of my only pregnancy, I popped one of my take-as-needed Gabapentin, which calmed the nerve. It would kick in before Stonehenge.

Piped through clear speakers, Milton was enlightening. Although the actual city of Salisbury was not established until the early thirteenth century, there had been a settlement in the area since prehistory. He pointed out antiquated green oak buildings and informed us that all the buildings would have looked like this in the 1200s.

Travel guides suggested visiting Stonehenge after peak hours and in precarious weather. Inadvertently, I had succeeded in both. The bus ascended a hill. On the other side, there it was. So used to seeing Stonehenge in books or documentaries, it took a minute to grasp that it was real. The site was well-organized, and the ticket line moved quickly. Emerging from a walking tunnel under the enormous parking lot, the crowd spread and thinned.

Somber Sunday skies created an otherworldly experience. We made our way around the stone circle, each at our own pace, in silence and awe. Low-lying clouds perfectly moody.

Thank goodness, wearing audio headgear further isolated tourists from one another. The British narrator was instructive. No written records remained, but many theories did. Radiocarbon dating indicated construction began in 2950 BC, completed in three phases over the next fifteen hundred years. The narrator helped put it into context. Stonehenge was constructed about the same period as the Minoan culture in Crete, one thousand years earlier than the Great Wall of China, two thousand years before Aztec constructions, and several centuries after the Great Pyramids of Egypt.

"Was it built as an astronomical observatory? An early calendar marking the seasons? A sun-worshipping cult? Was Stonehenge a place of healing—the primeval equivalent of Lourdes?" the audio's narrator asked. "Whatever religious, mystical, or spiritual elements were central to Stonehenge, its design functioned to observe the sky."[5]

The "road trip" in 1684 from Winchester to Salisbury had been James's effort to cheer Mary up. She had miscarried again a few months before. Maybe that August day, when the royal coterie stopped at Stonehenge with Mary clueless that she would be the queen in a mere year, she and her ladies sat among the mystical lichen-covered bluestones, a coven of striking, pampered enchantresses in their silks and satin, feasting without Celia Fiennes but with fine wine, sharing writing, wit, and conversations only women can share. I knew there had to be bluestocking—intellectual or literary women—societies before the term had been coined in the eighteenth century by Elizabeth Montague, founder of the Blue Stocking Society.[6] Women's intellectual circles couldn't have popped up in an instant. There had to be a progression, and I aimed to discover what part Mary played in its evolution.

Back in Milton's bus, I absorbed lush rolling countryside, winding roads, Queen Anne's lace, and willow trees. English gardens everywhere. Skies still ominous. Far away, low rumblings of thunder but no rain. Damn, it was a nice bus.

On the South Western Railway train returning to Oxford from Salisbury, again in a table group, I talked with a young mother knitting a blue blanket for her one-year-old son. She was returning from a three-day business trip in Bristol. She also had a four-year-old daughter. We talked about the universal dilemma of having children and juggling. We talked about how fun child-rearing was and how fast it went. We talked about chasing dreams and about the beauty of England.

When the train slowed down to stop at Radley, I smelled honeysuckle through the open window and saw clusters of wild daisies. I watched a boy feed his chickens, then a man with his bicycle running to catch the train. My mind wandered back to Mary and her ladies at Stonehenge. It reminded me of the Moon Circle, a sacred gathering of women, of which I was honored to be a member in Nashville, when Jesse was a toddler.

Teresa Rumbo, member of the Potawatomi Nation and the daughter of famed artist Tepper Rumbo, hosted the circle in her elegant Belle Meade home. Women came together to honor and celebrate the new and full moon. In ancient communities, this circle was used to call in the divine feminine, the spiritual concept that there was a feminine counterpart to patriarchal worship norms. The circle served as a way of grounding, centering, and receiving higher wisdom. Being in this moon circle was my first journey into mindfulness.

Teresa was the wife of one of American music's preeminent artist managers/agents. She befriended me when we first moved to Nashville. I hadn't yet gained my confidence, so, per usual, I was amazed she would honor me with a dear friendship. Teresa belonged in two polar worlds. First, there was the Teresa who drove me in her Jaguar to the upscale Green Hills boutique, Gus Mayer, where she urged me to spend big bucks on shoes and clothing. Second, she was a spiritual "Daughter of the Wind," who invited me into her sacred moon circle where women could renew their hearts, minds, and spirits.

I lost Teresa's calming friendship in my divorce.

I miss her. I think she is back in her native Oklahoma now.

I wore one of the Gus Mayer tops for a photo shoot for *People Magazine* when they did a feature on Manuel. My fifteen seconds. Now I wonder if maybe Manuel had asked Teresa to take me shopping! My tastes ran toward willowy vintage. When he dressed me, it was in impossibly form-fitting designs. Once he even tossed out a cherished, flowy vintage creation of gray silk chiffon with exquisite black bugle beading when I had asked him to shorten the delicate long sleeves. I don't think I expressed the anger I felt. I would today.

I will always remember one particular moon circle.

About twelve gathered in a circle on the floor, in Teresa's airy sunroom. Her hand reached into the cast iron chimenea, lighting sage to cleanse the space. After the opening prayer and guided meditation, Teresa asked us to share a fervent wish.

When the talking stick reached me, I said, "I want to give my daughter the gift of being fearless."

I desperately wanted Jesse to be unburdened from insecurity and fear.

She *is* the most fearless person I know, strong and successful, thriving in her professional and personal life. The only things that scare her are life-size Easter bunnies. Thank you, higher power. Thank you, Teresa.

IT WAS DARK BY THE TIME I RETURNED HOME to Painter's Cottage from the train station. I was physically tired but emotionally invigorated by the day. I had made good use of time, experiencing a magical Sunday. It felt good to have a familiar home base to return to. Tomorrow, I would continue my manuscript search.

I lay down to sleep. A guest in the adjoining room was sobbing.

Chapter Thirteen:

Queenie Parties

———⟨∘⟩———

MONDAY. I KNEW HOW TO SCAN MY READER card. I knew where the Special Collections' locker room was *and* how to work the lock's mechanism. Saturday's beginner feelings, like those from the first days of middle school, were gone. I still cringe at the memory of being laughed at in the cafeteria after spilling my lunch tray. It feels more like I belong today. Confidence forty years in the making!

Books ordered on Saturday before leaving Special Collections had arrived from their storage beds. I signed in. The circulation desk librarian brought my requests from the back. I picked up a braided coil weight (called a "book snake") used to keep pages in place and, being a creature of habit, beelined to the space I had used on Friday. The gray foam book cradle was ready. I connected my American plug to the UK jack, plugged in my laptop, turned on my light, arranged my "tools," and got to work.

I could photograph pages of manuscript, though I had to provide a slip for *each* one, deposited in a wooden box on the librarians' desk. No one talked in this library. Conversation was only through slight hints of smiles. The gray-haired, slightly built academic who worked in my row all week never registered my existence. I must have been wearing my cloak of invisibility, compulsory fashion for middle-aged women.

I was sensing a shift in focus regarding my work. *I paid attention to it.*

I saw life in grays, rarely black and white. Labels never worked for me. I used to pooh-pooh the feminist label. However, in the middle of my reading, I found offensive claims about women, by men, such as this quote from François Rabelais, circa 1494–1553, a major French Renaissance writer and humanist, doctor, monk, and Greek scholar. On the eve of the seventeenth century, his French treatise declared woman was not fully human, not endowed with soul, and not created in the male image of God. He decreed woman as the product of her animal side, her sexual nature:

> For Nature has placed inside their bodies in a secret intestinal place an animal, a member, which is not in man, in which sometimes are engendered certain saline, nitrous, boracic, acrid, biting, shooting, bitterly tickling humors, through whose prickling and grievous wriggling the entire body is shaken, all the senses ravished, all inclinations unleashed, all thought confounded.[1]

Animals in acidic-soaked female intestines causing orgasms? Sounds like QAnon to me. In all seriousness, I was reexamining my attitude toward the feminist label. I think I felt above labeling, an arrogance I am not proud of, similar to my condescension toward tourists—only worse. I am a Russian-Jewish descendant of resilient struggle, but it has always been vague . . . out there like a cloud. I was much more aware of civil rights for people of color than civil rights for women. How often did I use my looks as power? I regret that is my truth. But then I wonder, if that was a way to command power, was it wrong to use? I don't have the answer. I do know, though, that all the liberties and choices we women have are thanks to these ancient warriors.

As I skimmed and read, I found little detail about a woman's day-to-day, not to mention anything provocative concerning women's intellect. That was cause for such disappointment. Women weren't regarded enough to record their comings and goings, thoughts, or writing. Women could not initiate divorce or possess property, and upon a father's or husband's death, household property passed onto male heirs, the Mancini sisters wrote in their memoirs.[2] One of my favorite authorities on Renaissance writers, Harvard professor Barbara Lewalski, writes that since we have only recently begun to analyze these early women's texts, not much is known about how early modern Englishwomen "read and wrote themselves and their world."[3] Lewalski encourages research: "There is still much more archival and historical work to be done in this rich, comparative field."[4]

How would I find information on Mary's court? The only original correspondence from Mary of Modena that I found in Special Collections were thank-you notes and acceptances to invitations. (Thank you, former French teachers; I could loosely translate them.) Shamefully, I do not have a photo of even one of the letters. *And I am a scholar?*

Richard Braithwaite's rants in *The English Gentlewoman*, 1631, were equally as nauseating as Rabelais's:

Women are woe to men; No, they're the way, To bring them homeward when they run astray. . . .

What a furious and inconsiderate thing is Woman when Passion distempers her? . . .

If you (woman) cannot appease nor compose your inward Commotion, at least restraine your tongue, an inioyne [enjoin] it silence . . .

Now Gentlewomen . . . to enter into much discourse or familiarity with strangers, argues lightnesse or indiscretion: What is spoken of Maids, may be properly appllyed by an avfefull consequence to all women: They should be seene and not heard.[5]

But take heed!

Here is a counterpoint: Mary Astell's 1701 *A Serious Proposal to the Ladies for the Advancement of their True and Greatest Interest* is a fine response to Braithwaite's drivel:

How can you be content to be in the World like Tulips in a Garden, to make a fine shew and be good for nothing . . . For shame let's abandon, No longer drudge on in the dull beaten road of Vanity and Folly which so many have gone before us, but dare to break the enchanted Circle that custom has plac'd us in. Let us learn to pride ourselves in something more excellent than the invention of a Fashion, and not entertain such a degrading thought of our own worth, as to imagine that our Souls were given us only for the service of our Bodies, and that the best improvement we can make of these, is to attract the Eyes of Men. We value them too much and ourselves too little . . . if we . . . don't think our selves capable of Nobler Things than the pitiful Conquest of some worthless heart.

The Ladies, I'm sure, have no reason to dislike this Proposal, but I know not how the Men will resent it to have their enclosure broke down, and Women

invited to tast of that Tree of knowledge they have so
long unjustly Monopoliz'd. But they must excuse me,
if I be as partial to my own Sex as they are to theirs.

My own feminist arc is messy and roundabout, but what
the early feminists had to deal with is unfathomable compared to the modern fight for women's equality. Women were
property—they had *no* rights. Their voices were rarely heard
at this time. Women writers were uncommon and published
works by women rarer still. For most women, the only record
of their lives was in the registration of baptisms, marriages,
and funerals.

This makes Mary's court even more extraordinary.
Where had I been? The more I read, the more I felt com-
passion mixed with anger. Was that why I had cried when
the camera panned the *Treasure House* staircase, twenty-five
years before, when I sensed a past life? Had I been a woman
of those times without an identity, without any power of my
own, without self?

With my research path coming more into focus, I was
feeling loads of energy. I am not an authority of women's
studies, merely an explorer. My intent is to share my quest
with other women. Just as I have held dear and nurtured
my women writers' groups, my women's book groups, and
my women's social circles—past and present—I can imagine
millions of groups of women who treasure their own collec-
tives, as I am a part of the Queenies forever. We Queenies
have stuck together. Only sweet Fell is gone, after a valiant
struggle with cancer.

She had always wanted to be called Queenie; that's how we
got our name. Once she shared this tidbit with us, we presented
her with a tiara, which she wore proudly to every get-together.
During Fell's illness, we threw one of our Queenie parties in
her cozy log cabin on Flat Creek Road. She was bald from

chemo by this time, her dark straight pixie cut streaked with gray now gone. We propped her tiara on the front-room mantel, made from a poplar tree from their woods.

We may not get together often these days, but it doesn't matter. Our circle remains unbroken. They are my village. We raised our children together. We stayed strong—mostly—together. College buds, Meg and Taz, came to my second wedding. We danced for hours in the barn hayloft Tony and I had renovated for the reception. When we were proceeding down the grassy path to the wooden ceremony platform where our dear friend, an Episcopal priest, waited to begin the wedding ceremony, I saw Taz and Meg, screamed in exclamation, and left Tony standing in the aisle to hug them.

I know how important it is to have support of women friends: I hope my seventeenth-century counterparts had the same gift. Mary of Modena encouraged her maids of honor to translate Greek and Latin poetry and Italian romances. She wrote and spoke French and had a good knowledge of Latin, and she quickly learned to speak English, though she never adjusted to English spelling. Mary's support of the literary and artistic in court, through participation and patronage, allowed them a world of theater and art and an idyllic world of female friendship.

With religious controversy such a constant in her life, including political exiles to Scotland and Belgium, I am impressed that Mary's court thought about or created anything artistic. Kudos.

Who would I fantasize joined Mary's Stonehenge Queenie party? Which writerly women sat with Mary among the blue-stones? Which female artists would lunch alfresco with a queen determined to recover from the grief of miscarriage?

Chapter Fourteen:

Pretty Maids All in a Row

———— ❧ ————

I'D START WITH APHRA BEHN. DARK HAIRED with rounded brows deeming her more cute than pretty, she'd be a spicy addition to any party. While she was preceded by numerous female writers, notably Katherine Phillips and Margaret Cavendish, Behn was the first to consider herself a writer by profession, one "forced to write for Bread and not ashamed to owne it."[1] Other women of her time claimed their poetry was merely the product of leisure time in country solitude, designed only to entertain their friends.[2]

Born Aphra Johnson in Kent, near Canterbury, in 1640, possibly to a barber and wet nurse, little is known of Aphra's education. Biographical information is vague, and sources claim Behn wanted it that way.

As a young woman, Aphra likely lived in Surinam, on the northeastern Atlantic coast of South America. Returning to London, she married a Dutch merchant in 1664 who died a year later. Notably, she served King Charles II as a spy in the Netherlands for two years. In debt when Charles II failed to pay her for her services, Aphra landed in debtors' prison. How Trumpish.

Aphra Behn by Sir Peter Lely, c. 1670
CREDIT: Peter Lely, public domain, via Wikimedia Commons

Aphra Behn traded espionage for the theater successfully, writing increasingly political plays for the Duke's Theatre. More than once, she collaborated with Nell Gwyn, the famed actress and a mistress to King Charles II.[3] When Behn's plays grew increasingly suggestive, the public criticized her as a libertine. Though under attack for her assumed illicit ways and subject to seventeenth-century sexism, she continued to write. Behn's plays were well received by the public, but she continued to suffer criticism for the wild sexual content, tame compared to today.

In her early forties, Behn was arrested briefly for an epilogue that attacked the eldest illegitimate son of Charles II.[4] She turned to other forms of writing, including poetry, again successfully. Surprisingly, considering her reputation as a wild child, Aphra's favorite genre appears to be pastoral,[5] although she was primarily an urban woman. Pastorals allowed her to say what she wanted to say about love. When Charles II died in 1685 and Mary of Modena's husband, James II, succeeded to the throne, Behn was a loyal supporter. After John Dryden, she was the most prolific dramatist of the Restoration.

Behn was obsessed with Mary of Modena's beauty. Aphra devoted almost eight hundred lines in celebration of Mary as patron in her 1685 lyric poem.[6] She saw Mary's court with its relative freedom for women as empowering, since exceptional women, whether writers or artists, could flourish there. Even John Caryll, Mary's private secretary, was a scholar and poet. "Mary Beatrice was sung by the poets."[7]

Although Aphra Behn herself was not a member of the court, she wished to be rewarded with money and position there. There is little conclusive evidence that Behn moved in court or aristocratic circles; however, she was rumored to be the mistress of a fellow poet, the Earl of Rochester.

Aphra Behn was only forty-nine when she died. She is buried in the cloisters of Westminster Abbey in Poets' Corner. Today critics judge her on her merits alone, not her lifestyle. Her career broke ground for all women who came after, which prompted Virginia Woolf's now-famous lines from *A Room of One's Own*: "All women should let flowers fall upon Aphra Behn's tomb . . . for she earned them the right to speak their minds."

As long as I am fantasizing about a Stonehenge Queenie party, I must include gentle writer Mary Astell, born in 1666, hailed today because of her outspoken beliefs that focused on the education of women and her thoughts concerning marriage. Dubbed England's first feminist, Astell was from northern England's Newcastle upon Tyne. Her parents were members of the merchant class, so Mary was likely self-taught. By 1684, both parents had died. Mary moved to the Chelsea district of London. Philanthropist Lady Catherine Jones was her patron. Lady Catherine's prominence in court circles allowed Mary Astell to connect to several well-educated women interested in changing the status of women. Later in life, Astell and Jones created a charity school for girls. The school remained active until the late nineteenth century.

Mary Astell had more than Lady Catherine's connection to Mary's court. The unhappiness of one of Mary Astell's neighbors—none other than Mary of Modena's aunt, the Duchess of Mazarine, Hortense Mancini—compelled Astell to write *Some Reflections upon Marriage Occasioned by the Duke and Duchess of Mazarine's Case in 1700*. In it, Astell counseled women not to marry out of duty or to escape the hardships of life but to make their decisions based on reason. Hortense, the beautiful adventuress, was then thirty-eight years old, one of the richest women in Europe, and had no marital power.

It is not beyond reality to imagine that Hortense could have been part of the royal entourage passing through Stonehenge in 1684, with her niece, twenty-six-year-old Mary of Modena. Perhaps Hortense would have invited her young eighteen-year-old neighbor, Astell, to accompany the royal party and picnic with Mary that day at Stonehenge. An affirmed bisexual, Aphra Behn, in her introduction to her novella, *The History of the Nun*, implied a relationship with Hortense. At age thirty-eight and forty-four respectively, they would have been experienced mentors for Astell. So there were two connections between Mary Astell and the court of Mary of Modena. Ironically and sadly, Astell died from the predominantly female affliction of breast cancer, at age sixty-five.

Another woman writer of the time was fiction writer and poet Jane Barker (1652–1732), thirty-two years old at the time of Mary's trip to Stonehenge.

Jane Barker engraving, 1736

CREDIT: Reprinted with permission from Special Collections,
Kenneth Spencer Research Library, University of Kansas.

Jane was a devoted Jacobite and followed Mary and James into exile. She was one of the small number of individuals who maintained residence at Le Château Saint-Germain-en-Laye, outside of Paris; Louis XIV had turned over the chateau to the exiled James and Mary. Barker was born north of London to an unlanded Roman Catholic family. Fortunately, her brother believed she had an equal right to education. Edward, an Oxford student, taught Jane Latin, anatomy, and herbal medicine. Of course she couldn't attend university. It wasn't until 1920 that women were first admitted to Oxford.

Barker worked to alleviate the stigma of remaining single, to make it an acceptable alternative to marriage. Barker enjoyed her freedom from men in her own personal life. She established herself as a published female author, whose print works were primarily for a female audience. Relying upon income from her later publications for money, Barker had more freedom and independence than other female authors of the early modern period. Her work displays a strong feminist bent, writing about her alternatives to marriage, female education, and politics. I see her as too independent to blend in with Mary's court, but I'm willing to bet money that Jane came up in spicy conversation, along with talk about Margaret Cavendish.

Margaret Cavendish, Duchess of Newcastle, 1623–1673, died suddenly at age fifty, the year Mary and James married. Therefore, she would not have been at Stonehenge with Mary eleven years later, but Margaret was important as a precursor to the female writers who followed. She was twenty years older than Aphra Behn, to put them in context. Regal Margaret Cavendish, Duchess of Newcastle, was the most talked of "learned lady" of the Restoration period, 1660–1688.

Margaret Lucas Cavendish, Duchess of Newcastle,
by Sir Peter Lely, 1665
CREDIT: Peter Lely, public domain, via Wikimedia Commons

Margaret wrote in her own name in a period when most women writers remained anonymous. As with Mary of Modena, Margaret's mother was widowed young with a substantial fortune. In her autobiography,[8] written when she was only thirty-three in response to the criticism for her life-style choices, the Duchess of Newcastle describes a family life of splendor and luxury—so wealthy that a monument by the sculptor Grinling Gibbons was erected in Westminster Abbey, where she is interred. While only taught the basics of reading and writing early on, Margaret wanted to be known as both a wit and a beauty. She was determined to excel in literature. She yearned to be famous.

Margaret's family were devoted Royalists, eventually exiling to Oxford with the royal family when the civil war broke out in England in 1640. There, Margaret became a maid of honor to Charles I's wife, Queen Henrietta Maria, eventually fleeing with the queen and her court to France. Cavendish remained a maid of honor for two more years, until she married William Cavendish, Marquis of Newcastle, later made duke. The couple was able to return to England and the duke's ruined estates, Welbeck Abbey—now a restored vast country house—in North Nottinghamshire, one hundred miles north of London. Unsuccessfully, I tried to squeeze it into my itinerary. Next trip!

When Margaret returned to England, she wrote her first book, *Poems and Fancies, 1653*, a collection of poems, epistles, and prose. Cavendish, like authors such as Aphra Behn and William Wordsworth, stated her intended audience, writing purpose, and philosophy in prefaces, prologues, epilogues, and epistles. In her preface to *Observations upon Experimental Philosophy* (1664), the duchess wrote that "woman's wit" may equal that of man, and women may be able to learn as easily as men.[9] Cavendish argued that the only difference was that men had more opportunity to educate themselves. This caused a sensation. Critics thought her mad. They ridiculed both her writing and the outrageous and original costumes she wore in public. She enjoyed inventing herself through fashion. She disliked wearing the same fashions as other women. (Shades of Lady Gaga.) Margaret aimed to be unique in her dress, thoughts, and behavior.[10]

My kind of girl!

The duchess was capable of bold feminist statements. She expected criticism for her memoir, *The Life of William Cavendish, Duke of Newcastle, to Which Is Added the True Relation of My Birth, Breeding and Life,* and responded by declaring she was as justified in writing her memoirs as men were. Cavendish delighted in writing, connecting it to her desire for contemplation and solitude. She once compared women to birds in cages.[11] Cavendish wrote, "Women live like bats or owls, labor like beasts, and die like worms."[12]

Margaret Cavendish fought against the gender discrimination she faced but was able to publish twenty-two works during her lifetime and wrote one of the first works of science fiction, *The Blazing World*, in 1666. She was one of the most original thinkers of the age. Her modern reputation is of a truly remarkable woman. If I were on a quiz show and the emcee asked, *Who is a deceased woman you would most love to dine with?* my answer just might be Margaret Cavendish, Duchess of Newcastle.

Here's to you, "Mad Marge"!

So who *were* the women writers in Mary's court who would have accompanied her as she traveled?

Anne Kingsmill Finch, daughter of Sir John Kingsmill, was born at Sydmonton Court, Hampshire, now the home of Andrew Lloyd Webber. She is the most well-known poet from Mary's court and the thread that led me to Mary. (See chapter twenty-five.) Anne was maid of honor to Mary when she was Duchess of York.

Sarah Jennings Churchill, Duchess of Marlborough, is known today from the movie *The Favourite*. She eventually became one of the most influential women in British history, but at the time she was a good friend of Mary of Modena. She entered court as maid of honor to Mary of Modena and served until she married John Churchill, first Duke of Marlborough. When James and Mary as Duke and Duchess of York went into self-imposed exile in Scotland, John and Sarah accompanied them. Charles II rewarded John's loyalty by creating him Baron Churchill of Eyemouth in Scotland; thus Sarah became Lady Churchill.

Sarah Churchill, Duchess of Marlborough, by Sir Godfrey Kneller
CREDIT: Godfrey Kneller, public domain, via Wikimedia Commons

She was a strong-willed woman who liked to get her own way. The Duchess of Marlborough was a capable business manager, unusual in a period when men excluded women from most things outside the management of their household. She coauthored *Poems on Several Occasions*, published in 1738. She also had her memoirs published, *Memoirs of Sarah, Duchess of Marlborough: Together with Her Characters of Her Contemporaries and Her opinions*, as well as her letters, *An Account of the Conduct of the Dowager Duchess of Marlborough: From Her First Coming to Court to the Year 1710*, published in 1742, two years before her death, and *Letters of a Grandmother, 1732–1735: Being the Correspondence of Sarah, Duchess of Marlborough with Her Granddaughter Diana, Duchess of Bedford*.

During the rule of Queen Anne—Mary of Modena's stepdaughter—besides the queen, Sarah was considered the most powerful woman in England. Her wealth was so considerable, she hoped to marry her granddaughter, Lady Diana Spencer, to Frederick, Prince of Wales. Politics intervened. However, 226 years later, in 1961, Diana Frances Spencer, who *would* marry the Prince of Wales, was born to Viscount Althorp, the direct descendant of the first Lady Diana. Sarah Jennings Churchill, Duchess of Marlborough, was the ancestor of the Earls Spencer and thus of Diana, Princess of Wales. That is why one sometimes reads that Lady Diana, Princess of Wales, had more royal blood than the Windsors.

Facilitated by family connections, Anne Killigrew was one of six maids of honor to Mary of Modena, as Duchess of York. She was exposed to art and literature by her readerly family and was encouraged to pursue her creative talents. Growing up, she received instruction in both poetry and painting, encouraged by her mother, Judith Killigrew, a lady-in-waiting to Charles II's queen, Catherine d'Braganza. Judith was a talented lute musician. Anne's father, Dr. Henry Killegrew, was chaplain to Charles I and later James II, when he was Duke of York. Henry Killigrew published several sermons and poems as well as a play. Anne's two paternal uncles were also published playwrights. Uncle Thomas not only wrote plays but held a royal patent for his famed theater company, the King's Company. He also built the well-known theater now known as The Drury. The family's illustrious ties to the Stuart Court go back to James I, 1566–1625. Imagine their Christmas dinner conversations!

Anne Killigrew, self-portrait, c. 1685
CREDIT: Anne Killigrew, public domain, via Wikimedia Commons

Residing at court, Killigrew was a companion of strong, intelligent women who encouraged her writing career as much as their own. Skilled at portraiture, scholars believe Killigrew painted fifteen paintings. Both her poems and her paintings emphasize women and nature. Tragically, Anne died at age twenty-five from smallpox. Soon after Killigrew's death, a short book of thirty-three of her poems was published by her father as a memorial. Before 2009, none of her poems were known to exist in manuscript form, but then a small number were found among the papers of the John Evelyn family at the British Library. She is buried at Westminster Abbey in the Savoy Chapel monument.

Lady Isabella Wentworth was the daughter of Sir Allen Apsley, Treasurer of the Household to James, Duke of York, later James II. She became a lady of the bedchamber to Queen Mary of Modena. Isabella also grew up in a family that supported women's learning. Her paternal aunt, child-prodigy Lucy Hutchinson, was a noted poet, biographer, and translator.

Family encouragement is a repeating theme for these early female authors.

Catherine Sedley, Countess of Dorchester, daughter of poet Sir Charles Sedley, Fifth Baronet of Aylesford, in Kent, published *Poems by Anna Seward and Catherine Sedley, Countess of Dorchester, 1657–1717*. She was mistress to James II while he was both duke and king and mother of one of his daughters, Catherine Darnley. Becoming a mistress in the 1660s was almost a career choice. Sedley was independently wealthy but chose to become a mistress. Mary of Modena loathed Catherine. Sound familiar?

> *"Well, there were three of us in this marriage,*
> *so it was a bit crowded."*
> —LADY DIANA, Princess of Wales

Mary once said, "Give her my dower, make her Queen of England, but let me see her no more!"[13]

Catherine Sedley, Countess of Dorchester, by Peter Cross, c. 1685
CREDIT: Peter Cross (circa 1645–1724), public domain,
via Wikimedia Commons

Mary was so disturbed that James expelled Catherine from court, but later he put her in apartments nearby. That sounds familiar, too. Maybe it was her Lily Collins eyebrows.

Anna Scott, Duchess of Monmouth, Duchess of Buccleuch in her own right, was married to Charles II's eldest illegitimate son, the Duke of Monmouth. She was an attendant in Mary's coronation, leading the eight duchesses in Mary's coronation procession. Known for her literary and artistic patronage, she was one of the earliest patrons of the famed artist Godfrey Kneller.

Isabella Boynton, Countess of Roscommon, was maid of honor to the Duchess of York and lady of the bedchamber when Mary of Modena became queen. Isabella was the wife of Irish poet Wentworth Dillon, fourth Earl of Roscommon, master of the horse to the Duchess of York. Roscommon formed a small literary society, which formulated rules on language and style. They were very close to famed poet and court loyalist John Dryden, England's first poet laureate.[14] Isabella, though not a writer herself, would have been a part of the literary scene and most likely encouraged the female writers in Mary's court.

Not all of Mary's attendants were cerebral.[15] The famed auburn-haired beauty Frances Theresa Stuart, Duchess of Richmond, was one of the Windsor Beauties, the famous collection of oil portraits by legendary Sir Peter Lely.

Frances Theresa Stuart, Duchess of Richmond
and Lennox, by Sir Peter Lely, c. 1662
CREDIT: Peter Lely, public domain, via Wikimedia Commons

Nineteenth-century poet and historian John Heneage Jesse commented, "A beautiful simpleton . . . unfortunately, her head was as empty as its shape was classical and her amusements as frivolous as her face was beautiful."[16] She *did* love the theater, though, and Frances helped Mary of Modena appreciate British theater. Stuart was well-received at the court of James II and attended Mary during the birth of James Francis Edward in 1688, signing the certificate. Frances is buried in Westminster Abbey.

Mary and her entourage may have lunched at Stonehenge, but all of these women buried in Westminster Abbey, now *that* is a Queenie party.

So far, though Mary created an environment that encouraged the arts, it would seem her court was appointed through family connections. Not even a queen had that kind of power. However, I was not giving up in looking for feminist connections.

After one week working in Special Collections, it was my last day there. I found *unbelievable* seventeenth-century pencil sketches of the port of Calais in one manuscript. Imagine pencil sketches from four hundred years ago. Being on the short side, I stood up on a library stool to photograph the largest one and was promptly scolded by a librarian. I felt like one of my middle school students. It kind of felt good to be reprimanded. When I was young, I tried so hard to be the good girl.

I finished in Special Collections and decided to explore and take photographs to refer to for future oil paintings.

Approaching St. Paul's

CREDIT: painting by author

Saturday was the perfect day to watch Oxford unfold. People spilled out into the streets, mixing antiquity with the contemporary. I rested my aching feet in a bookstore and when I emerged, I found it had rained. I learned early on to keep an umbrella and hat in my backpack at all times. Six years before, the last time I had been there, England was suffering through an intense drought. I remember Peter saying that because of restrictions on watering gardens, he would take his plants into the shower with him. Not a problem this summer. The weather's moodiness suited me, as well as the cool temperatures. I don't think the thermometer reached seventy. I relished the afternoon.

Eventually making my way back to Painter's Cottage, I passed "the sobber" in the hallway before leaving. She was a small, pale woman with bleached-blonde hair. We shared greetings. What had made her cry so long and so hard? Her eyes were red-rimmed even now. What was her feminist arc, I wondered?

I hauled a pillowcase of laundry down Cowley Road to the laundromat about six blocks away. In the morning, I was taking a Sunday train into London for a five-day stay to visit palaces, return to the National Portrait Gallery, and hopefully spend a day at the British Library looking at a few more manuscripts. I planned on a Thames River cruise, as well, to Greenwich to visit the National Maritime Museum. I was hoping for a sense of seventeenth-century water travel, particularly how Mary might have escaped to France in 1688.

After a week in London, my plan was to train to Cambridge for a day or two before returning to Oxford and the Bod. Cambridge University had given me permission to read an unpublished dissertation I had been jonesing for. Following the intensity of a week in Special Collections, London was great timing. Online and using a good map of London, I had decided on lodging near Victoria Station. I reserved five nights at a small hotel off Belgrave Road, centrally located in Pimlico for most of my jaunts. When I returned to Oxford, I would devote more time to the Bodleian, a majority in the Duke Humfrey's Reading Room, before taking off to Kent to find the invisible footprints of Anne Finch, Countess of Winchilsea. Not only had the countess been one of Mary's ladies-in-waiting; she was also the most famous English woman poet of the seventeenth century.

But first, London beckoned.

Chapter Fifteen:

Loving London

———— ·⟨♥⟩· ————

I *LOVE* LONDON. IT IS A WALKING/SUBWAY city. Imagine the vibrancy of New York City with British flair. I packed lightly for a change.

The mellow train ride into London's Paddington Station was lovely. I talked to my tablemate, Glenn, a small-business owner. Pre-Brexit, we touched on the euro-dollar exchange rate and his interesting predictions. As an Oxford alum, he gave me some information about Oxford and travel. We also talked about how and why Brits love coming to the United States to visit and live.

"The same things you find intimate and charming get old," he said, "when you have to deal with them daily."

It was raining when I emerged from Victoria Station, having transferred trains at Paddington, so my walk to the Grapevine Hotel was under my ubiquitous umbrella, a cheap purchase from Boots pharmacy. You get what you pay for. The handle had already fallen off. Mary Poppins would not approve.

My hotel room was smaller than tiny—a twin bed and nightstand were all it contained—but it was ensuite *and* it had a ceiling fan, though it shook and rattled on high speed right above the bed. If it fell, I would be decapitated. Still, I was satisfied. The room also had a narrow casement window, overlooking the angled ledges from buildings across the way. Throughout the first night, pigeons cooed. They invaded my dreams, a nightmare of a huge black bird flying into my car and my ex-husband, Manuel, driving and scolding me for worrying. I was screaming.

I am phobic about birds. I stepped on a dead one once in my bare feet, walking home from school, and that was it. I can still feel the squish. I was afraid one would fly into the hotel room, so from then on, reluctantly, I closed the window to just a sliver at night.

I dropped my bags, turned on the precarious fan, washed my gritty hands in the miniature bathroom sink, and headed for Leicester Square in search of my reserved London Pass and Travel Card. Emerging to street level from the tube station, I smelled cigars and tuna fish. My first sight was a man wearing a Cleveland Indians ball cap. My hometown. My beloved team. Will I ever get used to "Guardians"?

I found the tourist office on Charing Cross Road and descended a narrow spiral iron stairway where two friendly, bouffant-haired young women helped me. Holding onto the iron railing—I am accident prone—I emerged again to street level, London Pass in hand. I was directly across from the National Gallery entrance.

Beginner's luck.

I entered the iconic museum with vivid memories of my last visit with Peter and the five others from my tutorial. I made a beeline through a wide rounded archway to Room 9. Herringbone-patterned golden oak floors, luscious cream ceiling trim, stately gilt-framed portraits on muted caramel walls. Yes, in Room 9, the members of the Kit-Cat Club[1] still gathered, though in life they met in Christopher (Kit) Catt's tavern on Shire Lane, now the Royal Courts of Justice.

Despite their lighthearted name and reputation for drinking, the Kit-Cat Club was the most sophisticated club in London. Sir Godfrey Kneller painted the member portraits over twenty years. They believed that Parliament should have authority over monarchy. Kit-Cats steadfastly believed a Protestant ruler should succeed to the throne. Definitely not in Mary and James's corner, pun intended.

Crossing through the next archway, in Room 8, a Lely portrait of James II shared a wall with Dutch master William Wissing's painting of Mary of Modena.

King James II, by Sir Peter Lely, c. 1665–1670
CREDIT: © National Portrait Gallery, London;
reprinted with permission.

Mary of Modena, by William Wissing, c. 1685
CREDIT: © National Portrait Gallery, London;
reprinted with permission.

The two royals were a striking couple, although James's portraits suggest that a sneer habitually marred his smallpox-scarred face. Writes Mary Hopkirk, "He was cold, haughty, and aloof."[2] Further, "James surrounded himself only with flatterers and was allergic to any expression of popular opinion, however courteously given."

Well, well, doesn't that sound—*cough, cough, Trump*—familiar.

I sat in front of Mary's portrait for some time, trying to "sense" her. She did not show herself. Next, I circled the galleries, searching for the ladies—the mistresses of Charles II, the notorious libertine and James II's more likeable brother, who fathered a hoard of bastards, called "natural children" back then.[3]

Six years before, Peter had lectured in front of many of the paintings. I was certain. I couldn't find them. I never asked a docent, though: I was wrapped in my cocoon of wonder and didn't feel like pricking it. Later, in the gift shop, I ordered a poster-sized print of Wissing's Mary painting and had it delivered home. She would keep me company as I wrote.

Reluctantly, I moved on.

Using the map supplied by the lovely ladies from the London Pass ticket office, I walked back toward Belgravia. Strolling through Green Park, lovers read supine and families laughed together on a Sunday. I marveled at extraordinary gilded gates in the distance—what could they be? They were the Canada Gates of Buckingham Palace! Once again, I had wandered unwittingly into majesty—and unveiled my ignorance. The palace was big and stark to me, not inviting. Through crowds, I snapped the obligatory shots of the queens' guards. Later though, during the days of Queen Elizabeth's funeral, I was grateful that I could sense the space.

The highlight of my walk was wandering by Westminster Cathedral,[4] just as Sunday-eve service was starting. I went in and participated in the hour-long service.

Jesus's large wooden cross was exquisite and haunting, his likeness painted on. Behind him, a massive *baldacchino*, or sculpted canopy, rose above the high altar made of white and colored marble, pearl, lapis lazuli, and gold. Though surprisingly dusty, the grand circular chandeliers were gorgeous, positioned on either side down the main sanctuary. The cathedral, the most imposing and most important Catholic church in England, was a "marvel of extravagant Byzantine style . . . one of the most striking and impressive examples of neo-Byzantine architecture in Europe."[5] It was the mother church of the Catholic churches of England and Wales.

The cathedral was much smaller and more intimate than I imagined. The priest was Italian with an engaging style of speech. During communion, an elegant Black laywoman, who at first did not know what to do with my closed Hebrew hands, blessed me. When I left the church, the homeless solicited worshippers, the juxtaposition jarring and upsetting. They were camped on the footpaths, English for "sidewalks."

Walking farther, I stopped at St. George's Pub, within a short stroll from Victoria Street at Vauxhall Bridge, for a dark ale, delicious calamari, and creamy tomato soup. They had me at calamari! Pub "protocol" dictates customers go up to the bar to order, find a table, and wait for a server to deliver the order. So easy.

Back in the hotel room, to my amazement, the small wall-mounted television worked. I watched England lose to Italy in the Euro Cup matches. Funny how quickly I started rooting for England. I had a scare when my blood sugar suddenly dropped—quickly my face glistened with perspiration, my heart raced, and I grew weak, all extremely uncomfortable sensations. I only had one glucose tablet left, a warning as a diabetic to always keep more and not go all day without eating. There were packs of sugar on the tea tray and I hurriedly downed them like whiskey shots. Phew.

I read myself to sleep, window closed, pigeons out.

MY THIRD DAY IN LONDON. I SAT IN THE SMALL hotel breakfast room, drinking my morning coffee and trying—to no avail—for internet connection. I needed to contact the British Library about spending a day there later that week, to study manuscripts and follow up with Cambridge about coming to look at the unpublished thesis I wanted to read.

I walked into Victoria Station. A long-haired blonde in a diaphanous blue-and-green gown was busking. The Monday-morning rush-hour queue into the tube was so long,

I decided to amble. Another sunny day so far. It was too lovely to follow my initial plan to start with the Banqueting House, the only building that remained from the original Westminster Palace. When I saw the glittering Thames, I knew I needed to boat up to Greenwich instead. The ride up the river was refreshing in the open craft. Most of the passengers spoke in subdued foreign languages. Only a few hands rose when the guide asked in English if anyone could understand him.

After arriving in Greenwich, I lunched at a French café, taking advantage of internet access while waiting for a menu. Does it taste better when it is offered in French? Decidedly yes!

Next, I headed to the Maritime Museum for information on Mary and James's barge transportation.

My "scolding of the day" was from a sour young exhibit guard, this time for taking a photo inside the exhibit of a piece of ship emblem embroidery from 1662.

"It is posted on the door," she admonished.

Hours later, in the Courtauld Gallery, I asked the guard for permission.

With an engaging smile, he said, "Take as many as you like."

What exactly are the rules? I wondered. That should be my epitaph.

I left the return boat at Tower Pier to conserve time for Somerset House, where dowager queens resided in the seventeenth century. Catherine of Braganza lived there after the death of her husband, Charles II, James's brother. I took the tube, jumping on a District Line train at Tower Hill. Four stops down to Temple. A quick zip.

Gaining entrance to Somerset House from the grand Victoria Embankment, I took a rickety lift, then passed through Seaman's Hall to the impressive fountain court. On the left was the Courtauld Gallery, and on the right was the

Courtauld Institute of Art, a foremost center for the study of art history.[6]

I took time to play voyeur in the fountain court, watching a striking Indian model in dazzling dress and a pampered professional poodle-model, posing in separate photo shoots in the stone courtyard. Fountain sounds delighted.

Past the courtyard, inside the gallery, I descended to a well-appointed bathroom and locker room. There was already a pound in the lock tray. A good omen. I zigzagged back to what I realized was the Nelson Stair.[7] Looking up from the bottom was overpowering. The dramatic, soaring staircase resembled a beautiful white snail shell, alabaster walls, treads, and risers as one. A living sculpture.

I ascended to Strand Level, where I enjoyed a flirtatious interplay with a couple in the Cezanne room on the first floor, something referencing the portrait of Cezanne's *Man with a Pipe* above the fireplace. Each room had its own treasures, be they Van Gogh, Manet, or Gauguin, set off by crisp light-gray walls and carved white moldings. *Ahh, Provence, will I ever get there?*

I headed back to the large courtyard, removed a light garden chair from its table set, and sat in solitude. The models were gone. The sun had mellowed. I sipped on water, watching a small blond girl delight in the dancing fountain. She was totally oblivious to the adults sitting along the courtyard's side. It was my turn to play photographer.

Two American women took seats at a nearby table, their loud Boston-speak jarring after quiet foreign voices.

Exiting back through to the Riverside Terrace, I sat and map-read, away from the chic, canopied bars and inviting extra-large square white umbrellas. I relaxed in waning afternoon sun, protected from strong breezes by the Somerset House's grand Palladian wall. Back down an elegant stairway to the Embankment, walking toward the setting sun, I was open to seeing everything and anything.

I slept the next day until after 8:00 a.m., after the high-intensity itinerary of the day before. Internet connected in the breakfast room that morning. Another good omen. That day, I would visit Westminster's Banqueting House and St. James's Palace, maybe others as well, if breezes blew me elsewhere.

I had a good laugh at myself over some idiotic mistakes I had made so far. The intimacy of Westminster Abbey that had surprised me? I thought it was the Abbey, when in actuality it had been Westminster Cathedral. The Abbey was *enormous*, with a constant line of tourists waiting to get in. And St. James's Palace? It was always closed to the public.

Another brisk, sunny morning. My angry leg nerve acted up. I popped a Gabapentin and sat on a bench in the park between Westminster and Lambeth Bridges. I helped a Japanese couple read their map, then opened the top of my yogurt, which squirted out all over my fresh white cotton tunic. I used my water bottle and napkins to scrub the strawberry stains away. Seemed like I was always looking for a trash can in London. In Oxford, they were everywhere.

Sufficiently destained, I made my way past Jewel Tower, built in the fourteenth century to house the treasures of Edward III. I walked past the front of Westminster, the metonym referring to Parliament and its big, important cars. Taking Westminster Bridge Road back to the Embankment for a few blocks, I admired statuary and the gardens of government buildings.

Hiking back to Whitehall via Whitehall Place, I suffered map confusion—rare for me. I love maps, and I have a strong sense of direction. I walked up, over, and down, passing Scotland Yard and multitudes of government offices before asking two testosteroned—and not in a bad way—policemen on horseback for directions. Even so, I had trouble locating the entrance to the Banqueting House, which turned out to be small, with an even smaller sign. Directly across the street from the nondescript entrance, two horse guards were on duty at the front of the Household Cavalry Museum. Gorgeous milk-chocolate-brown horses collected crowds of tourists attached to cameras. I had shied away from horses ever since my Mackinac Island debacle. One more on my "fear of" list. Still, the horses were beautiful. Majestic.

I was the first visitor of the day to the Banqueting House. First, I received my headset. Next, I sat alone in the vaulted cellar to watch a short video presentation. Afterward, earbuds in, I roamed, still the only visitor, and listened to the narrator explain the hall's significant part in British history. The ground floor felt medieval with whitewashed stone walls, low rounded archways, and standing wrought iron candelabras. Indeed, in the thirteenth century, Cardinal York bought the property on King Street, renaming it York Place. Three hundred years later, Henry VIII took York Place from Cardinal Wolsey as punishment for failing to grant the king a divorce. Henry VIII moved in and started the never-ending restorations that would become Whitehall Palace. I signed the guest book, fascinated by the building's history. I was in part of Elizabeth I's palace!

Upstairs, I entered a completely different world than the medieval one below, this one an elegant Italianate Renaissance world that had caused a sensation when James I commissioned famed architect Inigo Jones to renovate the hall in 1622. The audio continued. Inspired by the classical architecture of ancient Rome, it had been ahead of its time. The Banqueting House would have been a stark contrast to the Tudor style of the rest of London.

Again, it is the only original building left of the original Whitehall Palace.

Although the main palace was Whitehall, the largest royal palace in Europe in the seventeenth century, court culture was polycentric, meaning it had many centers, including rural retreats. A queen consort's household had its own lord chamberlain, the most senior official, with parallel salaried roles and similar responsibilities as the king's court.[8] Often husbands and wives were given respective positions in the king and queen's household. An "average" day for court ladies would start with a stupefying number of social engagements. Public theaters had reopened after the end of the conservative Protectorate. Pleasure gardens, lavish dinner parties, and grand balls were the thing. For courtiers, dining meant sitting before the king and queen and admiring the royal couple as they were served on literal bended knee. Entertainment would ensue in the Banquet Hall,[9] where champagne from France was the latest treat. The marriage of Charles I and his French princess Henrietta Maria had been ratified in the Banquet Hall. Their oldest sons, James and Charles, attended masques there when they were old enough. Poor James II was only sixteen years old when his father was executed outside this room. And Prince Harry thinks he has it bad.

I was completely dumbfucked—yes, I know, very scholarly— when the audio's narrator explained the incredible ceiling murals above the balconied great room were by Peter Paul Rubens. After Rubens's ceiling panels were installed, masques stopped. Wisely, Charles I didn't want to risk lit candles and torches damaging Rubens's masterpiece.[10] Twenty years after Rubens installed the panels, Charles I would step out to the execution scaffolding from the Banquet Hall window. The panels are the only Rubens canvases that remain in their original location, although during the London air raids of 1940 they were cut out and hidden in the British countryside.

When Mary of Modena arrived in London in 1673, the city was still in the grasps of rebuilding after the Great Fire of 1666, building now more in the Italian style, leaving Tudor architecture behind. Today the Banqueting House hosts events ranging from fashion shows to state dinners. Fortunately, there was no event that evening.

Once again, I had fallen into the right place, my senses combined with enough knowledge of British Restoration history and enough luck to help me make efficient decisions. Fortunate to be alone in the Banqueting Hall for most of my time there, I rejected the option of looking into mirrored high tables to view Rubens's murals. One hundred ten feet long by fifty-five feet wide—and two stories high—I alternated sitting on each side of the hall, looking up from each side of the room for long periods of time. I changed seats often, imagining Mary of Modena and James II on thrones similar to the threadbare, crimson velvet ones at the head of the room, on a slightly raised dais. The thrones were probably used now as props during the fashion shows. Especially because I was alone, though, I felt a strong sense of place in this only remaining building of the original Whitehall Palace. A sense of the past remained.

The fantasy of luscious masques that James's father, Charles I, and his mother, the French princess Henrietta Maria, so loved served as a metaphor for his monarchy: the King was oblivious to a civil war looming. I struggled to believe that they walked him right through this room—wearing an extra shirt so he wouldn't look as if he were shivering—out the window that now loomed above the staircase.

And now it is a venue space.

I was visiting the house because it was the only surviving building left from the original Westminster Palace. I hadn't remembered any readings about a direct connection to James II. Naturally, when I stood in the hall listening to the audiotape guide and I heard not only the story of the Rubens ceiling but also the story of James's father being walked to his execution in that spot, I was once again amazed at how interconnected the royal monarchy was and how they were connected to the streets of England.

After leaving the Banqueting House, I walked past the Churchill War Rooms building, toward St. James's Park. Children were on a yearlong schedule and I found myself in a gaggle of young school children, who were touring London and heading to the park for lunch. I had a quick, friendly conversation with one of the teachers, but I knew from experience she did not need any distractions.

ALONG BIRDCAGE WALK, COMING FROM Buckingham Palace, horseback guards in full regalia were on the move toward Wellington Barracks. I delighted in watching and listening to the marching music, along with other overjoyed tourists. Beginner's luck again! When I faced west on the bridge that would take me to the Mall, the splendor of Westminster from a distance astounded. I gasped. It looked like Disney's Magic Kingdom. I reveled in people watching. A potbellied woman enjoyed an ice cream cone; a bald-headed man cozied up with his chocolate lab.

On my way to sight-see St. James's Palace, one of London's oldest palaces, I felt sheepish because I had unknowingly walked by it the day before.[11] I'd thought it ugly, though I had admired its chimneys and weathervane and taken photographs, not realizing, with its blackened redbrick exterior, that it was a major palace. Beginner's folly. Again. It hadn't looked like much from Cleveland Row when strolling by. Author Daniel Defoe called it "low and mean," but apparently from damasked-walled and tapestry-laden rooms, there were views of groves, meadows, Westminster Abbey, and beyond.

Henry VIII commissioned the building of St. James's Palace on the site of a former leper hospital. He used it as a hunting lodge. Now it is across from the London Eye. Elizabeth I was said to have spent the night there while waiting for the Spanish Armada to sail up the channel. Charles I slept rather less soundly, as it was his final bed before his execution. James II lived there as a widower, preferring it to Whitehall, especially in the summer. Here he brought his new bride, my Mary of Modena. No sovereign has resided there for almost two centuries—though Princess Anne resides there when in London—but it has remained the official residence of the Sovereign and it is the most senior royal palace in the UK. Its Proclamation Gallery is used to announce the passing of a reigning monarch, as seen after Queen Elizabeth II's death.

AFTER FINALLY FINDING THE BRITISH LIBRARY to get my reader card for the next day's research, I had enough time for Kensington Palace. I took the Circle Line to High Street and walked the rest of the way. James II's successors, daughter Mary II and son-in-law/nephew William of Orange, bought the palace in 1689, then known as Nottingham House, as a newlywed country retreat. As long as I was in London, visiting the palace made sense, but I assumed there wouldn't be a link to my search. When would I learn? In a seemingly forgotten room, dusty and dark, I stumbled upon—and was able to photograph—the bed in which Mary of Modena gave birth to James the III, which started the end of their short reign.[12] It was a four-poster bed draped in chintz from India, popular with the wealthy at that time.

And I thought there would be no connection.

The room looks and feels like a palace version of an ordinary guest room that becomes a catch-all storage unit. I didn't stay. Bad vibes. I followed the enfilade procession, a room-by-room progression, explained later in more detail. A female guard told me how spooked she was recently. She thought she saw and heard the ghost of the nanny of Mary II's children. I believed it. It was creepy there.

The queen's staterooms were dark, dreary, and depressing, but the king's household was elegant and well appointed. *So much* sexism, as I read and visited. I could see how it took Prince William and Catherine, the Prince and Princess of Wales, more than a year to renovate their apartment before Prince George's birth.

Sipping from my water bottle, I sat outside on the Orangery patio overlooking Hyde Park Gardens. Who could forget the days following Diana's tragic death and the cascades of flower memorials at the Kensington gate? I left the palace, strolling down the wide avenue toward High Street. I was enormously tempted to take photos, but *everywhere* there were postings that none were allowed. Walking past a row of embassies, including Israel's, I understood that security on this road was at its maximum. Gatehouse guards on Palace Avenue at High Street operated bollards that disappeared into the road at a button's push. The security risk felt very real.

I returned to the Circle Line, took the underground at rush hour to Sloane Square, and walked toward my hotel. My feet were burning. I sat on a bench in a small triangular patch of park at the juncture of five points, including Pimlico Road and Ebury Bridge Road. I removed my shoes, rubbed my aching diabetic feet, and people-watched for a long while, gaining strength for the push home. I was so relaxed and content to sit there in the waning, breezy afternoon with trees as my canopy. Back home in Tennessee it was boiling, the summer air too thick to enjoy being outside.

I gathered my might and stopped at a quaint pub close to my hotel. Descending three stone steps, I sat at a wrought iron table for two in a lush, small patio garden. *Ahh*, a Pimm's and lemonade—delicious—and an "ultimate burger," not so good, but it served its purpose. An old drunk flirted with me when I bellied up to the bar. *That doesn't happen too often anymore*, I rued good-naturedly. I must have left my cloak of invisibility back at the hotel. I was still adjusting to the invisibility that comes with middle age. At least it meant no more trouble.

Chapter Sixteen:

Popcorn, Parkinson's, and Party Girls

———·❧·———

1970s.

"Su-sa-an . . . phone ca-all."

The high-pitched, shaky voice was a bit garbled through the school's antiquated PA system.

"Take it in the teachers' lounge," she warbled.

Like every school secretary, Wilma Jerrard was the glue that kept everything and everyone intact at Shaker Heights elementary school.

I put my chalk down, wiped my hands on tan corduroys, and walked down to the lounge, next to my second-grade classroom. A few minutes later, I wiped my tears, channeling calm but questioning why my mother had to "pull a Jackie" so bright and early? And why I had allowed it? *What a way to start the day*, I thought, taking a deep breath.

With the first bell ringing, before returning to my classroom, I forced the cheerful face my beloved students expected.

On my way home, another tediously winter-gray day in Cleveland, I stopped for gas at one of the few full-service stations left in town. No credit card slots here. The attendant serviced my beat-up fifteen-year-old yellow VW beetle. It was my first car, $460, rusted through to the road beneath and no heater.

Damn, he looks good. Always a sucker for blue eyes, I expertly assessed the young man. Probably about my age. Quiet. Didn't encourage small talk. He looked familiar. *I'll bet you say that to all the guys.*

Climbing the steps to my Winslow Road attic apartment, I heard my landline ringing. I rushed up the remaining steps to answer.

"What took you so long?" my sister, now sixteen, asked on the other end.

Before I could answer, she continued. "Guess what I just heard? Jake Morrison and his wife are separated. He's perfect for you, Sue. And Mom and Dad would approve of this one!"

Choosing to ignore my sister's playful jibe at my tendency to be attracted to men who walked with one foot on the wrong side, I laughed ruefully to myself. Indeed, Jake was well-educated, wealthy—and blue-eyed. I hadn't forgotten how easily we had clicked the summer before at the club. He had been with his children while I had been swimming, making feeble attempts at reading texts for summer graduate classes. We talked easily about a gamut of things, from wine to Watergate. I had already heard about the Morrisons' breakup earlier that winter and had a strong sense he and I would eventually hook up. But next summer would be soon enough.

"How about we wait until the ink is dry on the papers!"

I would look forward to next summer.

The following day, my car gave me trouble again. I returned to the same gas station. Blue-eyes was there. He fixed my car easily but still said little.

"Thanks. My first car. I guess you get what you pay for."

He smiled slightly. *Man, what a looker.*

"I know this sounds like a pickup line," I continued, "but you look familiar. Am I crazy?"

"No, we were in contemporary history together. Eleventh grade. Mr. Dress."

He reached out his hand.

"Michael Levitt."

More silence.

Then, "You were the only one to stand up for me when I defended President Wilson's Fourteen Points."[1]

Trying hard to remember without success, I replied, "Well, I'm glad I had it in me."

Before leaving the station, I discovered he was home for the semester from Baylor in Houston because of illness but was planning to return in a few months. I was all of the following: attracted to his mysterious air; sympathetic to his illness; enticed by the "safety" of his leaving town soon. And he was hot!

Shallow, I know. Sigh.

Despite the all-proverbial red lights, I decided to go full speed ahead. Interminable Cleveland winters were isolating. I felt like I couldn't suffer this one alone. But when Michael left town in early spring, there was relief on my part mixed in with some sadness. His intensity had become overwhelming. Turned out his illness was schizophrenia.

Sigh.

Immediately, though, I was sidetracked, busy moving to a new Willoughby Hills apartment away from town. I was ready for privacy, away from the scrutiny of students' parents. Nothing worse than Saturday-morning coffee and a toke, then running into a parent at the grocery store. School teachers were only a half-step behind pastors in ethical expectations.

Sure enough, on Memorial Day, at Oakwood Club's posh tree-lined swimming pool, instead of on the golf course, Jake was there with his two young daughters. Immediately, he came over to me. He was in his midthirties, attractive, and dynamic. Behind mirrored shades, like a John le Carré spy, I had been reading with one eye and following his tracks with the other. Just as I knew we would, we fell into easy conversation. Before he went back to his children, we made a date for the best ribs in town. I was leaving the week after for a summer trek cross-country in my new MG with my old college buddy, Taz.

Our date was magical. So were the ribs. I regretted parting in the Cedar Center parking lot. But I knew Jake and I would pick up right where we left off when I returned.

"The Summer of '76"
(Sung to "The Streets of Laredo")

There was a young teacher on the back roads and highways
Driving cross-country with her dear, dear friend Taz.
In her new MG they started each morning
With coffee, a joint, and a full tank of gas.

Playing Fleetwood Mac each morn as they wandered
With the top down they sang to the tunes of the day.
From the lakes of Wisconsin, following signs for Wall Drug Store
To Mount Rushmore, the Badlands, and cheap inns on the way.

They cruised through the Rockies and then through the desert.
The plan was to hook up with Taz's cuz Wyn.
He happened to be a Cal State law school flunky
Newly released from the state loony bin.

Atop Griffith Park the three sat back and toked up.
They spoke of their futures and the mysteries of life.
Wyn talked Carlos Castaneda and peyote buttons.
Then they left a huge roach for hikers weary from strife.

Hitting the bars on Melrose the night of July fourth.
The bicentennial summer with parties full swing.
One LA stud after another tried to pick up the travelers.
Neither one was attached, why not have a fling?

Two drinks too many, Naftali approached her,
an Israeli rejoicing, Entebbe captives sent free.
Taz left with a playboy, teacher parted with Jew boy,
thinking, "He's one of my people, how much safer
could I be?"

Poor judgment beset her and not for the first time.
He stripped down to his brown socks and demanded
she suck.
"What's with these men and their sucking?" she
asked with a panic.
She ran out of the room before he'd want her to fuck.

Out on the street now, she ran quickly thankful.
She'd been blessed with strong legs; the right way
she'd select.
When she finally found her way to Wyn's roof
apartment,
All she saw when she walked in was his penis erect.

For there on his bed, he slept naked as a jaybird.
Once again she ran out as fast as she could.
Until she came to an In-N-Out Burger
And comforted herself with some greasy fast food.

Clearly it was time to leave the City of Angels.
She sensed someday she would once again return.
But for now the backroads and highways called her.
She had Frescas in the cooler and bridges to burn.

Jake and I did pick up where we left off. Summer turned to fall. I was back for my third year teaching second grade, this time deeply and truly smitten with Jake Morrison.

"Hi."

Startled, I looked up from unlocking my car door in the school parking lot.

"M-m-Michael! What are you doing back here?"

"I'm here for you. I left school. I missed you."

The intensity in his vibrant blue eyes, once so thrilling, now frightened me.

"Uh, Michael, I'm sorry, but I never—"

"Never what?"

"Uh, I never meant for you to get the idea that—"

"That what?"

He came as close to me as he could without touching.

"Michael. I'm sorry. I met someone else. I'm—"

Michael gripped my forearm.

"I haven't."

"M-m-Michael, please." I tried to disentangle my arm. "You're hurting me."

He dropped his hold but didn't move away. In a voice quiet but chilling, he warned, "We're not through."

He walked to his steel-blue Pontiac Firebird, backed out, and left the parking lot.

Shaken, I fumbled for my key. I sat in the car for minutes before pulling out of the parking space.

Over a period of days, Michael harassed me by phone and by hanging around the school. Then, as abruptly as he'd appeared, he was gone. However, he continued to write accusatory letters daily, and he harassed me by mail and phone. Sometimes he hung up; sometimes he talked. Sometimes he would have the operator interrupt other phone calls.

In the meantime, Jake and I grew closer, but the intimacy we shared also scared him away for days and weeks at a time. When he was feeling really threatened, he would pick up other women. To get even, I'd match point with Don Strater, the stunning assistant the new school superintendent brought with him. Between Michael's harassment and Jake's erratic behavior, I grew more tense. Jake and Match Point lived in opposite directions but both a Virginia Slims smoke away from my apartment.

ON A GRAY SATURDAY, A LATE SPRING rainstorm off Lake Erie caught Jake and me while wandering verdant paths at Squire's Castle. With incessant rain and wind beating down, we hurried into the front vestibule of my high-rise. An elderly couple ahead of us unlocked the front door. We all shuffled in, making our way to the elevator.

On the seventh floor, apprehensive and drawn, jeans, tweed blazer, and Frye boots soaked, I fished for keys in my backpack. Hearing the phone ring inside the apartment, I visibly jumped. Jake, in faded jeans and ivory cashmere sweater, equally sodden, took the key and opened the door. We hurried into my inviting living room, lots of art and plants and a big sliding glass door left half-open, leading to a balcony. Because of the wind, my students' workbooks and papers had scattered from a glass-top dining room table.

The phone stopped ringing before I could reach for it.

Click. Then only a dial tone.

"Damn."

Slamming down the receiver, I turned to Jake, who silently acknowledged my frustration. I went to the front-hall linen closet. I threw a towel to Jake.

"Here. You want to shower?"

"No, I'll just towel dry. I need to call my service."

As he took off his wet sweater, I gave him a look of slight exasperation but rolled my eyes affectionately. Half joking, I said, "How could I forget? I'll go change."

I stopped at the front door to bolt and chain it before leaving the room. In my bedroom, white with colorful accents, I disrobed. Someone knocked on the apartment door. I jumped, then relaxed.

"Jake, get the door? I'm undressed."

I heard him talking to his service. "This is Morrison. 5003. Any messages?"

With a heavy sigh, I cursed, "Damn phone."

I reached for my China silk robe and hurried out of the bedroom. With my robe barely on before reaching the door, I looked through the peephole before unlocking two locks and a reinforced chain. A short, perky, dark-haired woman about my age stood there, with a light dusting of flour on a delicately freckled face. She wore masses of gold and diamond jewelry, despite running shorts and a tank top.

"Hi. I'm Sarah Kitt. I moved in across the hall a few days ago."

She peered around me. Even at barely five foot three, I was taller.

Winking at me but looking at Jake, she continued, "Nice place."

Understanding Sarah's reference, I laughed, "I think so too. Come on in."

"Sorry to barge in on a Saturday afternoon, but I'm in the middle of a cake—well, not in the *middle* of a cake—in the middle of *baking* a cake. It's raining and I don't have enough sugar for frosting. I bake when I'm depressed. My boyfriend and I broke up."

It was jarring to hear cheer mixed with heartbreak, and I was surprised a stranger would share so much. But there was something endearing about the spunky brunette.

Jake's voice, in the background, distracted me. I absently fingered my chai chai—meaning "life" in Hebrew—on a delicate gold chain around my neck. Sarah took note of the charm.

"*You're* Jewish?" she asked. "Me, too. Funny, you don't look Jewish."

I was used to the comment. People who are not Jewish think we all have large noses or else we've had rhinoplasty. I pulled Sarah inside the door, locking and bolting it again.

Sarah noticed and raised her eyebrows. "Am I being held captive?"

I laughed and pointed to Jake. "He's the one held captive— by his little black beeper. I'll get the sugar, be right back."

I strained on tiptoes for the ceramic sugar canister on the top shelf of a kitchen cupboard, glimpsing myself in the mirror that hung inside the cupboard door. I gasped at my weary mirror image. My damp long hair was frizzing as it dried. Brown eyes, normally big and wide, were red from lack of sleep.

"Christ. How much more stress can this puss take?"

I stuck out my tongue. "Funny, you don't look Jewish," I mimicked.

I headed to the front door and handed the sugar to Sarah. "Just like Mayberry."

Jake hung up the phone and came to stand next to me.

"Jake, this is my neighbor, Sarah Kitt. We're just meeting now."

The phone rang. I jumped and said too tersely, "I'll get it."

Sarah raised an eyebrow as I took the ringing phone into the nearby bedroom, staring at it as if it was a mortal enemy.

I picked up the phone. "Hello. Hello. Hello!"

I slammed down the phone. While chewing on a thumbnail, I looked out the bedroom window at steady, driving rain.

I reentered the room. Flatly, I stated, "Him."

Jake coldly replied, "You ought to change your telephone number, Suze. This has gone on too long. You're only playing into his hand."

I bit my lip, searching for a reply.

Sarah awkwardly spoke up. "Well, uh, I'd better be going. I'm a flight attendant and have an early call tomorrow. Thanks for the sugar."

Jake unbolted and unlatched. Sarah backed out of my door, holding the canister up high. She mocked a Shakespearean actor, bowed, and bid us goodbye. "Sweets to the sweet, farewell!"

Jake closed the door and turned to me. We laughed.

The phone rang again. This time Jake disappeared into the bedroom to answer it. Returning, his expression made clear who had been on the other end. I closed my eyes for a few seconds and then walked to a table drawer and pulled out the top envelope from a rubber-banded pack of envelopes.

"This one came yesterday," I stated limply.

Jake glanced down at the opened letter and read, "I know you well enough to realize that you are laughing at me but someday I'm going to find your resonant frequency and break you apart like it happened to me so many times before. You set me up, then you let me fall, and afterward, you wanted some remittance of the aftermath to gloat over."

Jake read more to himself. When he finished, he said, "What the hell does 'resonant frequency' mean?"

"He's probably not taking his medication. He hated taking it. Said it made him fuzzy, drowsy.

Jake replied, "He's back in Texas. He can't hurt you."

Running fingers through my hair, I asked, "And when he comes back? His mother still lives here."

I stared at Jake while rubbing my temple.

"Come on, Suze. You've gotta unwind. This is what he wants. For you to get upset. Come on."

He reached out and untied my silk sash. He took the robe off, bent over, and began licking my breasts. It drew me into his lovemaking. We fell to the floor. The sound of thunder in the distance and rain pounding on my balcony gave way to the phone ringing again and again and again . . .

This time when the phone rang, we didn't pay attention.

FOR THREE WEEKS THE PHONE REMAINED silent and the mailbox empty.

I was thinking about it after work as I trudged into the apartment building from the connected underground garage. Hot and irritable from muggy weather, I heaved opened the heavy door to the lobby and walked a few steps into the mailbox alcove. A bath and a good book were all I had in mind for the evening. But as soon as I saw the Houston postmark among my bills and junk mail, I knew a quiet Friday night was not remotely possible.

Only the deafening silence in the crowded elevator kept me from screaming as soon as I opened the envelope. My heart pounded. My ears rang. Actions time-lapsed into slow motion. Seventh floor. The elevator opened. Thick humid air. Suffocating. I felt like I was clawing my way on all fours.

I don't remember screaming. Apparently, I'd left the front door wide open.

Sarah Kitt came rushing over. We had passed each other only once in the hall since that rainy Saturday. I had had all four wisdom teeth removed and had been hiding my Jackie Gleason jowls behind layers of scarves for days, so I had hurried by Sarah with a mumbled "hello" when I saw her.

Although I hardly knew Sarah, I felt kinship. I handed her the envelope. Silently, she read the newspaper clipping and the typewritten paragraph from his family.

LEVITT, Michael J., age 24. Survived by parents, Mrs. M. J. Levitt, Shaker Heights, Mr. M. J. Levitt, Houston; sisters, Anita and Wendy. Services and internment 1:30 p.m., Thursday, Rosecrest Chapel and Cemetery, Houston, Dr. C. B. Bevy officiating.

Among Michael's possessions was this letter. We decided to send it to you. Please under no circumstances contact us. You would just compound the pain. We have read the letter and think it speaks for itself. We see Michael as a kind and sensitive person. The way you put him down was so malicious and selfish, we simply cannot understand the reason why. Of course, we don't blame you. What happened, happened. Please try to keep the matter to yourself. We are certain no explanation is necessary. Again, do NOT contact us.

Sarah read part of a five-page suicide letter addressed to me, also included in the envelope. Sarah looked up from the letter. I was trembling. I shuddered, trying to picture Michael cold and still. Dead.

"I cared. Really. But he was sick. I couldn't handle it. Didn't want to. I started up with Jake and couldn't be bothered." I sobbed. "Shit, I can't believe it."

Wrapping her arms around my shoulder, Sarah responded, "This is the guy you were so tense about when I borrowed the sugar, isn't it?"

I nodded.

"This isn't your fault. It was probably inevitable. A troubled soul at peace now."

"No. There's always a chance. He gave up. He was young. Bright. He'd wanted to study medicine, but his illness kept interrupting his schooling."

I started to cry again.

"So, we talk," Sarah proclaimed. "But first, let's get some air in here; it's a hot mothafucker tonight."

She went to the window and pushed it open, allowing moist breezes to filter through the apartment. Sarah looked at my bookcase, stacked solid with academic texts.

"Aren't we a pair!" she laughed. "How different could two women be?"

I was in baggy jeans and a vintage top. Sarah dressed like a disco queen, a ball of Jewish princess energy, dripping in gold chains and diamonds. Her father was a jeweler.

"Well, you are definitely the better friend. I don't think I would have canceled a date with Jake for someone I'd only met once, like you just did," I admitted.

Thinking about Michael's remarks, I continued to cry. "I *am* selfish and uncaring, just like he said. He tried to break it off once because he couldn't handle a relationship, but I wanted him and that was that."

"Who was Michael, and what were you doing with someone so unhinged when you have that gorgeous curly-headed lover?"

"Jake? He'd only disappoint me if I saw him now. I'd want him to hold me. He'd interpret it as a request for a lifetime commitment."

I leaned forward and looked at Sarah.

"In January, I was house-sitting at my folks', staying with my little sister Kathy while they were in Florida. A very close colleague at work had died unexpectedly—massive heart attack. I was upset. Her name was Sadie Sartz—what a character—just how you would imagine a Sadie Sartz to be. She taught my older brother, too, when he was in sixth grade at Malvern, so she and I had a kind of history. She looked out for me. Grew to be 'the mother I never had,' you know? I asked Jake to come over. I needed a shoulder. He came over, all right. A shoulder? Not quite. Right in front of the fireplace, with my kid sister upstairs, he pulled out his dick and said, 'Suck me.' Thank God I didn't."

"Well, that's pitiful. But who's in worse shape, you or Jake?" Sarah continued, "Stunning or not, why are you with a man so emotionally unavailable? Not that I'm any less screwed up. Dr. Levy would say you only fall for men you can't have."

"Dr. Levy?" I asked.

"Eli Levy. My shrink. I have my own demons, believe me."

I raised my eyebrow.

"Your shrink would probably say I am as threatened by commitment as Jake."

"Because your chimney-sweep father left when you were three, leaving you and your mother destitute on the streets?"

"No, but you're close."

We burst out laughing.

"Well, you won't do a valium, so how about cake? That's what I do. I go to Fazio's bakery and buy unclaimed birthday cakes. And play racquetball, see my shrink, and continue my quest for my first orgasm—not necessarily in that order. I told you. I have demons."

"I don't have cake. But how about popcorn with 'caramel' sauce, and I'll do some listening for a change?"

We went into the galley kitchen, gabbing, and made popcorn with melted butter, sugar, and a splash of vanilla. Coming back to the living room, we lit a joint.

Taking in a big hit, Sarah laughed, "Now this is better than dick anytime."

"Almost," I lamented.

After a long chat, Sarah stretched and yawned. "Well, kiddo, it's almost morning. Think you can sleep now?"

"I'm okay now. Thank you. I would have gone crazy if it hadn't been for you. I'll never forget it."

Sarah gave me a hug and scooted across the hall.

For the next few weeks, I dealt with the power of both hurting and being hurt. When Sarah wasn't flying, we spent evenings together, front doors left open, reminding me of college-dorm days with Taz and Meg. Slowly I improved and adjusted. Started sleeping again.

A few weeks later, one weeknight, Sarah was on a Cleveland–LaGuardia turnaround. After a quick pizza and beer with friends in Little Italy, I drove home, feeling relaxed. I put on a nightgown, grabbed a day-old *New York Times*, and crawled into bed.

Minutes later, I thought I heard the lobby buzzer ring. I wasn't sure. I put down my newspaper. I waited. It rang again. I looked at my clock, nervously. It was late.

I padded to the intercom next to the front door and held down the "listen" latch. I heard breathing in the lobby vestibule.

Too afraid to ask, "Who is it?" I waited. Motionless.

Moments later, a group of people came into the lobby vestibule. Drunk. The lobby door clicked open. Movement and voices faded. The lobby door clicked shut.

Whoever had been waiting for me to answer the intercom was in. I waited at the peephole of my apartment door. Frozen. Through the peephole, I looked at the closed door across the hall.

Of all nights for Sarah to be away.

I briefly laughed to myself, visualizing my short friend trying to overtake an intruder with her eggbeater.

In my head, I imagined how long it would take to walk to the elevator, ride up to the seventh floor, and walk to my door. Right about the time I finished, the knock came.

I looked through the peephole. Distorted by the lens, it was hard to tell who it was. A beard. He knocked a few times. I was still. Not my heart.

He finally left. I ran to my phone. I called Jake to see if it had been him with a friend.

"No, dear. I'm here at home doing some work."

"I thought maybe you stopped by with Stephen." He had a beard.

"I wish I were there, but no."

Next, I called Match Point, though he was smooth-shaven. Same thing. I even called Gene, a bearded colleague. No dice. I put the phone down.

Who am I trying to kid? I'm not crazy. He is.

I waited for the phone to ring. I was numb. It rang. I picked it up.

A voice, soft, gentle. "Hi."

For me, everything that happened next happened in a blur. I said no when he asked to come up—the first few times. But I knew I had to see him. In my dazed state of mind, it was as if he had come back from being dead.

The knock on the door was a quiet one.

"Michael."

I embraced him, feeling relief, not anger.

A small voice in the back of my head hollered, *Red light! Red light! Red light!* But we sat down on the love seat. The irony.

All of my senses detached from my body. My movements time-lapsed again.

"What happened? I don't understand."

"I wanted you to remember that you cared. I had a phony obituary printed in the paper. It was easy."

His blue eyes were clear and penetrating. The beard was becoming. I was confused. He looked like a Poussin painting of Jesus. Beautiful.

"I'm sorry. I didn't mean to hurt you. But that's over now. I'm back."

I knew I should have been outraged and thrown him out. But I was not in control of my actions. I had honestly thought he was dead. I had honestly blamed myself.

He led me into my all-white bedroom and removed my nightgown. I tried to protest, but I hadn't the will. And he knew it. I lay passive. He penetrated. My mind was on autopilot. *No* echoed in my brain. No sound emerged. Afterward, silence.

Michael spoke first, angry now. "You want to destroy me, don't you? You shouldn't have hurt me like you did."

A chill went through my spine and snapped me out of my fog. I turned on the light and got up. He continued speaking. I put on my nightgown.

He said, "Maybe I meant to hurt you. Maybe I will. Before you hurt me again. I'm going to break your spell. I'm not a scarecrow you can tire of."

I was smoothing down my nightgown. He spun me around and slapped me hard across my face.

"Listen to me when I'm talking."

Stunned, I looked at Michael. His eyes had clouded over. I knew the signs. Part of me was paralyzed, just like the old days with my mother. But the survivor in me knew I had to get him out of the apartment.

"You're right, Michael. I'm sorry."

I convinced him to leave by promising to see him the next day. At the front door, he stopped and grabbed my shoulders. He shook me again.

"I'm not a scarecrow."

He walked out.

I shut the door and locked it.

I leaned against the door.

He started knocking.

"Night, Michael. I'm going to sleep now. It's a school night. You need sleep too. See you tomorrow."

It took a half hour more of his beating on the door, calling from the lobby, and buzzing on the intercom before he left.

I had no intention of seeing him the next day—or ever. I took an overnight bag out of the hall closet, not sure where I was going, but I knew I couldn't stay in the apartment until it was safe. I took a long hot shower, scrubbing, as if I could wipe my mistakes away with soap and water.

I was so screwed up. If I appeared on *Jerry Springer*, the title of the episode would be, "What Kind of Fucking Idiot Are You?"

I toweled my hair dry and fell into bed, exhausted. Angry with myself. It was 3:00 a.m. I slept the few hours until morning.

I woke up and dressed for work, my actions mechanical. I grabbed the overnight bag and took the elevator to the lobby, expecting Michael to jump out of every shadow. Thankfully, he was nowhere in sight. I threw the bag into the trunk of my MG and got in. Emotionless. On the outside.

Friends reacted more to Michael's reappearance than they had to his suicide. Upon seeing me show up at school with a suitcase and my complexion the shade of paste, the school secretary insisted that I must stay with my parents, despite my objections.

"My dear," Wilma declared in her scratchy voice, "Those are the only ones you can count on."

Yeah, right.

I expressed no outward signs of agitation. I didn't go to Jake for help, so he wasn't scared off this time. I knew he felt guilty, too, that he hadn't responded to my phone call the night that the whole awful incident had occurred. I continued through the motions of my life. Why wasn't I reacting?

Even my father, normally detached, got involved. He called the county prosecutor first and Michael next, threatening him with legal action if he contacted me again.

One afternoon, after I had been back at my apartment for a while, my father called to see if he could come by the apartment on his way home from his office. Sipping his customary Canadian, three ice cubes, and soda, he explained some family background, including the bombshell that my mother had been under *daily* psychiatric care all of my young life and still saw the same doctor regularly.

This information only bewildered and numbed me further.

I knew my father's side of the family had a history of violence and mental illness. My bubbe had struggled with depression. When she was a girl in Russia, her father had tried to kill her by throwing her down a well. She had tried to overdose on her sleeping pills when I was a young girl. During that time, every Sunday, before my sister was born, my brothers and I would have to wait in the car while my parents visited Bubbe at Windsor Psychiatric Hospital past Chagrin Falls, where one of my aunts told me Bubbe had received electric shock therapy. But I never knew about my mother's psychiatric care.

What do I do with this?

A few weeks later, our apartment front doors open, Sarah and I were having a regular night in, eating our favorite popcorn concoction.

Munching, Sarah chimed in, "Dr. Levi says the brain has a way of protecting the psyche. It will know when you're ready to handle the trauma."

"And what would he say is going to happen when the dam breaks?" I asked.

A few weeks later, it did.

Slowly, at first.

My summer graduate class at Case Western Reserve University initially helped me keep my act together, as did my friendship with a nun who was taking the same course. I can still see Sister Mary Joseph in my MG, top down, her nun's habit blowing in the breeze as we drove down Mayfield to the convent.

Once the course ended, I started crying, a lot, often uncontrollably. I stopped sleeping. Soon, thoughts became fragmented. Next, I had difficulty completing sentences.

One night in the shower, I found myself repeatedly and *violently* pounding my head against the white subway tile. *Bam. Bam. Bam.* Hysterical tears mixed with the hot water streamed down my face and body. I knew it wasn't only the ordeal with Michael causing me to unravel.

"I'm tired . . . I'm tired . . . I'm so tired . . . taking care . . . myself."

I sank down to the bottom of the shower, curled in a fetal position, hot water continuing its cascade, resilience be damned. Only when the water turned cold did I collect myself enough to get out. Exhausted, I grabbed a towel and the telephone book.

That weekend, miraculously, I ran into my old friend, dear Joanne Lockley, on the seventh fairway of the Canterbury Country Club golf course during the annual Fourth of July fireworks display, a Shaker Heights tradition. I had mechanically walked over to the golf course, wandering and half watching the display. Joanne, seeing the state of nonfunction I was in, urged me to drive down to Columbus, where she was dancing with a small company and lived with her musician boyfriend.

I incurred strong "phone wrath" from my mother for not joining her for a Detroit, Michigan, wedding of a cousin that I hadn't seen in twenty years. I finally talked back to my mother for the *first* time in my life—even slammed down the phone. I drove down to Columbus and spent a few rest-less days there, rekindling the steady low light of my oldest friendship and trying to regroup.

A day after returning from Columbus, still fragmented, still agitated, still sleepless, I left my Willoughby Hills apart-ment and headed west along Lake Erie, on I-90. Exiting the expressway, I traveled farther west, then south, and found the address I had written from the phone book and ensuing phone call the week before. I looked at my watch. *Right on time.*

I walked into a two-story plain limestone building in front of a strip mall. Minutes later, a short, rotund man with frizzy coarse gray hair and the most unusual bushy sideburns I had ever seen opened his office door.

"Susan? Come in."

He took off his thick black-rimmed glasses.

Nervously, I shook the nubby hand extended across an enormous paper-laden desk.

"Dr. Postini?" I paused, then said, "I'm sure you've been expecting me for years."

I attempted a weak laugh, standing across from my mother's shrink, and closed the door behind me.

SOMEHOW, WITH THE BOOST OF COUNSELING and Ativan, in one small moment of clarity, I found the strength to break it off with Jake. He would always be emotionally unavailable. I knew I needed—though I didn't yet know I *deserved*—someone who could give me that.

A defining moment in my life.

Even years after, I missed him though. Eight years after the breakup, I was walking along the Gulf of Mexico, at my folks' place. My eye caught an unusual shell. I picked it up and sobbed. *Eight years.* After a long, long cry, I promised myself that would be the last time.

In my twenties, using "my power" coupled with an honest ambivalence toward "relationships" attracted men like a scent. I knew when I walked into a room that I attracted attention. I knew eyes were on me. I knew that if I was interested, I pretty much had my way. I used it. How arrogant. But underneath that level of confidence, how much self-respect was there? *Some* of "my wild" was the exhilaration of freedom, but loads of it was a manic search. Underneath, I was a needy little girl still searching for approval from people who couldn't give it. My messy roundabout feminist arc. Now older, I am ultimately a better person, I think. I value quality aspects of life. Respect for women is one of them. If I did anything right, it was bringing up my strong, fearless girlie that way. Both her father and I wanted that for her.

The old flirt in the quaint pub waved goodbye. I continued my walk toward my Belgravia hotel. New carpeting in the foyer and stairwell. Nice. I watched some first-round Wimbledon coverage and read myself to sleep, window closed, pigeons out. No dreams this night.

JAKE MARRIED A PARTY GIRL AND MOVED TO the Keys. She proved to be an alcoholic, and they split after he was diagnosed with Parkinson's. He died unable to speak.

Sarah committed suicide when she was thirty-three.

Chapter Seventeen:

Palaces and Politics

I SPENT MUCH OF WEDNESDAY LOOKING AT manuscripts in the British Library ordered the day before. The first artifact in the folder was a cartoon by a well-known caricaturist of the time, showing how dogs were used to turn the roasting spits in the kitchen chimney. How appropriate: the bottoms of my feet were *on fire* from all the walking, though I slept better than the night before. I hoped to complete my readings today. There was still so much to see before I left London.

The second manuscript arrived, part of the Althorp Papers—yes, the same Althorp estate where Diana, Princess of Wales, spent her childhood and is laid to rest as a descendent of the first Earl of Sunderland, Henry Spencer. A fine example of the inbred nature of royal courts, the Spencer family is one of the oldest and most prominent noble families in Britain that currently holds the titles of Duke of Marlborough, Earl Spencer, and Viscount Churchill. Again, noble Spencer ancestors include the legendary John Churchill, first Duke of Marlborough, and his equally famous wife, the powerful Sarah, Duchess of Marlborough.

The first Earl of Sunderland married Anne Digby, a lady-in-waiting for Mary of Modena. Digby was present at the birth of the Prince of Wales. She was the one who signaled to the king that his new child was a boy. Sunderland's mistress was ancestress to *both* wives of Charles III: Diana, Princess of Wales, *and* Queen Camilla.[1] One thread of a complicated monarchial tapestry. How interesting that the world viewed Lady Diana as a commoner when, really, she was part of a very long line of impressive, powerful British aristocracy, centuries before the Germanic Windsors came on the scene.

In my cache of ordered books, I found the slender worn brown volume *Rules of Household for James II*, dated April 1685. So damn cool. I ended my readings at the library with handwritten letters from Mary of Modena. Since she wrote in French, I could translate a bit. Thank you, again, Mr. Wolf (third through sixth grade), Mr. Keys (seventh through ninth grade), Miss Siegal (tenth and eleventh grade), and my French graduate assistants at university. Mary's letters were desultory thank-you notes and inquiries, nothing informative. Disappointing. Therefore, I relied on other sources.

Mary was only fourteen when she arrived in England, yet despite her youth, upon first sight, Lord Peterborough described her as poised and elegant: "Such a light of Beauty, such Characters of Ingenuity and Goodness. Her Eyes so full of light and sweetness that they did dazzle and charm."[2]

All her life, Mary suffered grief from losses and frustration due to a myriad of illnesses that dogged her reign as duchess, then as queen. People thought she would not live into old age. Early twentieth-century British scholar Martin Haile wrote, "The Queen remains with a complication of disorders which the Doctors and the general public believe will not give her long life."[3] Haile wrote that her Catholicism was forgotten because her candor, grace, and goodness captivated the people.[4] The public also adored her generosity: she once paid all small debts under £5, releasing eighty from Newgate prison and many hundreds throughout the realm.[5]

Don't be deceived. Mary was used to her luxuries, and James set about to provide them. Immediately after their coronation, which was obscenely decadent,[6] he commissioned Sir Christopher Wren to rebuild her apartments. English royalty loved color. Scarlet, blue, green, yellow, and ebony Oriental cabinets stood on carved and gilded stands, showcasing silver-mounted tables, sconces, and candelabras. The estimate for Wren's remodel in today's money would be three million dollars, not including the new Roman Catholic chapel. Famed masters provided the labor: Verrio painted the ceilings,[7] Gennari provided the paintings, and famed Dutch woodcarver Grinling Gibbon did the extraordinary carvings.[8] The bed's ceiling had a mirror in the center surrounded by Gibbons's leaves, flowers, and husks and surmounted by the royal arms, gilded with burnished, gold-draped swags. There were paneling and moldings in gold, colored marbles, a Grand Staircase, a Great Bedchamber, taffetas, satins, and damask.

Mary grew deeply in love with her husband, but she revealed strength and pride when dealing with his mistress, Catherine Sedley. Mary demanded James remove Catherine, "not at all a good girl," from court and held fast until James acquiesced. I'll bet he gifted her something expensive for that too. He was known for it.[9]

Back near my London hotel, I relished a quiet dinner at an airy Thai restaurant on Hugh Street. Ordering my standard Pimm's and lemonade, I eased back, enjoying the teak woods and fresh décor, sea blue on white. I wrangled with how to rationalize writing about characters so flagrantly and wastefully wealthy. Mary's staff numbered over one hundred. In addition to her ten maids of honor and bedchamber women, she had a full-time doctor, ushers, waiters, pages, coachmen, footmen, grooms, chairmen, watermen, postilions, cooks, a seamstress, a starcher, a laundress, and a lace mender. But it was my literary quest, and it was just so damn fun to read, visualizing the luxury and beauty, the colors and textures. Spending time in England, even if only in my mind, is my delight.

If I ever need to reconcile sharing Mary's story, I only have to remind myself that despite the excess and decadence, no matter how acceptable it was for a queen to be subjected to public birth, it is humiliating and denigrating in any century— the ultimate show of power and powerlessness.

What started out with four close women witnesses ended with a circus filled to standing room with members of the king's court, including the Privy Council. There had been no screen around the bed and the side curtains were open. Mrs. Dawson,[10] the first to arrive, shared that in full labor Mary asked the king to "hide her face with his head and periwig,"[11] which he did, for she said she "could not be brought to bed and have so many men look on her." All of the (nineteen-member) council stood close at the bed's feet and the lord chancellor on the step. At the king's ensuing enquiry, *forty-five* witnesses, some very embarrassed, gave evidence. *They* were embarrassed? Politically, James II needed the birth to be well-documented. Mary would have known this. But shit. Indeed, the ultimate show of power and powerlessness. Poor thing.

Padma, the Thai restaurant's owner, strolled by. She told me I was beautiful. *Will this be the last time I hear that from someone besides my sweet Tony?* I guess I *was* still coming to terms with the aging process and the invisibility it brings. I'll get there. I expect it is a gradual thing. It bothers me that I care.

Exiting the restaurant, I found a pay phone—yes, in an iconic red telephone box—around the corner and called Tony. It was *great t*o talk to him. He sounded well. *Damn, I love the sound of his voice, sweet and southern.*

One of his brothers was helping him move furniture. Tony was replacing disgusting dog-dirty carpet in our bedroom with hardwood floors—a major item on his honey-do list. Having a man who can build a house is very sexy.

I returned to my hotel room too tired to write, so I enjoyed winding down by sitting in bed at my laptop and editing some of the day's photos. Wimbledon this week. I listened to the tennis coverage in the background. I didn't even have to read myself to sleep.

Thursday morning, after another nightmare, I was off to Windsor Castle. *What is it with these dreams?* I was wandering through London with my heavy backpack and I ran into a former difficult student with his family. The shy older brother ignored me, the younger sister had her hair straightened and dyed purple, and the father's face was plastered with white zinc oxide due to sunburn.

I rose to a guidebook challenge that Windsor Palace, southwest of London, and Hampton Court, in Richmond—twenty miles away—were difficult to see in one day, not because I wanted to rush but because I only had five weeks to gather information. I needed to be focused on what I saw and why I saw it. I was lucky in London with the weather; the summer was proving to be a wet one.

Rain dodging.

The train to Windsor was quick and easy. I changed once at Slough (pronounced "sluff").

I walked up Castle Hill to Windsor Castle. Since it was a weekday, the mood was mellow. The breeze was perfect. Windsor had a special, charming vibe. Raising my face to the sun, again I felt moments of gratitude. The royal family was not in residence, having departed the week before after celebrating Garter Day.[12] Had the queen been there, Windsor Castle would have been closed to the public. I would have missed my chance to take in exquisite staterooms. No inside photos were allowed here.

Windsor Castle is the oldest and largest occupied castle in

the world—from Norman fortress through medieval expansion, from Protectorate headquarters and military prison to home for Charles II after eleven years in French, Belgian, and Dutch exile. What would it feel like to return home—home, the place where your murdered father was laid to rest, a place redesigned into an English Versailles? Diarist Samuel Pepys called it "the most Romantique castle that is in the world."[13]

Walking up Castle Hill, past gardens restored for Queen Elizabeth II's Golden Jubilee, I listened to the now-familiar and pleasing introductory narration by Charles, then Prince of Wales, that opened each audio tour. He had found a niche in celebrating ancient architecture and sounded genuinely sincere, welcoming those who shared his passion for antiquity.

Architects designed Baroque (1600–1750) palaces according to rituals of etiquette. Called "enfilade," the design was a common feature in grand European architecture from the Baroque period onward, though there were earlier examples. Doors of all the rooms were aligned along a single axis, providing a vista through the next rooms—the presence chamber, privy chamber, withdrawing room, great and little bedchambers, and closet.

The enfilade remains a common design in contemporary museums and art galleries because it facilitates movement of large numbers of people through a building.[14] Royal palaces had separate enfiladed state apartments for the king and queen.

Windsor Castle was stunning. I was in love. Imagine Italian murals by Verrio on twenty-three ceilings, black-and-white marble floors in a new great hall, and dazzling compositions in carved limewood by Gibbons. The richness remains everywhere—expensive textiles, fringed velvets, gilded ceilings, magnificent tapestries laden in color, and works of art by master painters. Both Charles II and James II spent their childhoods in exile. The French influence was ever present in all of their palace renovations. Imagine elaborately carved and gilded stands, silver-mounted sconces, ebony and laburnum candelabras, and fine veneering and marquetry.[15]

James's daughter, Anne—later Queen Anne—was born by his first wife, Anne Hyde, at Windsor, and James felt distinct affection for the castle. It is my favorite, too, of the ones I visited. Mary and James spent time at Windsor Castle. It was a part of the revolving-palace-door policy that dogged the Catholic couple during Charles II's reign. On brief occasions, depending on the political/religious tone of the country, Charles would send them off to Holyrood House in Scotland or Hampton Court, southwest of London. The Stuart court of James II spent the summer of 1685 at Windsor Castle, returning to Whitehall in October. They returned to Windsor again the following May.

James II could be applauded for his honest devotion to his religion, although how he justified all of his mistresses tastes bitterly of hypocrisy. As a political animal, however, James's actions were unsavvy and blatantly stupid. He was cold, haughty, and aloof. Had he been more likeable, there would have been less opposition to some of his actions. He was his own worst enemy, unpopular with his Protestant public. Instead of playing down his Catholicism, James was dogmatic. Therefore, Mary of Modena's pregnancy in 1688 had consequences. Brits were reluctantly willing to accept a Catholic king, but the thought of a Catholic heir to the throne was *unacceptable*.

I sat in the narrow St. George's Chapel at Windsor Castle as students on a field trip tried to keep still and listen to their docent. I stayed for quite a while after they exited. I thought about the religious controversy surrounding Mary and James in this room. Crests of deceased knights mounted the walls, and flags of the current hung above the chapel benches. The nave's west window featured stunning sixteenth-century stained glass . . . a perfect place to sit and think. Who knew that this spot would become known worldwide when the Duke and Duchess of Sussex married there?

Knowing the chapel's revered and ancient history,[16] I would have been miffed, too, if I were the late queen and the duchess had pushed for air fresheners. It showed little regard for history. Now there is added poingancy since it's where the funeral of Prince Philip was held, where the queen sat alone in black, Covid-masked.

I ran into the field-trippers outside of the chapel. Their harried middle school teacher begged for attention. I giggled to myself, grateful I was just a tourist today and not in charge of unruly twelve-year-olds. Later, as I was leaving the Middle Ward Shop, I watched her scolding four or five preadolescent boys. *Long day*, I mused sympathetically, remembering a local field trip to Andrew Jackson's Hermitage outside of Nashville. Some of our students had behaved so terribly, we teachers feared we were added to their shit list, asked never to return. It happens.

Before leaving the Windsor Castle grounds, I watched a palace gardener at work in the once-moated area. The castle's grandeur took a homey spin. I relished my time there. There *was* a reason why people visited. I walked back to the Windsor train platform. Leaning against a metal railing, wind the only noise, I lifted my face to the sun and waited for the next train back to Waterloo Station and Richmond, home of Hampton Court. I felt good. I felt strong.

HOW DO YOU EXIT A TWENTY-FIRST-CENTURY South West Railway train, walk through a few turnstiles, and find yourself five hundred yards from the sixteenth century? Hampton Court was clearly older than other palaces, rougher and partially medieval. Visitors here, as at other historical sights, seem stunned, thus subdued, while walking through history, especially in the waning of a busy day.

It hits you hard.

I was lucky to arrive in the late afternoon. As time went on, more of the manor became my own, except for docent guards. I roamed from the Great Hall, with its hammerbeam roof and incredible hanging tapestries, to Henry's vast kitchens, once serving six hundred people twice a day.

The kitchens at Hampton Court Palace were the largest of Tudor England. They were a central part of palace life. Two hundred cooks, sergeants, grooms, and pages worked to produce over twelve hundred meals a day for a hungry household. The kitchens were divided into a number of departments, each controlled by a sergeant and a team of yeoman and grooms. Working in the kitchens could be a sweaty and dirty job. One million three hundred thousand logs burned in hellish fires every year. Three master cooks oversaw the roasting, one for the king, the queen, and the rest of the court. Fresh water for drinking and cooking was piped into the palace from springs three miles away. Barrels of wine were sent from Europe and kept in cellars next to the kitchens, while beer was stored close to the Great Hall. I traipsed through the labyrinth of kitchen rooms for quite some time. Not sure why. I *hate* to cook. I think it was because the rooms were so authentic.

In the Chapel Royal, a glorious chapel in continuous use for over 450 years, my eyes were instantly drawn upward. Photos couldn't replicate the vivid blue ceilings vaulted with gilded oak timbers, nor could they capture how the gold-painted stars shone in fields of indigo blue.

In the shaded Fountain Courtyard—one of twelve—young girls rehearsed for a maypole ribbon dance.

I walked on.

Halfway through map-designated staterooms, I found closed double doors and a spotlight aimed at an easel that posted an exhibit placard reading, "The Wild, The Beautiful, and the Damned."

Curious, I opened the door. Darkness.

I moved forward.

Black cloth-bound walls and dimmer spotlighting dramatized portraits that weaved through a mazelike exhibit.

My ladies. I found them!

In Hampton Court, in Queen Mary II's former state apartments, where wooden floorboards creaked and smells of the ages were caught between their timbered cracks, my ladies from the National Portrait Gallery had reunited for a six-month visit. The mystery of their disappearance solved. Kismet.

However, not all my searches ended as successfully.

Chapter Eighteen:

Red Lantern

"SUZE. WHAT'S THE RUSH?"

A chunky middle-aged redhead cloaked in navy-blue wool caught up to me. We were both heading toward the teachers' parking lot. It was difficult to hurry while dodging puddles of melted ice, chunks of rock salt, and boulders of hardened snow.

Crunch.

"Hey, Annette."

I slowed my pace to accommodate my dear friend, who today slightly resembled the Little Engine That Could.

"What's your hurry, girl?"

"I have a dentist appointment." I looked up at the threatening sky. "Can't say I relish the thought of getting snowbound in a dentist's chair."

"Depends on the dentist."

I snapped back my head and let out a full-throttled laugh. My poor, stifled, married friend. "So, what's up?"

"I wanted to know if you had plans for your birthday."

I glared at her.

Annette grasped my arm. "Don't tell me you're still upset about turning twenty-six? Look at me. For God's sake, twenty-six is nothing."

"It's a sore spot."

Hurts more than my tooth, I thought, remembering my vow last year, amid my depression, to be out of Cleveland by thirty. *One year closer, but I'm not closer.*

"Listen, sorry to end this delightful conversation, but I've got to run."

I crunched to my car, then weaved in and out of traffic, through slush and past snowbanks crusted black from automobile exhaust, only to be kept sitting in the South Euclid waiting room. I hated dental appointments as much as I hated February in Cleveland. Gray, gray, gray—the sky, the dead branches on barren trees, the air. I pulled on a strand of hair and examined it.

"Even my hair."

An old man in a shabby topcoat stared at me. I pulled my camel-hair coat closer around myself. He was still watching. I stared back.

He shrugged and went back to reading his *Cleveland Jewish News*.

I rummaged through my pocketbook to avoid his glances. I weeded out useless receipts and expired coupons. *It's a wonder there's room for money in here*, I thought, and giggled, rolling the trash into a ball. *Not that there's much money to put in it.*

The old man looked at me again. Managing a weak smile, I returned to my cleaning. I checked a small pocket in my wallet. An aging piece of yellow paper, folded in half, was stuck to the back of my zoo pass. Every once in a while I came across the small note, read it, and put it back into the deep recesses of my wallet. I never threw the paper away. *Just in case*, I'd say to myself. Then I'd promptly forget about it.

I took out the worn paper and opened it.

I gasped, "It's time. Holy—"

Again the old man looked up. He coughed, then returned to his newspaper. I returned to the note, printed with red ink in neat block letters, though the ink had bled a bit over the last five years.

Susan and Robin solemnly swear to rendezvous five years from now, on the Saturday night following Susan's 26th birthday, Red Lantern Inn, Beverly Shores, Indiana, 8:00 p.m., in the bar—NO EXCUSES!

—signed in earnest (and sworn with a long, wet kiss),
SUSAN & ROBIN, INDIANA UNIVERSITY, BLOOMINGTON

Robin Inham. *Hmmm.* I examined my hair again until I found the gray one. Sighing, I yanked it out. *Ouch.*

The old man put down his *Jewish News.*

"Young lady," he said with a strong Yiddish accent. "Von gray hair is all you've got? Look at my het. Now dis iz gray hair. And mine teeth? Vat you tink I'm doink here? Dis doctor has mine teeth in ze ozzer room. Now dat iz olt. Enjoy yourself vile you can. Pleeze."

The nurse came to the waiting room door.

"Mr. Stein?"

The old man stood up and walked toward the nurse. He stopped and turned around. He did a quick little bow and disappeared behind the door. I slapped my hand to my forehead and laughed.

Did I dare? Hmm.

But what would I be missing here in Cleveland? In February. Alone. I glanced out the window. Gray, gray, gray. I read the note again.

"Susan?" the nurse had reappeared at the waiting room door.

"That's me."

"Come this way, please."

I refolded the yellow paper and tucked it back in my wallet. I threw the ball of trash in the wastebasket and followed the nurse.

An adventure. Maybe my birthday wouldn't be so depressing, after all.

"YOU GOTTA GO FOR IT, SUZE."

Annette took a bite of her chicken-salad sandwich.

"But what are the odds he'll be there?"

"Who cares? You'll have another vicarious adventure for me!"

"Shh, not so loud. Eloise is right there."

"Oh hell."

Annette glanced around the teachers' lounge, then whispered, "She's just jealous, married to that tiresome preacher."

"Jealous. Hmm."

I thought of the painful recent breakup with Jake. Although it had been a healthy move, I missed him desperately.

"Annette, I am tired of defining myself by the men in my life."

"Oh, pish. Tell me about your torrid college love," she coaxed, with a mouth full of chicken and mayonnaise.

I laughed.

"The usual, I guess. Pretty serious for about a year and a half."

I thought back. *I scared him away.*

"Robin was charming. He lived in a rickety old house off campus with a Vietnamese roommate who spoke little English. Tang would scurry around the dilapidated kitchen, making exotic dishes for us to sample."

I continued, "There were cockroaches everywhere. At first, I hated getting up in the middle of the night to pee. The roaches would scramble all over the bathroom sink when I turned on the light. But I got used to it. We named them."

Annette looked squeamish. She stopped chewing.

"I asked about your lover. You describe Asian roommates and arthropods. Quit stalling!"

"Just creating the mood," I teased. "Robin had a wonderful skylight right over his bed."

"Now you're talking."

I laughed.

"He was the morning DJ on the campus station. I woke up every morning to his voice over the clock radio. 'Hi, Robin Inham here. WIUS radio.' We had a secret code. He'd say dirty things to me over the airwaves. Nobody knew."

Annette leaned forward. "What kind of dirty things?"

I bit the inside of my lip. "I can't remember."

Annette looked disappointed.

"Sorry." My eyes brightened. "My nickname at school was Cabbage." I smiled, remembering.

"It was a great way to wake up. 'Robin Inham, here. Time for all Cabbage roses to rise 'n' shine.'"

Listeners wondered if it was from an obsolete poem. Or Victorian novel? It became a feature of the show, to try to figure it out. Robin never told.

"Cute. Not sexy. But cute." Annette urged me on. "Go on. How d'you meet him?"

"My roommates were from his hometown. They invited him to a party in our dorm room. I went with him on a beer run. He drove a '48 black Cadillac. He was as classy as his Caddy. I was hooked."

"Come on, I'll look up the phone number. American? United?"

"I have no way of contacting him. I tried last night after

I found the note. I even called the old college radio station. The guy thought I was crazy. He was right."

"C'mon, now. Where's my adventurer? Show up and take it from there." Annette wiped the breadcrumbs off her skirt. "When was the last time you saw him?"

"We split up our junior year. I scared him away. I took it hard. But we ran into each other at the library, the night before our last senior exams. We studied late together. He walked me home, past the old dorm where I'd first met him, past the drugstore where I'd bought my first pack of cigarettes. Thirty-five cents a pack. He spent the night. It seemed right. I can still conjure up the melancholy as I watched him walk away, in his obligatory turtleneck under an open flannel shirt, tails flapping in the light breeze.

"That last semester had been difficult. I had returned to school after winter break. After a night at Taz and Meg's on Washington Street, I took a shortcut through Dunn's Wood. Normally, I would have walked around campus, sticking to the roads, but it was the coldest night of the year. The bank clock on Kirkwood Street froze at seven degrees. Crossing through the wooded campus, I remember thinking, *Nobody in their right mind would be out.* Well, nobody in their right mind *was* out, but a man *not* in his right mind was. He grabbed me from behind at the Adam and Eve statues and tried to force me to suck him. His dick was huge. So was his bulbous nose. The rest of his face was hidden behind one of those Russian ushanka hats, you know, the furry ones with the earflaps."

"Oh, Suze, no."

"Yeah. But in that split second, I decided I would rather be shot in the back. I kicked him in the shins as hard as I could and ran for it. Man, you never know how you will react. I remember expecting the shot. I kind of kept to myself for the rest of the semester."

"I can imagine," Annette sympathized.

"I read that the Eve statue had been damaged and stolen since then but recovered. She also has endured. An apt metaphor."

I picked at the remnants of my sandwich.

"That was one reason why my tryst with Robin that last night on campus was moving. The next morning, watching him walk away—" I swallowed. "Wow, emotions are rushing back. I had been watching my past walk away, with the future staring me down. I wasn't ready to return to Cleveland, but I wasn't prepared to do anything else."

"You gotta do this." Annette wiped her hands with a "World's Best Teacher" napkin. "So why the Little Red Steamboat?"

I laughed. "I'm not the only one who's been teaching too long. It's the Red Lantern Inn. An Indiana dunes resort outside of Chicago on the Lake Michigan shore. Robin worked there every summer. I surprised him there one weekend."

"Tell me what I want to know!"

"Let's see. Well, late one night we tiptoed into the cavernous hotel kitchen. By candlelight, Robin cooked two filet mignons in a massive restaurant broiler."

"Come on. I'm not asking about two pieces of meat in an oversized oven."

"Give me a chance to warm up. I didn't know I'd be doing story hour today. We ate in the dining room overlooking Lake Michigan. By candlelight. The only two people in the restaurant dining room."

I stopped and glanced around the lounge to make sure Eloise wasn't listening.

"I can't remember having a more romantic weekend. The sound of Lake Michigan hitting the rocks as we slept wrapped in the breezes and each other. Delicious. And I'm not talking about the steak."

I lowered my voice. "The next morning, we took a jug of wine and walked for miles along the shore. Until sunset.

We would make love in the sand dunes and then rush down to Lake Michigan to wash and cool off."

"Bull's-eye!"

"Shh." But I laughed.

"We thought we'd walked miles? Well, the next day, sober—and very sunburned—we discovered it had only been a few hundred yards!"

"Yes!" Annette jumped out of her chair like a cheerleader after a winning touchdown.

Eloise glanced up from her bifocals. I grabbed Annette's hand and pulled her back down. Good thing I hadn't added the post–Mackinac Island episode with Robin. She would've lost it.

Annette cleared her throat. She whispered, "Sounds like a perfect place to rendezvous."

"If you think I'm frolicking on a beach in the dead of winter, you're nuts," I joked. "But you and the little Jewish man are right."

"Huh?"

"Never mind. I'll do it. It's crazy, but what the hell? If he's not there, I'll drive back to Chicago and pamper myself at the Mayfair."

Annette whistled. "Yummm."

"You've inspired me. A birthday splurge."

The bell rang. Annette threw her trash away.

I picked up my stack of ungraded papers and walked toward the door.

"He was dreamy, that's for sure. Damn, I loved him."

My voice sounded lighter than it had all winter, forgetting that Robin had broken up with me because I had scared him away.

O'Hare had hardly changed in the few years since I had flown in for a wedding in Evanston. The concourse was still under construction. Still claustrophobic. A reckless skateboarder dodged in between wall-to-wall clusters of irritated travelers. *Do these same weary people wander back and forth for eternity?* Under my breath, I hummed the first few eerie notes of the *Twilight Zone* intro.

I left the airport terminal with rental-car keys tucked into my gloves. Frigid Chicago winds blasted my slight frame. I wrapped my coat around me and walked against the wind. The high color in my cheeks wasn't only from the chill factor. I was having no more luck keeping calm than a youngster today waiting for the next *Guardians of the Galaxy* movie. I knew the odds of Robin showing up were less than slim. *But maybe*, I thought, buckling my seat belt and readjusting the mirrors. One last look at the map. A glance at the clock on the dashboard. Dark at six fifteen. I was off!

I plunked coins into the tollbooth basket, waving to the buxom Black woman inside, who waved back in surprise. *At least there's no snow tonight.* There were plenty of potholes, however. Craters, some of them.

The tollway ended three miles from the Indiana border. I waved at the woman in the booth. This one didn't respond. My left foot tapped the floorboard. "Welcome to Indiana" flashed before me. I flicked the radio buttons like a distressed woodpecker.

This is a big mistake. How did I get talked into it? I'll turn around and head to the Mayfair. Drink a vodka gimlet in front of the fireplace. That was my drink of choice with Robin. I fondly remembered the back booths at Mother Bear's and the nerves that came with using a fake ID.

I tapped my bag, hotel confirmation number safe inside, written on the back of a leftover workbook page of second-grade story problems.

"Susan is driving at fifty miles per hour and needs to travel a distance of ninety miles. Robin is on a magic carpet driving at ninety-five miles per hour. Who will get there first?"

I laughed. Nerves were making me giddy. I gripped the steering wheel.

I smelled Gary, Indiana, before I saw it. Rotten eggs. High school chemistry class. However, the steel mills, oppressive by day, were smoke and crystalline sculptures by night. It was like landing in a NOVA documentary.

The landscape changed after leaving Gary. Gone were the big-city lights. A brightly lit farmhouse appeared now and then. About thirty minutes outside of Gary, I spotted the sign that read, "Indiana Dunes, next right." I flashed my turn signal and exited the freeway.

At the bottom of the ramp, I took a deep breath. Had I been breathing at all?

I turned at Old Highway 12. In the almost-full moonlight, I saw pine woods on the right and marshland on the left. Moon-lit white sand salted the asphalt on each side, and train tracks paralleled the road. At every crossroad, I slowed down to check the street signs, recognizing some surroundings. Each mile of sand-bottom forest took me farther back in time. Waiting for Robin at Showalter Fountain. Two a.m. eggs and hashbrowns at the Hour House. IU basketball games at Assembly Hall.

Broadway. Funny name for such an isolated road. I turned and headed toward the shore. Lake Front Drive. The Red Lantern would be just ahead, on the right. My insides felt like they did one spring break when the night the manager of a Fort Lauderdale motel caught me hiding naked in Robin's closet. I'd been shaking so hard I'd made the empty hangers rattle.

I drove a few blocks. Something was wrong. I noticed remnants of road-repair work. I drove up and down the road several times. On the dunes' side, old wooden stairways still led up to elegant beach-cliff homes. But the beachfront was void of any structures. I continued driving back and forth like a duck in a shooting gallery. I started to sweat.

There was no Red Lantern Inn. How could this be? Cinder blocks and boulders marked where the resort had been. Only old parking spaces remained.

Erosion caused by Lake Michigan had swallowed the inn.

I parked between two faded lines. Seven years before, in my excitement, I had nearly jumped out of my car before coming to a stop. But now, staring out into darkness, I was as still as the solid ice formations on Lake Michigan.

The lake stared back. I was numb. What do I do next? Running fingers through my hair, I flicked on the radio and sat back, stretching my arms and legs.

"Happy birthday," I muttered.

Fidgety, I leaned forward and started with the radio buttons again, looking for a good oldies station.

What I need now is a great song from the past to make me feel really miserable.

I had prepared for Robin to be a no-show. I would have walked into the cozy Red Lantern bar. Ordered a drink. Maybe talked to the bartender or some of the regulars. Told my story. They'd have enjoyed it. I would have driven back to the Mayfair to toast my twenty-six years. It had seemed fitting to spend the weekend looking back.

But I hadn't prepared for this empty feeling in my chest.

"Where's a damn song?" I pounded once on the dashboard.

A melody caught my ear, and I stopped pushing buttons. "In My Room." Of course. How cheesy. How right.

I closed my eyes and pictured a waterbed rolling under a wooden skylight . . . an alarm sounding . . . a bare arm from under the sheets reaching for a dusty, old clock radio . . . *Cabbage Rose, wake up.*

The hollow in my stomach filled with the aching of many lonelinesses.

Chapter Nineteen:

Bermondsey or Bust

───────·⌒⌒⌒·───────

ROBIN AND I NEVER REUNITED, BUT MY scandalous court ladies had. I had solved the mystery of their disappearance from the National Portrait Gallery. Here they were, in a darkened room in Hampton Court, lit only by spotlights. At Hampton Court, the home of Henry VIII, the ultimate misogynist. Oh, the irony.

When I think of these paintings, the word "zesty" comes to mind. On display together were the famous Windsor Beauties of Sir Peter Lely and their later rivals, the Hampton Court Beauties by Sir Godfrey Kneller, all of them "gorgeous as ripe peaches and just as pampered."[1] Normally, these women were the fashion icons of the day and wore splendid, bejeweled, brocade gowns, embroidered, braided, and fringed—with stiff bodices, elbow-length cuffed sleeves, and skirts pulled back into gathered trains to reveal silk petticoats, also adorned. The height of Restoration women on average was five foot one, men five foot seven. Most who were on the tall side were likely to come from the well-nourished sectors of society.

A tall man like his elder brother, Charles II, James II was described as being "two yards high." Mary was known to be "tall and admirably shaped."[2] Height was status.

A woman's principal undergarment was her thigh-length smock or shift, with bunched sleeves closed around the upper arm and cut low over the breast, often perfumed to help negate the ripe stench of pervasive body odor. Waistcoats, a form of vest, were made of linen and worn for warmth over the smock. Petticoats were similarly meant to keep someone warm, sometimes visible under the open section of an overskirt or gown, which was made of silk or taffeta. Striped patterns were considered fashionable, perhaps with a slight train and trimmed with lace. Bustles were an innovation of the 1680s. Women's clothing was restraining. Diarist Samuel Pepys wrote that women were "so pent up that they could not so much as scratch their heads for the necessary removal of a biting louse."[3]

The early 1500s marked the arrival of the corset among women in France. At this time, most corsets had a long piece of wood or whalebone sewn into the casing. Can you imagine the feeling of relief these women felt when taking off their undergarments?

The early corset pushed the breasts up and together, causing the tops of the breasts to spill out of the tops of dresses for a shelflike bust effect. The corset would live on as a popular woman's undergarment for nearly four centuries. There wasn't an option of a brassiere until 1889, when French designer Herminie Cadolle cut a corset in two, creating two separate undergarments. The top section supported the breasts by means of straps, while the lower piece cinched and shaped the waist. I haven't worn a bra for twenty-five years. Thank God for perky pointers.

In the 1660s and 1670s, the typical style was a bodice and skirt. The bodice was the predecessor to a pair of stays but worn as an outer garment, lavishly decorated with ribbon and lace. Sleeves, which could be detachable, were worn full to the elbow or decorated with lace just above the wrist. Though bodices and gowns were cut low, showing bare arms above the elbow was considered risqué. Go figure.

Changes in women's fashion occurred frequently. A major new trend in London around 1680 was wearing a gown instead of a bodice and skirt. Stockings were brightly colored knitted wool or silk. Shoes were leather and pointed with a high heel. Slippers and mules were velvet or embroidered cloth with silk and satin for the linings, also often perfumed. To walk through the mud and muck of city streets, a patten, which was an iron frame, raised feet to avoid the dung. Hats fell out of fashion by the 1670s. Cloaks were voluminous and reached to the feet, tied at the throat.[4] However, in the portraits at Hampton Court, by the masters Lely and Kneller, the beauties were clad in revealing loose gowns they may have worn in the morning before dressing for the day.

In that darkened room in Hampton Court, I stood in front of the oil painting of auburn-haired Margaret, Lady Denham, whose husband was rumored to have poisoned her. No court would be complete without a little intrigue.

Next, regal raven-haired Barbara Palmer, first Duchess of Cleveland, Countess of Castlemaine. She had five children with Charles II and was aptly draped in soldier's cloth.

Even in her portrait, Henrietta, Countess of Rochester, though fair-haired with porcelain skin, looked haughty. Strong-minded and acquisitive, sometimes ruthless, she was sister-in-law by marriage to King James II. Was that why Lely painted her in the most delicate blue?

And seductive Carey Mordaunt, Countess of Peterborough and Monmouth, might have been innocent looking, but she had a secret marriage in her past.

Chased, abused, using looks as power. Hmm, sounds familiar.

Both brothers had a thirst for infidelity. Claire Armstrong Jerrold wrote, "The restoration was a wild carnival played out by a delirious people and an irresponsible king." Charles II's brother James was cold at heart, but he "belonged to his time and felt he needed to show princely luxury and abandonment."[5] I'll translate: Neither Charles nor James could keep their dicks in their pants.

Some of Charles II's mistresses have been forgotten, but many are still known, for instance, the famous actresses Moll Davis, witty, warm-hearted Nell Gwyn, and sensational, promiscuous Hortense Mancini, Mary of Modena's aunt. She arrived much to Mary's dismay at court in 1676, "on the run from her husband, scandalous reputation preceding her."[6]

Hortense's marriage proved miserable. She was married at fifteen years old. Her husband was abusive, depraved, and pathologically and dangerously jealous.[7] I thought of Jimmy Murray, my steppingstone to California, who had beat me with a ceramic tureen as I'd slept in our Hollywood studio.

Hortense had four children by the age of twenty-two before she ran away to her sister in Rome at the age of twenty-nine. Running away for a woman in the seventeenth century was nothing like today. There were no online pages advertising Safe Haven or Women Are Safe. Hortense wrote in her memoir that they traveled like Roman heroines—an abundance of jewels but no clean panties. Sounds like my beloved, panty-less great-aunt Ann, who opted to save that step to avoid mishaps in her older age.

Hortense and Maria's escape sparked discussions across Europe concerning the legal rights of husbands. "Aunt Hortense" eventually settled in England, much to the embarrassment of Mary of Modena, now Duchess of York. Hortense's memoirs were published that year. She lived elegantly in her house in Chelsea, surrounded by books and art. Like her sister's in Paris, it was a salon of witty and intellectual friends. The British dubbed her The Italian Whore. Hortense was only fifty-three when she died. Diarist John Evelyn claimed that she had drunk herself to death.

By her own account, Hortense enjoyed England.[8]

I'd say!

Though vivacious, Maria Mancini was considered the least beautiful of the sisters, yet she won the love of Louis XIV. Both Mancini sisters were among the first women to publish memoirs, in part to give evidence of their abusive marriages. Hortense and Maria were pioneering free spirits, feminists long before the word existed.

In all, Charles fathered *nineteen* children.

Hortense Mancini, Duchesse de Mazarin, and her sister
Marie Mancini, by Jacob Ferdinand Voet, c. 1661
CREDIT: Jacob Ferdinand Voet, public domain, via Wikimedia Commons

Not as prolific but equally profligate as his elder brother, James had his own list of infidelities: sharp-tongued Catherine Sedley, Arabella Churchill, Frances Jennings—shared by both brothers—and vivacious Susannah Armine, Lady Bellasys—the same Lady Bellasys who became a close confidante to Mary of Modena.

I continued my meandering through the portrait maze, contemplating infidelity.

Chapter Twenty:

This Is What
Hell Must Be Like

———————— ·⟨⟡⟩· ————————

H E LOOKED UP AT ME FROM WHERE HE WAS crouched on the floor, removing carpet tacks with a hammer claw. Sounds like a line from a country music song.

It was as if I'd been stun gunned.

"Susan," Manuel introduced, "this is Tony. He's working for Darren."

Manuel had bartered clothing for trade. I probably said hello, but an initial, visceral reaction to warm but penetrating eyes took me by surprise. They matched the blue brilliance of the Royal Chapel ceiling at Hampton Court. Uh-oh.

A month before moving from LA to Nashville, a man had burst through our back door, having been shot in the arm, in the park across the street—a drug deal gone bad. Thank goodness it was one of the few nights that Manuel was home because Marty Stuart was our houseguest for a few days . . . the only man I knew who took more time to dress than a beauty pageant queen. He was Jesse's godfather, though it was his manager who took care of any gifting. Thankfully, we moved to Tennessee with three-year-old Jesse to open a shop in Nashville and live a higher-quality life than we could in LA. We found a beautiful Tennessee home in rural Williamson County.

I had grown numb in my marriage—for various legitimate reasons—and had hoped the move from LA to Nashville would bring me back to it. Our plan was to open a boutique in town, in an elegant brownstone on Broadway. Manuel commuted from Nashville to LA, where he still had his studio and original workshop.

Over weeks and then months, while Manuel was away, Tony and I talked easily as he worked on the house. Our friendship blossomed. There was a warmth that enveloped him. I assumed someone was loving him. I looked forward to his truck driving up our hill every day. Oh dear.

I invited him to my sister's wedding, for which he was currently building a back deck.

"Bring your wife," I said.

"There isn't anyone," he replied.

Uh-oh.

Our lives would never be the same. We were drawn to each other, filling lonely, perilous holes of our past.

And honestly, I had the *hots* for him. Those eyes, the smooth rich skin, his rough edges, his soft insides. The honesty with who he was, totally unpretentious, completely natural. Manuel was a peacock, as a dear friend had labeled rather accurately.

Ah, the pendulum swings again.

For over a year, I wrestled with what to do. I assumed once the secrecy dissolved, Tony would be gone, so I had to be 100 percent sure leaving my marriage was something I chose with or without him. I had wanted my daughter to have the perfect childhood, the one I didn't have.

Manuel once said to me, "*El amor va a donde quiere ir.*"

Love goes where it wants to go. How ironic. After months of emotional torture, I finally decided if I did not leave my marriage, I would get cancer and die.

Tony stayed for the long haul. He cares for me as if I am the exquisite porcelain lamp that I inherited from my great-aunt Ann, the aunt with "an abundance of jewels but no clean panties."

"*Por cada cordero su compañero.*" For every lamb, its mate.

I have never been proud of breaking my vows, but I have always been honest about it.

My guilt over Jesse remains too. There is an anger within her that wasn't there before the divorce.

"TRAIN, MOMMY, TRAIN." JESSE JUMPED AND pointed.

I feigned a shared excitement. "Yes, sweetheart. Chug-a-chug-a-chug-a-chug-a."

I enjoyed a quick snuggle with my three-year-old girlie. My eyes were stinging. Breathing was difficult. Overcome by the pungent smell of fires burning out of control, I hurried Jesse toward the hospital door. *After this, will I always associate the stifling September Santa Ana winds with death and decay?*

A whistle blew. A train passed by, it's locomotive silhouetted against the darkening San Fernando Valley sky. I glared at the distant flames that framed LA's vast San Fernando Valley on three sides. Most of the country was looking forward to autumn's cool breezes. LA braced for the hottest month of the year. This edge of the valley had always depressed me.

In the midst of industrial wasteland, my brother-in-law lay comatose, all vestiges of dignity stripped away, like the once-majestic trees burning in the surrounding canyons. Bits of ash flew helter-skelter.

This is what hell must be like. The caboose faded away, taking its noise too. I took a deep breath and poised my hospital smile. With Jesse clutching one hand and my nightly contribution of home-baked goodies in the other, we walked through the automated double doors to a sparse lobby where family and friends waited. And waited. And waited.

My eyes searched for my sister-in-law, Rosie. How strange to become familiar so quickly with this nightly pattern. The first night Manuel and I had pulled into the hospital drive, not knowing where to park, which door to enter, what to say or do. Now we were pros at the tortuous waiting game.

Had it only been a week before? The disorienting, dreaded, middle-of-the-night phone call. When the phone rings, you expect the worst. It's usually a wrong number or a teenage stepson with a flat tire and no money. This time, though, it was the worst.

"Come quickly, Manuelito," said his brother, Jorge. "It's Luis. An embolism. He's not expected to last the night."

We drove without speaking much. I wanted to feel close to Manuel. I tried to will it. Maybe this tragedy would help me feel closer to him. What a terrible thing to think. But I had been moving further away from him emotionally. I didn't feel married at all.

"Did Jorge say if it was the heart or the brain?" I asked.

"If he did, I didn't catch it."

"I hope it's the heart . . ." I trailed off, shuddering at the thought of Luis and Rosie's ten-month-old daughter growing up never knowing her father. She was the youngest of five children. Luis was only thirty-six.

The interstate was empty.

"Too bad you have to wait until 3:00 a.m. for rush hour to ease," my husband remarked in his thick Spanish accent.

I nodded agreement. In spite of the circumstances, with the car windows down, I was enjoying the first refreshing breezes in weeks. I'd never get used to the oppressive San Fernando Valley summers. Like a mythical beast, heat terrorized my day until retreating to its cave at the stroke of midnight, only to surface the next day stronger and more menacing, with no visible signs of weakening.

"Where should we park?"

We had reached the hospital.

"Emergency?"

Then we saw Rosie, sobbing on a back stair, a priest by her side. My husband had ten siblings, five of them sisters. I was the closest to Rosie. The youngest, she was the most modern of the six lovely sisters from Michoacan, Mexico, and the one most open with me. We shared a strong sense of morality. We both suffered when others didn't live up to our high expectations. Her need for order and tendency to worry frustrated me sometimes. How many times had I pleaded, "Rosie, loosen up!"

"You get exasperated because they're qualities you dislike in yourself," Manuel teased.

Rosie thought I was laid back, which really gave him a chuckle. What cruel irony. The sibling who most craved order was the one whose life was irrevocably turning upside down. I hurried to Rosie and placed an arm around her trembling shoulder. Her eyes were swollen shut.

"Oh, Dios mío," she moaned. "So many things unsaid. You see, Father, I was the affectionate one. It was hard for Luis to—"

"Rosalie, you need to be strong now," the priest interrupted.

We still didn't know if Luis was alive. Manuel walked toward the emergency room to find out. I clutched Rosie's hand, not a time for words. I resented this priest who thought wearing a white collar gave him the right to tell my sister-in-law how to handle her grief. I would have made a lousy Catholic.

Another sister brought her a can of Diet Sprite, her favorite.

"Rosalie," urged the priest, "you've got to go in there. You must be with your family now. Come back inside."

We filed inside. The waiting room was filled with family members. Manuel came over to me.

"It's his brain. He's in surgery, a last-hope effort. He's not expected to survive."

I didn't know what to say to anyone. For the first time in my years with my in-laws, my skepticism toward organized religion made me uncomfortable. I had no pet phrases or Bible verses to lean on. I thought, *Luis will fight this. And we will help him with whatever rehab is necessary.*

I found an empty seat. Luis's mother sat across from me. We smiled, the language barrier not keeping us from communicating with our eyes. She sat stoically for hours while family poured into and overflowed the waiting area. We all tried to keep Rosie distracted.

Luis survived the surgery. Manuel and I left the hospital as the doctors were conferring with Rosie, who was agitated and exhausted. The priest had left hours before.

At first daylight, the air was clammy. My eyes were parched from being open all night, as if I had been studying for a final exam. My mouth was dry and foul-smelling. I needed a couple Advil. Manuel, ever the gentleman, opened my car door for me. He tossed a cigarette and stepped on the stub. When had he started smoking again?

I rubbed my temples.

"He'll make it. I can sense it. We'll pull him through."

I never doubted my words for a minute.

We returned that afternoon. Rosie was a different person.

"It's time to grow up," she said, her voice a dull monotone. "I don't have time to cry. There is the business to take care of. And my children."

She was distant and detached. My heart broke to hear her voice so heavy.

Luis lay in a coma in ICU. The doctors claimed half his brain was dead. By the third week, a specialist was called in.

"The hospital staff never should have saved him. He could last like this, on machines, forever." He turned to Rosie. "Don't hope for much."

I heard what he was saying, but the brain had unlimited and untapped potential for recovery. There were always stories about miraculous recoveries from comas. Luis would be one of those stories. We would put our positive energies toward that end.

In the weeks that followed, intense heat stagnated the valley. Rosie went through mood swings like changing patterns on Doppler radar.

Euphoria. "Luis squeezed my hand. He can hear me."

Dejection. "The doctor said it was only a reflex."

And I felt no closer to my husband.

"Here, Rosie." I had found a lovely hardbound journal for her.

"When Luis is better, you'll have a record of this time for him. Maybe it will help. The kids could write in it, too, or draw him pictures."

Ever the teacher.

We embraced. I was family and yet I wasn't. She could share her gut feelings with me and not feel guilty.

"People keep saying, 'I know how you feel.'" She ran her fingers through her short bright-red hair, the color of autumn. "I want to scream, *no you don't!* They say I'm so strong. I'm not. I'm scared to death. Have you seen him? How he looks?"

"No," I admitted. "To be honest, I want to picture him like the last time we were together, at Lexa's quinceañera. And I feel, I don't know, like he wouldn't want us gaping. Seems like an invasion of privacy."

"Thank you." Rosie breathed a sigh a relief. "I get so angry when the old ones go in there with their negativity. They talk about him as if he were already dead."

"Like old Jewish grammas in a sewing circle."

Rosie laughed. "Luis would love that."

Rosie's oldest daughter came in with handpicked garden flowers for her father.

I left the air-conditioned hospital and headed for my car. Damn thing wouldn't start in the heat.

The following Saturday night, I showed up as usual. The lobby was empty. I phoned the waiting room upstairs, next to ICU. No answer.

"Where Tía Rosie go, Mommy? Jesse asked. "Where everybody go?"

I sat down, my spirit limp. I looked at the plate of brownies in my lap. I'd let up some. I'd stopped baking homemade and had switched to Betty Crocker.

I phoned Manuel at the store and cried into the phone. Jesse and I walked back to the car for the long, miserable drive home, both of our shirt backs still soaked from the ride there.

The weather shifted during the night. Rains finally came, cooling off parched pavement and clearing the smoke-choked sky. Manuel, Jesse, and I were at our front window, watching the rain fall when the phone rang.

Luis was dead.

And I was forced to accept . . . that so was my marriage.

Chapter Twenty-One:

Upscale

INFIDELITIES TRANSPIRE FOR MANY REASONS. Authors have written copious fiction and fact about Charles II and James II's mistresses. However, my focus was Mary of Modena and her coterie. Mary never displayed any of that kindly tolerance toward her husband's mistresses that so marked the character of Charles II's wife, Catherine de Braganza. James had been astonished when Mary threatened to enter a convent if his mistress, Catherine Sedley, created Countess of Dorchester by James, was not forced to leave the court. Sedley was banished to Ireland after Mary declared she would not suffer the humiliation of a public scandal.

You go, girl.

However, Sedley was put in apartments nearby not long after.

I walked through the blackened Hampton Court maze, each evocative portrait glamorous, sensual, and sumptuous. Just as at the Banqueting House, I felt a current, but this one was dark. One of the last visitors, I had walked through the empty redbrick Tudor gatehouse, from the present back to echoes of the past. I was grateful. The Wild, the Beautiful, and the Damned exhibit was only six months in duration and I had fallen into it—into the middle of Power with a tinge of Discomfort.

Understandably, neither James II nor his brother Charles II visited Hampton Court often, preferring Windsor Castle. Hampton Court held sad memories for the two brothers. Their mother and father had honeymooned there twenty-five years before, and their father, Charles I, was imprisoned there for three months before his execution. Had I planned further ahead, I would have arrived at Hampton Court a tad earlier to return to London via river launch, but I had just missed the last launch departure. I would have pretended it was a royal barge returning to Westminster Palace after weeks of country entertaining.

It was my last night in the hotel. I would be spending the next night, my last in London, with Tisha Sarnes at her upscale Bermondsey flat on the south bank of the Thames. Our children had attended school together. I enjoyed her quick British wit. Now that her children were grown, she stayed half the year in her native England. Tisha had planned a visit to a neighborhood gallery opening, then dinner. Finally, Borough Market on Saturday morning before I trained up to Cambridge to read Barclay's thesis on Monday. Afterward, back to Oxford, to read in the Bod and regroup.

By now, my diabetic feet were swollen and on *fire*. The tennies I had purchased days prior in a High Street Oxfam weren't doing the trick. I needed a damn good pedicure before joining Tisha—with a damn great foot massage. Checking out of The Grapevine, suitcase rolling behind me, backpack filled to the brim, I went in search of Victoria Station–area salons gleaned from an internet search in the hotel breakfast room.

Rain was intermittent. On my third umbrella, I balked at the price at the first salon on Wilton Road. Determined to find a better value, I walked farther along Victoria Street.

None were walk-in available, and none were cheaper. Tail tucked under, I returned to the first place and got a pedicure I'll remember for life, not as exuberant as Meg Ryan in *When Harry Met Sally*, but close. "Ooooh . . . this is unbelievable . . . this is perfect . . . this is soooo wonderful."

I had booked myself on a picturesque narrow boat ride along Regents Canal, from Little Venice to Camden Locks before heading to Bermondsey. I had trouble pretending to be back in the seventeenth century. A teething infant cried in front of me for most of the hour. How I longed to scream at her unfazed Italian parents, *Will you give her a damn finger to suck before I do?* But I held it in. I guess there would have been seventeenth-century screaming babies, but it definitely spoiled the ambiance.

We exited the narrow boat to find the festive weekend markets of Camden Town at full tilt. I lost myself among the dealers' booths. I bought Tony a small blue-and-green glass water pipe. The rough biker vendor was taken aback by a late-middle-aged woman traveling alone, sizing up drug paraphernalia. I loved blowing his mind. *Hey, I'm not my mother yet.*

Tisha was a delightful hostess. We wound through the cobbled narrow streets of Bermondsey and along the wide Thames promenade to dinner at Magdalen's and back, catching up on our children and school gossip. I treated myself to champagne at dinner. As a diabetic, if I'm gonna cheat, it's normally with pasta or potatoes, though I had been dabbling pretty regularly into the Pimm's bottle. Hopefully, all of my walking served as a healthy counterpoint. On the short walk home, we stopped at Potters Fields Park and people-watched along the south bank of the Thames.

Borough Market the next morning was colorful and bustling, from the yellow knee-high rubber boots and crisp aprons of the cheese-shop clerks standing behind piled-high cheese wheels to the white-haired fishmonger setting his catch on ice. Tisha was charming, enlightening me on the history of the market, a market on this site dating back to the eleventh century. We roamed past booth upon booth of flowers, resembling the opening scene of Covent Garden in *My Fair Lady*, and bought lunch at Tisha's favorite coffee counter.

I wonder, now, exactly where in Borough Market the three jihadis struck, wearing suicide-bomb vests and terrorizing the city of London in 2017, killing eight and injuring forty-eight. Nowhere is safe anymore, sadly, not even a harmless outdoor food market.

At Magdalen's, Tisha had talked about estrangement with her children. She wore its pain in every wrinkle. I am blessed to have a funny, loving relationship with my Jesse, who at the time was living in LA, wrapping up a year of work and fun in the sun—a chip off the old block—before heading to Chicago for law school. Tisha and I talked about motherhood. I rarely talked about my mother, but Tisha was open and kind.

"I always wondered how I would react when she died. How would I grieve for a woman void of the ability to communicate meaningfully with her children? Christ, I never had one conversation with her. Ever. But I think she loved me."

I reached into my wallet and pulled out a photograph. My mother and my sibs cuddled on the front lawn, a rake projecting upright from my mother's hold.

"Since I found this, I keep it with me. See? Something's there, right?"

Tisha took the photo and looked at it. The restaurant was noisy, but I was still.

"Oh, Suze, you are just snuggled up in there, aren't you?"

I sighed. "When she died, I had to clean out her home. She was a depression baby, and she had kept ev-er-y-thing."

I sipped my post-dinner decaf.

"Each time before opening a drawer or cabinet, I would pray that it would not be stuffed to the gills."

Saybrook Road, autumn
CREDIT: photo from author's collection

I looked at Tisha. "I had worked my way up to their bed-room. Leaning against her antique highboy, I gazed out of her bedroom window at the moon over the Gulf of Mexico and began sobbing uncontrollably."

Tisha reached across the white-linen-covered table for my hand.

"It wasn't for her dying, but for what I never had with her, what I had wanted so badly from her. I just couldn't stop crying. That night is what I remember when I think about losing her. But I never had her to begin with."

"Oh, darling, I'm sorry," Tisha consoled.

What else could she say?

Chapter Twenty-Two:

Final Days

"I THINK YOU'RE LEAVING TOWN BEFORE WE explore issues regarding your father."

It was a Parker Burbey understatement. In therapy, I'd come far in resolving impacts of my mother's abuse. She was ill. She couldn't help herself. She'd done the best she could. Her own mother had been cold and unforgiving. As a result, my mother had the self-esteem of dust. I maintained, too, that she was stifled, a creative woman born in the wrong time.

But my father? What excuse did he have?

As a child, I worshipped him, proud of his national reputation as a brilliant legal mind. People assumed I had inherited at least a chunk. I relished the respect. He was detached but kind, even when my mother forced him to scold me whenever I was banished to my room. His footsteps would drag up the stairway. I could practically count the steps. He was never angry, just resigned. The only time he ever raised his voice at me was when he was teaching me to parallel park.

He had been the safe parent. Every night, I would go down to his study to say good-night, clinging to him for dear life until, finally, he would break the hold I had on his neck.

But in my late twenties, while housesitting, I discovered his stash of porn paperbacks, *all* father-daughter themed. Afterward, forever, he repulsed me, the famous attorney whose volumes of legal tomes graced the shelves of every American law school . . . his endless ogling, paralyzing . . . his fatherly touches, stomach-churning.[1]

In my thirties, I was visiting from LA when I found the framed collage of sexy photos resulting from a chaperoned photo shoot by a Cleveland photographer. It was sitting *above the toilet in my father's bathroom.* I gagged into the bowl. Can you say "ephebophilia,"[2] boys and girls?

My folks thought Uncle Noah was funny when he'd kiss me, forcing his tongue deep into my mouth every damn summer in Toronto, starting when I was a preteen. I would spend the ritual cocktail hour in my cousin's elegant Yorkville garden, evading Noah, dodging between stylish, wrought iron lounge chairs as he slithered closer. Funny? No wonder my perception of parenting is skewed. Facebook homages on Father's and Mother's Day? Wistfully beyond comprehension.

No, Parker, at this point, I don't care enough to put in the work.

"Parker, Cleveland's toxic. It's time for me to live my life and stop talking about it."

Eventually, aging was my armor. My father lost interest. He shriveled down to nothing.

But the panic remains.

As conflicted as I am, I wonder, *How will I handle his death?*

I FLEW TO BE WITH MY MOTHER during his final days. She was mean to him in the end. He was no longer the right version of himself. She obsessed over keeping his diaper clean, scolding him like an irresponsible toddler when he didn't. Poor guy. I could relate. With poorly functioning heart valves, helping him in the bathroom was difficult for her. In case she needed me, I would stand outside the door, forced to listen to her scolding, praying she wouldn't need me.

Please. Please. Dear. God.

One night, my mother insisted on cleaning him up. A part of my brain was screaming, *No, no, I can't do this*, while helping her take his pants down. He was leaking diarrhea. She insisted on wheel-chairing him up in their small elevator, so we could shower him off in the master bathroom.

I expressed my doubts, faintly, but I was never a match for her bullying. The shower had a step, so we could not wheel him in. It was up to me to lift him up, naked, into the shower.

My worst nightmare.

I picked him up, lifted him over the step, and held him up, his front against my front, while my mother—grasping the shower door for dear life with her right hand—took the showerhead with her left hand. One part of my brain was screaming, *How can this be happening?*

His penis.

I can do this. I have to do this.

Though silver-headed, he had a big bush of reddish pubic hair. Its color amazed me at the same time I was panicking that I would drop him.

At this point worry took over. How on earth would we do this? He was semiconscious, dead weight. We were in over our (shower) heads. I was beyond worrying about how I would handle his nudity.

"I can't hold him any longer." I pleaded with my mother to stop.

She acquiesced. Finally.

I tried to drag him back over the step and into the wheelchair, but I didn't have strength left. Instead, I had to lay him down on the cold marble floor, his feet still dangling in the shower's watered-down excrement.

My mother used her Life Alert to call paramedics. I covered my father with the largest towel I could find, "Toes in the Sand Drink in My Hand" monogrammed in ludicrous lettering. My mother went downstairs to wait for help. I was alone with this man who had invaded my psyche for years with his gawking and worse. He was lying naked, semiconscious, on a stone floor because his wife didn't want a soiled diaper.

Suddenly, miraculously, my anger dissolved. Somehow, I was given the gift of grace.

He opened glassy eyes. "You're my daughter? You're my daughter?"

"Yes. I am your daughter."

He drifted back into unconsciousness.

I sat next to him, silently, on the cold marble floor until the paramedics came. They were wonderful. And hot. Why are firemen always hot? Gently, they carried him down on a stretcher to one of the guest bedrooms.

He never regained consciousness.

My mother never went into the bedroom, ironically referred to as "The Honeymoon Suite."

Though still uncomfortable, I couldn't bear for him to be alone. There wasn't a chair, so I curled up, tightly coiled, in the farthest corner of the king-size bed for two days, reading a David Baldacci novel. A few times, he sat up and reached up toward the heavens. Was he reaching for a loved one?

Those last two days were a gift. An angel? Fairy dust? *Something* washed over me. Washed away decades of dread and anger.

Hospice delivered a hospital bed. Now he was in the great room with us. Riveted to her beloved cooking shows, my mother never went over to the bed or spoke to him.

Fifteen minutes after the hearse took him away, my sister and me sobbing, my mother insisted we go out to lunch. For Greek.

For thirty-plus years, I panicked at the thought of being left alone in a room with my father.

I was afraid of my mother until she died.

BACK AT TISHA'S AIRY SOUTHWARK FLAT FOR tea and biscuits, we sat on the well-landscaped stone riverfront patio shared with top-floor tenant Patrick Stewart, whom I had drooled over six years before, when he was the lead in Stratford-upon-Avon at the RSC's *Antony and Cleopatra*. He was incredibly, engrossingly, sexy. To hell with *Star Trek*. Damn. Tisha thought he was full of condescending pomp. Now that's what I think of whenever I see him on television. Another fantasy crushed. Sigh.

Tisha called a driver's service to pick me up and take me to Liverpool Street station for a straight shot to Cambridge. It had been fun to be pretend wealthy for a night—I was thirty years from my pampered, privileged county-club days—but I was ready for my next adventure, chasing Andrew Barclay's PhD thesis, "The Impact of King James II on the Departments of the Royal Household." Tisha and I hugged genuine farewells, promising to meet in Nashville in the fall. I enjoyed a good get-together, but solitude was *fresh* air. Necessary.

As the train edged closer to Cambridge, I imagined lives beyond the train stations—Tottenham Hale, Cheshunt, Harlow Town, Sawbridge Worth, Audley End. I was in a Beatrice Potter watercolor, with a touch of Dickens for balance. Captivated.

Please refer to Appendix IV for child sexual abuse statistics and referrals.

Chapter Twenty-Three:

Cambridge

———— ✦ ————

IN CAMBRIDGE, BY THE TIME I SETTLED AND wandered out, the town was locking up for the night. I crossed Clare Bridge in misty dusk. Like Oxford, Cambridge had a collegiate system that enabled its colleges to be completely independent, with a centralized administration. The earliest Cambridge University college was founded in the late thirteenth century. I was staying for two nights at Clare Memorial Court, founded in the seventeenth century. The taxi had mistakenly dropped me off at the contemporary college, Clare Hall, a twentieth-century steel, glass, and brick eyesore.

The guard flagged down a professor wandering by and asked him to escort me to Clare Memorial. An insufferable ten-minute walk ensued with the obliging former professor, socially unable to conduct a personal conversation. Hunched over, in tedious monotone, he lectured on Cambridge history. When we arrived at the correct gatehouse, the professor cowered and backed out, having suffered some kind of past unbearable humiliation by the porter on duty.

My ground-floor suite in entrance M was spare but spacious after six days in my cramped London hotel space. There was competition between Oxford and Cambridge. Colleagues usually had powerful feelings about one over the other, so I was curious to see for myself. My connection to Oxford was so strong, I didn't quite connect to the centuries-old college town of Cambridge. I think I was also drained, so I missed an opportunity to take in more.

I passed the majestic, gothic King's College several times, the subject of three of Wordsworth's sonnets. Unfortunately, I did not take the time to visit Trinity College's Wren Library. The master architect was surfacing in *all* of my reading. My walk reminded me of one of our "Peter jaunts," roaming the streets of London in search of Wren treasures. Among the special collections housed in the Wren Library at Cambridge are 1,250 medieval manuscripts, early Shakespeare editions, books from Sir Isaac Newton's own library, and A. A. Milne's manuscripts of *Winnie-the-Pooh* and *The House at Pooh Corner*. How much more fun it would have been if Peter had been there with me.

It was Sunday. Clearly worn-out, I indulged in a day off. I crossed Queen's Road and wandered the path over the River Cam to the Buttery in the English Gothic Clare's Old Court for my breakfast coffee. Returning to my suite, I read and fell asleep for two more hours. Once awake, I showered and went out to roam Cambridge. I came back and read some more. Peanut butter and crackers with a cold glass of milk for dinner was the perfect comfort food. I read some more . . . a cozy indulgence. Tomorrow, I planned to read most of the day at the Cambridge library. When finished, I'd take a direct bus to Gloucester Green in Oxford to begin my second full week of reading there, at the Radcliffe Camera.

I finished reading *The Elegance of the Hedgehog*. Truly elegant.

My feet were feeling a bit better.

G'night.

I SPENT ABOUT FIVE HOURS IN THE Cambridge University Library, after time in the admissions office obtaining my reader card. The notes from Andrew Barclay's PhD thesis, "The Impact of King James II on the Departments of the Royal Household," in a worn thin brown tome, proved more valuable to me than I realized they would. Barclay's writing serves as reaffirmation of how "small world" the inner workings of court were. But the more I studied, the more I was forced to admit Mary of Modena had little to do with appointing women to her court, try as I might to make that part of my research work.

Andrew Barclay belittles Mary's advancement of the arts, crediting her with little beyond the patronage of Italian musicians and fine artists. Though conceding that these Italians helped introduce the court to a wider range of literary works from the continent, Barclay maintains it wasn't so much Mary's interest in the arts as her coterie of friends.

That is coming from a man.

I prefer the literary research of Carole Barash in *English Women's Poetry, 1649–1714: Politics, Community, and Linguistic Authority*. It energizes me each time I reread it. She speaks of the wide range of women's writings during this time, a "royalist" or "late Stuart women's poetic tradition" and the need to research these writings.

In the 1680s, feminine rituals at the English court of Maria Beatrice enabled several of the authors to participate in European literary culture as actors, translators, and authors. Mary of Modena recreated at the English court a sense of female community associated with European convents. Mary of Modena's arrival at court stimulated the arts. She came by it honestly: her paternal grandfather was known as one of the most enlightened and educated Italian patrons of the time.[1]

The train ride home was relaxing. Returning to Oxford was like coming home now. A new guest was staying at Painter's Cottage. With wild, frizzy graying hair, Dmitri was a Russian émigré, comically professorial with a pinch of put-on. Though tall and slender, he had a little stomach pooch. He bowed every time we passed, reminding me of the nodding contestants in the Strasburg folk festival scene from *The Sound of Music*. I was glad I had stopped in Cambridge. I would have wondered, always, what I might have missed.

Chapter Twenty-Four:

Patient Patient

MY LIFE HASN'T BEEN ALL CHAOS AND calamity. There have been periods of genuine grace and calm. For instance, when Jesse was four years old, one Sunday afternoon, she and I were invited to a grill-out hosted by a family we had gotten to know in our charming country community. Faith Hargrove was one of my queenies. She had an adorable family. Her eldest of three, Marlee, was Jesse's babysitter on Saturdays while I was at work. Already at fifteen, Marlee was a talented artist and writer, perfect for my inquisitive, creative daughter who thankfully hated when I returned and her time with Marlee ended. Thankfully because I never felt bad for leaving all day on Saturdays. I already suffered enough guilt.

Contrary to Manuel's admonition that I couldn't make it alone, my timing was perfect. I was hired to start a branch of the Williamson County library system in the old Bethesda School, up the hill from the "new" school Jesse attended. Every day, she walked up after school with my friends' children. I would seat them at a round table next to the circulation desk for a snack, and then they would finish homework and play outside until picked up by their moms after work.

We were a village. I was making enough money to get by, supplemented by my work as a proofreader for a court reporter who lived down the road. I also taught art once a week after school in our quaint farmhouse dining room to a handful of Bethesda children. I never shook the feeling that my friends enrolled their children to help me out financially. But it was fun.

That Sunday, Jesse and I drove down an idyllic gravel road that wound down and around to a hollow, where a hundred-year-old small yellow farmhouse nestled. Rolling hills enveloped the property, rocky ledges on one side providing habitat for Faith's tribe of goats. A beat-up-but-functional chicken house stood just behind the back door. Road Island Reds pecked, a few Plymouth Rocks strutted, and a handful of good old Leghorns roamed the hilly eighty-acre property.

When we stepped up to the Hargrove's porch, Faith was contentedly sitting on her husband's lap, in a wide rocking chair. Jay's Martin acoustic leaned against the farmhouse porch wall. He would strum bluegrass later with other Bethesda musicians. It all seemed so perfect. A cozy house, a hot husband, a little yellow farmhouse.

Dolly Parton, have at it.

Fate intervened. Faith and Jay were renovating their huge barn at the turn of the drive for their residence. Guess who ended up renting the cozy little farmhouse with her darling daughter? Yes. For the first five years after I left my marriage, Jesse and I lived a sublime life on the Hargrove farm, until I realized I should probably consider buying my own house to build equity. Jesse grew up pretending with precocious Penny, the youngest Hargrove. They spent hours outside, sharing "Rock Land" with the goats, using Well House, Chicken City, and Hargrove Hills as settings for their escapades, pretending they were black panthers—the leopards, not the superheroes.

One night, after a heavy snowfall, unusual for middle Tennessee, Tony built a bonfire at the top of the steepest Hargrove hill. He and I sipped Crown Royal by the fire while the children sledded down the hill, ecstatically, time and time again. Tony and I were so happy on Lane Road, making love every night, our bed in front of the rustic stone fireplace surely made from rock harvested on the property one hundred years before. It was a double fireplace; the other side, in the living room, had a potbellied stove insert where we queenies congregated once a month. At that time, we called ourselves The Twisted Sisters. Faith was the only queenie without a sordid past, but we allowed her anyway! On Hargrove Farm, I blossomed, independent and in love— shades of Hortense Mancini.

Jesse adored Tony. Until one Saturday. She and Marlee found letters from Tony in the back of my dresser. That was how my dear daughter learned of my infidelity. She never let Tony in again after that, feeling fierce loyalty to and protection toward her father. An anger emerged in her and a sadness and guilt in me that, as I have mentioned, has never left.

Something else that never left? My propensity for accidents.

IT WAS TERRIFIC TO BE BACK AT THE BOD from London. I looked forward to a solid week of discovery. I planned on switching to the grand Duke Humfrey's Reading Room the following day, so I was determined to finish up with books on my list from the Gladstone Link underneath the Radcliffe Camera. A perfect rainy day for a library.

Midmorning, not wanting to test the limits of my diabetes, I stopped to eat a banana. Naturally, no eating was allowed in the centuries-old library. I stood outside the entrance door, under the overhang, to avoid getting wet from steady rain. Before returning to my seat, I asked the guard if

I could throw the banana peel in the trash can immediately behind her stool.

"No, you must throw it away in the can just outside the gates," she insisted in her clipped British accent.

"But the rain," I pleaded.

"Sorry, can't help."

"I don't see the can."

"It's just past the gate on the other side of the entrance."

I was looking for the mystery trashcan as I descended the steps. Both flip-flopped feet slipped from under me. I fell—hard—down *all* twelve rain-coated iconic flagstone steps, one by one by one by one. The pain was quick and strong. I know I groaned repeatedly, loudly. People came from everywhere to my aid.

I was completely embarrassed and angry.

Unbelievably, the guard came out and said, "Can I help you?"

It took a while to catch my breath and find my voice. It took all my composure not to shout at her, *You could have let me throw my fucking banana peel away in your goddamn trash can.*

Humiliated, I curtly shooed everyone away and slowly, painfully rose. I climbed back up the stairs, tenderly. I kept on reading, but after about two hours of discomfort, including an aggravating headache, my lower backside was now rock hard. I started feeling dizzy, faint, and nauseous, and I was covered in sweat.

I tried to make it to the door for fresh air but I couldn't, so I hobbled, really frightened, back to my seat and tried to will it to go away. Eventually, through my confused state, I realized it could be a diabetic sugar low, so, hands shaking, I reached into my backpack for my emergency glucose tablets and slowly regained some normalcy. I read a bit more but eventually closed up and excruciatingly made my way home.

Back in my room, I lay on my tummy with a homemade ice pack on my back—knickknack paddywhack. I was freaked out about the low–blood sugar attack and wondering if it was related to the bruising, or maybe I hadn't eaten enough before taking my diabetes meds, hours before. Except for my Pimm's-and-lemonade fix, I had been eating healthily. Damn. I had found some great reading material and hoped I could make it back to the library in the morning. The next day was the Fourth of July. On Independence Day, six years before, I'd had my last period in Oxford. Yeah! I don't think that is the independence that Martina McBride was belting about, but I'll take it.

Next morning, on my way to the library, I stopped at the Boot's Pharmacy on Cowley and purchased a bottle of paracetamol—the Brits' version of acetaminophen. I was encouraged. At first. But after an hour or so, the pain was glaring. My lower back continued to swell to major proportions, to the point where I couldn't localize where the pain was generating. I realized this was beyond me. Had I broken something?

I packed up my books and shuffled to High Street, catching the number-thirteen city bus for John Radcliffe Hospital on Headley Way. It was the A & E—accident and emergency—for me. I could barely sit in the bus's seat. I thought back to Julia-from-the-train-to-Bath and how we talked about Britain's National Healthcare System. Little did I know then that I would need the NHS a mere few weeks later.

I was the only passenger. The considerate bus driver dropped me off as close to the glass-plated entrance as possible. I shuffled in, found the check-in window, and answered the obligatory questions.

Oh, the irony. The hospital is named after the same Radcliffe—John—as the library.

"Good afternoon. What seems to be the trouble?"

"I slipped and fell down the steps of the Radcliffe Camera. I fell very hard on my . . . uh . . ." I whispered, "backside."

She couldn't hear me.

"I fell on me bum," I grimaced, a bit louder.

"Excuse me?"

This can't be happening again, I thought, remembering a much more comical waiting-room visit.

Middle Tennessee hills can be snow crested in March or blooming with daffodils. Miraculously, the week before our late-March wedding day, Tony and I were blessed with daffodils, tulips, redbuds, and early vestiges of white flowering dogwoods. Our ceremony would be on our sweet Piney River's bluff. For our hayloft reception, Tony and I had painted its floor, hung miles of twinkle lights, and restrung an heirloom chandelier, dormant in storage for a year. It was early in the season, so I hadn't given a thought to spraying myself against insects. Stringing twinkle lights along the road, I should have worn hiking boots, not glitter flip-flops.

I was beyond exhaustion by the morning before our wedding. A nice, long, morning-before-the-wedding shower was just what I needed before spoiling myself with a luxurious manicure at the Sassy Scissors, before dinner for family and out-of-town guests at the landmark Miss Mable's Tea Room and Fine Dining Establishment—as it was posted on the interstate exit sign, along with signage for the Waffle House, Taco Bell, and Pepé's Pizzeria.

I soaped up, my head filled with images of how beautiful the property looked and how exciting it would be to walk through the field to where—*Oh my God, a lump*. A large lump. On the right lip of my "bagina," as my ex would pronounce it.

I felt sick to my stomach. I finished my shower quickly. Grabbing a hand mirror, I hoisted my leg up onto the nightstand. *Damn, where are my reading glasses?* Okay, now I had them. I feigned a chuckle, remembering my need for a mirror to insert a tampon until I graduated from college. Sure got teased for that!

Oh my God, there it is. A gnarly lump; a repulsive, engorged tick. Nausea and panic combined. *Blast those flip-flops!* I grabbed tweezers, but after a few tries, I knew it was hopeless. Now part of the tick was out and part was dangling. My stomach dropped lower. Disgusting.

"Extra!" my students would say.

I felt more like Lucy Ricardo than a bride-to-be at fifty-three. The phone rang.

"Hello," I yell.

"Hi, hunney, whatcha doing?" my sexy, southern husband-to-be whispered in my frantic ear.

"I can't talk now. I have a tick on my bagina. I'll call you back." Slam went the receiver.

Relatively new to the area—I commuted fifty miles to work now—my doctors were still back in Nashville. I had no clue where on a late Friday morning I would find a clinic, never mind a tick-removal specialist. I paced madly before deciding to head for the Yellow Pages. Flipping through the directory pages, I could feel the lump and visualized half a tick, squirming.

No ob-gyn, no internist—all I could find was a children's clinic. *This will be interesting.*

I dialed, still pacing.

"Good mornin', Children's Clinic," a sweet southern receptionist drawled.

"Okay, get ready for a story you've never heard before," I began, nervously. "I am getting married tomorrow, and I have a tick stuck on my vagina. Can you tell me where I can go to get it removed?"

"Sweetheart, you can't be serious," she sympathetically drawled.

"Never more," I replied.

"Hold on, dear. I'll ask." She put the receiver down.

I could hear her in the background: "Charlotte, this here lady has a tick on her privates, and she is getting married tomorrow. Can we help?"

A minute later she returned to me.

"Honey, we can't help you here. We are a children's clinic. Go to the Family Medical Group. It is right across from the hospital . . . and . . . good luck, y'hear!"

Okay, so . . . do I stop and get my nails done first? How ridiculous is that? But I had taken the only appointment I could find in town at short notice. After all that planting, my nails looked like the "before" picture in a back-cover magazine ad for nail strengthener. I got dressed in a hurry and barreled off towards Highway 70 and the Sassy Scissors, next to Ruby's Wings 'n Things.

Every stereotype you could possibly think of for a southern small-town beauty salon was bottled up in the Sassy Scissors—big hair, bleached hair, big-hipped women. All there. Cardboard Easter bunnies in the front window, plastic armchairs covered with orange UT Volunteer blankets in the waiting area.

"Hey there, darlin. Can I help you?"

I wanted to scream, *Yes, I am getting married tomorrow, and have a tick on my twat*, but sanity prevailed.

Demurely, I said, "I have an appointment with Darlene for a manicure."

"Follow me, sweetie." I was led to a tiny cubicle and Darlene.

Darlene looked like a female trucker drenched in makeup and loaded with cubic zirconia from wrinkled neck to shiny toe. A two-inch sparkly French-scripted "D" nestled between her ample bosom.

She took one look at my nails and boomed, "Honey, I

don't have enough time for *this*. Can you come back later this afternoon? You're gonna take a while, sugar."

"Well, actually, it *is* a relief. You see, I am getting married tomorrow and I have a tick stuck on my vagina. I really should be sitting over at the clinic right now, but—"

"Honey pie, you can't be serious."

"Sadly, yes." I didn't know whether to laugh or cry.

"Hey, Virgie!" hollered Darlene with a capital "D" between her breasts. "This here darlin' is gett'n' hitched tomorrow, but she has a tick stuck on her privates. Can we squeeze her in later today?"

Squeeze? Ouch, too close to home.

Double ouch, as all the matrons in the shop put down their issues of *Us* and *Star* magazine to see the pathetic victim. I made a new appointment and scurried out of there as quickly as possible.

Now instead of big hair and small cubicles, I had a shy young clerk behind a glass partition.

"May I help you?" the timid creature asked.

As quietly as I could and yet still be heard, I stated my case. "I am getting married tomorrow, and I have a tick stuck on my, uh," I paused. Even softer, I said, "Genitalia."

"Excuse me?"

I glanced over my shoulder at a full waiting room of rednecks and Latina mamas.

"Uh," *Oh, please let her hear me this time*, "uh, I . . . I'm getting married tomorrow, and I have a tick stuck on my privates."

"Again, please?"

A little louder this time. "I'm getting married tomorrow and I have a tick stuck on my vagina."

She turned a shade of pink before stammering, "H-h-h-hold on a sec."

Shy Young Clerk turned on her heels and whispered to another just-out-of-high-school clerk at the copy machine.

Eventually Shy Young Clerk returned.

"Ma'am, you need to go out the door to Paxton Medical Associates immediately. Next door to the left."

She couldn't close the partition soon enough.

I did as told, finding myself in an identical waiting room a little less congested, with an identical glass partition. Fortunately, the receptionist looked to be about my age.

"May I help you?"

Again, as quietly as I could, I said, "I am getting married tomorrow, and I have a tick stuck on my vagina. The folks from next door sent me here."

She gave me a sympathetic look. You could tell she'd been around long enough to have heard just about everything.

"Hold on a second, hon."

My-Age Receptionist disappeared over to the previous clinic, which connected behind the partitions. The logic in all this escaped me. It was like the gatekeeper scene in *The Wizard of Oz*.

Shy Young Clerk was going to be queried, I was sure. Poor thing.

My-Age Receptionist returned and instructed me to have a seat.

"We'll work you in, somehow."

Fine.

Grateful.

I sat.

And watched.

And squirmed.

Finally, they called me back.

A young mother whined, "Why is she going in before me?"

At this point I had no pride.

I bellowed, "Because I'm getting married tomorrow and I have a tick stuck on my goddamned twat."

Mustering all the grandeur I could, I went through the Golden Doors.

Much to my surprise, the female PA who entered the examination room was sophisticated and our conversation delightful. If it weren't for my feet up in stirrups and the fact that she was going at my vagina with monster tweezers, we might have been meeting for coffee in a chic Manhattan café.

When she instructed me to bathe daily, I laughed and said, "Duh."

"Believe me, you never know," she laughed back.

I left with my dignity intact and a prescription for antibiotics. By evening, I was feeling no pain and sipping champagne at Miss Mable's Tea Room and Fine Dining Establishment. Let the wedding rumpus begin!

I SPOKE MORE FORCEFULLY TO THE WOMAN behind the Oxford Accident & Emergency admissions window. "I fell on my ass down the Radcliffe Camera steps!"

I leaned against the Oxford hospital's emergency room counter, putting my weight on my forearms.

"Just have a seat," the buxom admissions clerk replied clearly unimpressed.

Easier said than done, I ruminated, looking at the rows of plastic waiting-room chairs, screwed together. Nothing good comes of polyurethane, I rued, remembering my all-nighter in a plastic chair at Newark International.

When was I going to learn not to wear flip-flops? For I am the English teacher who left school during an open period and while walking over to the drug store fell hard on her face after tripping over her never-shortened harem pants in front of Bruegger's Bagels, which caused two black eyes—à la LA Jimmy. And I am the teacher who had to take a ridiculous ambulance ride, literally across the street, to the Vanderbilt ER, after falling down wet back steps in my school's fine art wing, holding a just-kilned ceramic piece instead of the railing. Clay piece in hand, I had tumbled down the remaining stairs into a cinder block wall so hard that my left pinkie finger contorted sideways and backward, making a kindergarten child sitting in the nurse's office howl when the sculpting teacher rushed me through the halls, screaming, "Oh my god oh my god oh my god."

Blasted flip-flops. Again. You would have thought I'd learned my lesson. *Maybe* that *should be my epitaph*, I thought, thinking of all the mistakes, all the backward and forward that my insecurities had shaped—all the metaphorical rain dodging. I'd been a human metronome.

But I am proud of myself for ever trying to move forward, to affect change in my life when I thought it was necessary. My own feminist arc smooths.

"You have strong intuition. It gave you courage when you needed it," my latest counselor applauded. "You are resilient."

I liked her.

I tried to sit in the damn emergency room chair.

The LED message board flashed.

Average wait . . . three and a half hours. No matter what health-care system, playing the waiting game was part of the process. Also playing? Wimbledon was still taking place on the mounted television above the center of the long narrow room. The men's final.

At first, there were no empty seats close to the telly, but by the time a nurse called me back to an examination cubicle—four and a half hours later—I had the *best* seat in the waiting room, inching closer and closer to the telecast over the hours. I alternated between leaning to the left, leaning to the right (stand up, sit down, fight-fight-fight), standing on my knees, leaning against a wall, just plain standing. At least the match had been a long one. Three and a half hours, plus a thirty-minute delay. The roof closed for the first time in Wimbledon finals history. When you watch tennis for that long, you learn a lot. By the way, Federer defeated Murray, 4–6, 7–5, 6–3, 6–4.

Dr. Juene was young, lovely, and sympathetic. She gasped when I pulled down my pants enough for her to see the damage. Immediately she had me lie facedown on the padded patient table. She told me that if I wanted the swelling to subside, I would have to lie still for "several days." Thinking of the time I had left and how much I had planned to do, I started to cry.

Everything had unfolded so beautifully to that point. I saw days in the library and further travels disintegrate. My once-in-a-lifetime chance to succeed with this project— smithereens. Frustration mixed in with pain. I kept crying.

Dr. Juene offered comfort before leaving to get some pain medication for the swelling and bruising that covered the entire width of my back.

"Perhaps you could extend your stay?" she encouraged.

"I was thinking about that while you were out. I wasn't *just* sobbing, you know," I tried to joke.

I blew my nose.

I have a small nose but a loud blow. My students used to tease me.

"I'll have to see if it is possible and how much the airfare penalty would be." At least it brightened my outlook.

"Here are your antibiotics and a codeine pack. Avoid ibuprofen; it can cause more bruising. Call me if the pain persists."

"Basic amoxicillin?"

She nodded her head. I thanked her for her kindness and asked where I paid my bill.

"It's free."

"What? But I'm an American."

"Just go." She winked.

I thanked her again and found the taxi phone. I was home in a few minutes.

I walked into the Painter's Cottage living room, where Emma was watching television, reclining in the cozy love seat. I told her that I was injured.

"So am I," she responded flatly and showed me her sore ankle.

I feigned sympathy and limped up to bed, realizing I was really on my own with this one and wondered what to do about food. Emma obviously wouldn't/couldn't lend a hand. I dropped off my heavy backpack, still laden with laptop and books. Opting for cash in my pocket, I winced back down the stairs and stopped to ask Emma if she needed anything.

"No."

Very slowly, I edged to the small co-op market around the corner and stocked up on peanut butter and rye crisps, flavored water, tuna, a head of lettuce, an onion, and some soup. Damn. Oxfam farther down on Cowley at James Street was too far for me to buy some paperbacks to kill time. My back was tightening up.

I hope I can find a few paperbacks in the house.

I hiked back to my bed and passed the bowing Dmitri along the way. I was so stooped over, he probably thought I was bowing back. I took another dose of codeine and eventually fell into a drug-laden sleep.

How did I pass the time? *Lots* of BBC radio on my laptop and Emma's paltry collection of morbidly depressing mysteries. *Why am I not surprised?*

The codeine helped. I was amazingly patient. Probably drug induced, but I had accepted that the only way I was going to have a chance to travel was to be a patient patient. Maybe I needed the rest.

Not once in five days did Emma knock on the door to check in. *Can you say "bitch," boys and girls?*

Thanks to my injury, instead of five to seven days, I only had one more at the Bodleian before leaving for Kent. I sucked it up. I would spend one more day in the Radcliffe Camera, one goal to gather a strong reading list for my future back-to-interlibrary-loan days in Nashville.

When I came back from Kent, I would also have only one day in the legendary Duke Humfrey's Reading Room.

Chapter Twenty-Five:

Kent or Bust

———————⌒⌒———————

On the road again: Love it. Train to Reading, changed to Paddington underground to St. Pancreas. Fire alarm so subway entrance closed. Along with throngs of other commuters, I walked from Euston. Blocks and blocks. No problem. Now on Southeastern Highspeed train to Ashford, Kent. New territory. Looking forward.
—from my journal

OFF THE TRAIN IN KENT, MAP IN HAND, I walked in a strong breeze, only having to ask once for directions to the car rental. Thankfully, the car was small—most British vehicles were. No room for big cars on the narrow, barely two-lane roads. Thank goodness for roundabouts. I could keep going round and round until I figured out what to do! Tenderly, I settled into the car, testing my backside. Very sore but livable. It took a bit of time to figure out car etiquette, and it didn't come all at once. My first stop? A little market/post office in Hothfield. I bought nan and cheese and mailed a few postcards at the village post office in the back of the store.

Driving on the left side of the road, with the steering wheel on the passenger side of the car, was nerve-racking. I practiced for a while, making a loop on the back roads— Great Chart, Snodhill, Pluckley—a few small warehouses, but mostly rolling farmland. Got hard-honked twice. Finally feeling brave enough to leave my little loop, I gingerly crossed over A20 in search of Eastwell, Anne Finch's homeplace.

My Oxford paper titled "Nighttime Is the Right Time: Anne Finch, Countess of Winchilsea and 'A Nocturnal Reverie'" is the research that led me to discover Mary of Modena's literary court. Anne Finch (1661–1720) is known today as one of the most gifted poets of her generation. Her poetry is Augustan (1660–1760), meaning that it reflects upon nature and the search for both an emotional and a religious relationship. She had a vast range as a writer and translator, attaining a modest amount of notoriety during her lifetime. However, her large body of work would earn greater attention after her passing at only fifty-nine years old. While Finch also authored fables and plays, today she is best known for her poetry: lyric poetry, odes, love poetry, and prose poetry. Later literary critics recognized the diversity and intimacy of her poetry. She drew upon her own observations and experiences, offering insight into the Jacobean social and political climate.

Anne struggled with depression throughout her short life. She recorded private thoughts running the gamut between joy and despair, playfulness and despondency. Anne's poems also revealed her spiritual side. In *A Nocturnal Reverie*, the speaker addresses the beauty of nighttime and the disappointment when it ends. Finch uses night and day to create a serene metaphor rich in imagery, comparing the busy world to peaceful solitude. This is a quiet poem, as gentle as the wind it mimics.

"A Nocturnal Reverie"

In such a night, when every louder wind
Is to its distant cavern safe confined;
And only gentle Zephyr fans his wings,
And lonely Philomel, still waking, sings;
Or from some tree, famed for the owl's delight,
She, hollowing clear, directs the wand'rer right:
In such a night, when passing clouds give place,
Or thinly veil the heav'ns' mysterious face;
When in some river, overhung with green,
The waving moon and the trembling leaves are seen;
When freshened grass now bears itself upright,
And makes cool banks to pleasing rest invite,
Whence springs the woodbind, and the bramble-rose,
And where the sleepy cowslip sheltered grows;
Whilst now a paler hue the foxglove takes,
Yet checkers still with red the dusky brakes
When scatter'd glow-worms, but in twilight fine,
Shew trivial beauties, watch their hour to shine;
Whilst Salisb'ry stands the test of every light,
In perfect charms, and perfect virtue bright:
When odors, which declined repelling day,
Through temp'rate air uninterrupted stray;
When darkened groves their softest shadows wear,
And falling waters we distinctly hear;
When through the gloom more venerable shows
Some ancient fabric, awful in repose,
While sunburnt hills their swarthy looks conceal,
And swelling haycocks thicken up the vale:
When the loosed horse now, as his pasture leads,
Comes slowly grazing through th' adjoining meads,
Whose stealing pace, and lengthened shade we fear,
Till torn-up forage in his teeth we hear:

When nibbling sheep at large pursue their food,
And unmolested kine rechew the cud;
When curlews cry beneath the village walls,
And to her straggling brood the partridge calls;
Their shortlived jubilee the creatures keep,
Which but endures, whilst tyrant man does sleep;
When a sedate content the spirit feels,
And no fierce light disturbs, whilst it reveals;
But silent musings urge the mind to seek
Something, too high for syllables to speak;
Till the free soul to a composedness charmed,
Finding the elements of rage disarmed,
O'er all below a solemn quiet grown,
Joys in th' inferior world, and thinks it like her own:
In such a night let me abroad remain,
Till morning breaks, and all's confused again;
Our cares, our toils, our clamors are renewed,
Or pleasures, seldom reached, again pursued.[1]

Yes. The relief that twilight brings.

Anne Finch, Countess of Winchilsea, by Peter Cross, c. 1690–1700

The countess was important to me. She started this quest, and I related to her beneath-the-surface melancholy, the chaos in her life, and her resilience. Finch's book, *Miscellany Poems, on Several Occasions*, was the first artifact I was blessed to handle. I ordered it as I ordered all the texts at the Bodleian circulation desk. But when I picked it up, wrapped in archival board tied with brown archival ribbon, I could barely breathe. Copyright 1713. *What I am holding is three hundred years old.* Sacred. I thought of my childhood rabbi removing the Torah scroll from the ark while chanting, tenderly undressing the Torah.

The ritual. Remove the silver-gilded pieces for the handles. Take off the pointer, bare hands never touching the Torah. The breastplate, also silver gilt, lovingly removed. Finally, the mantle cloth made of velvet and silk and lavishly embroidered with metallic thread, as an honor to God.

Yes, I was so nervous I had to go for a walk before I could begin to use *Miscellany Poems* for my research. I asked the librarian to hold it for a bit. This time I did not fall.

In my 2006 research paper, I write that Anne Finch was born Anne Kingsmill in 1661—making her Mary of Modena's contemporary—in Sydmonton Court, Hampshire, currently the country house of Andrew Lloyd Webber and home of his summer arts festival. She was the youngest of three children, though Anne never knew her father. He died only five months after she was born. Extraordinary for the times, in his will, Sir William Kingsmill specified that his two daughters receive financial support *equal* to their brother for their education.

From my vast reading I learned family was a common thread among the writerly women in Mary's court. What a concept. The Kingsmill sisters received a comprehensive and progressive education, exceptional for females at the time. Anne learned about Greek and Roman mythology, the Bible, French and Italian languages, history, poetry, and

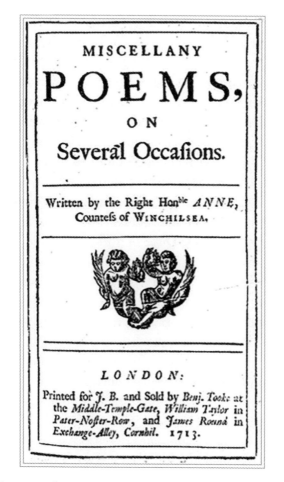

Title page of *Miscellany Poems on Several Occasions*, 1713

CREDIT: Anne Finch, Countess of Winchilsea (1661–1720),
public domain, via Wikimedia Commons

drama. Tragically, she was only three years old when her mother died. Family-custody lawsuits ensued. The sisters bounced from grandmother to uncle until their uncle's death. When twenty-one years old, Anne Kingsmill went to live at St. James's Palace, in the court of Charles II. She became one of six maids of honor to Duchess of York, Mary of Modena.

Anne had an affinity for the pastoral life. She genuinely loved the countryside and associated the rural with writing poetry. Her friends included Sarah Jennings Churchill and Anne Killigrew, two other maids of honor in Mary of Modena's court who shared poetic interests. The court provided Anne Finch with plenty of opportunity to write.

She was also encouraged to publish by her supportive husband. While residing at court, Anne met Colonel Heneage Finch, a courtier and soldier, appointed groom of the bedchamber to James, Duke of York, two years before he ascended to the throne. The Finch family had strong Royalist connections to the Stuart dynasty. Initially, Anne resisted Finch's romantic overtures. However, Heneage proved persistent, and the couple was finally married in 1684, when Anne was twenty-three. Upon her marriage, custom dictated that Anne resign her court position, but she remained close to Mary of Modena. Heneage retained his own appointment and would serve in various government positions. Therefore, the couple remained involved in court life.

Anne must have appreciated the chance to be settled after her tumultuous upbringing. The Finch marriage proved to be enduring and happy, in part due to the aspects of equality in their partnership. Indeed, part of Anne's development as a poet was due to her ability to express joy and love for Heneage. She had his complete support. Her early works, many written to her husband, celebrated their relationship and passion, therefore quietly defying contemporary social conventions. In other early works, she had satirically disapproved of prevailing misogynistic attitudes, but, just like my Tony, Heneage strongly supported her writing activities. She was lucky.

So am I.

The couple demonstrated great loyalty to the king in what turned out to be a brief reign. James II was deposed in 1688 during the "bloodless revolution"[2] and fled England for exile in France. Heneage Finch lost his government position and retreated from public life. The loss of position meant loss of income. Once again, Anne's life was uprooted. The Finches were forced to live with a variety of friends in London for a period. While living in the city, the couple faced harassment, fines, and potential imprisonment.

In 1690, Heneage was arrested and charged with Jacobitism for attempting to join the exiled James II in France. Heneage and Anne Finch remained separated from April until November of that year. Understandably, the circumstances caused the couple great emotional turmoil. Living with friends in Kent while her husband prepared his defense in London, Anne often succumbed to depression. Writing helped ease the pain. Writing was a means of objectifying her inner world of imagination. Writing freed her from the helplessness and passivity that were her lot as a woman. There was liberation in the act of writing.

Yes.

The poems that she wrote during this period reflected Anne's mental state. Other poems involved political themes, all noticeably less playful and joyous than her earlier work. After Heneage Finch was released and his case dismissed, his nephew Charles Finch, the fourth Earl of Winchelsea, invited the couple to move permanently into the family's 2,000-acre Eastwell Park estate in Kent. The Finches took up residence there. Anne and Heneage found peace and security on the beautiful estate, where they would live for more than twenty-five years in the quiet countryside. Terraces and formal gardens surrounded the mansion. Ancient oak and beech groves, hills, valleys, and fields dotted with gazing sheep remained. The sea was just visible on a clear day. For Anne, Eastwell provided a fertile and supportive environment for writing. Peace and seclusion at Eastwell fostered the development of her poetry. Retirement in the country provided her with her most productive writing period.

For me, as well. I related to her, powerfully. I gravitated toward her, strongly. Melancholy childhood. Educated. Chaos. Bouts with depression. Preferring the country life. A husband who supported her need to write. A survivor.

Resilience.

By the early eighteenth century, the Finches moved back to London, where influential friends, including renowned writers Jonathan Swift and Alexander Pope, encouraged Anne to publish under her own name. She was reluctant. The social and political climate remained oppressive for women.

In her poem "The Introduction," initially privately circulated, she reflected on contemporary attitudes toward female poets. Women were writing about this over three hundred years ago. The first lines:

"The Introduction"

Did I, my lines intend for public view,
How many censures, would their faults pursue,
Some would, because such words they do affect,
Cry they're insipid, empty, and uncorrect.
And many have attained, dull and untaught,
The name of wit only by finding fault.
True judges might condemn their want of wit,
And all might say, they're by a woman writ.
Alas! A woman that attempts the pen,

Such an intruder on the rights of men,
Such a presumptuous creature, is esteemed,
The fault can by no virtue be redeemed.
They tell us we mistake our sex and way;
Good breeding, fashion, dancing, dressing, play
Are the accomplishments we should desire;
To write, or read, or think, or to inquire
Would cloud our beauty, and exhaust our time,
And interrupt the conquests of our prime;
Whilst the dull manage of a servile house
Is held by some our outmost art, and use.
Sure 'twas not ever thus, nor are we told
Fables, of women that excelled of old;
To whom, by the diffusive hand of Heaven
Some share of wit, and poetry was given.[3]

Even twelve years later, when she published the book that I had been blessed to handle, *Miscellany Poems, on Several Occasions*, in 1713, the cover page of the first printing indicated the collected works—which included eighty-six poems and a play—were "Written by a Lady." However, on subsequent printings, Finch—as Anne, Countess of Winchilsea—received credit as the author. Wordsworth himself complimented Anne in his legendary *Preface to Lyrical Ballads*. He found in Finch's writing, "genuine crystals of poetic language." Further, he singled her out as one of the "few Augustan poets to use genuine imagination in describing external nature."[4]

Anne Finch became Countess of Winchilsea upon the sudden and unexpected death of nephew Charles Finch in 1712. As Charles had no children, Heneage Finch became the Earl of Winchilsea, making Anne a countess. The Finches had to assume Charles's financial and legal burdens, which took years to settle in court.

Renewed strains resulting from the Jacobite Rebellion in Scotland in 1715, initiated by James and Mary's son, Edward, further aggravated the tense political situation. Other Jacobites had been sent to prison. The stress took its toll on Anne's health, which deteriorated. She became seriously ill. Her later poems reflected her turmoil. She died in Westminster, London, at age fifty-nine, her body returned to Eastwell for burial.

Nearly a century after her death, Anne's writing had been largely forgotten until William Wordsworth's praise. Contemporary literary scholars acknowledge Finch's distinctive voice and her poems' intimacy, sincerity, and spirituality.

In 1929, centuries after the countess's death, in the classic essay *A Room of One's Own*, Virginia Woolf, one of my favorite twentieth-century authors, expressed grief that Finch was so unknown. Woolf wished to know more about "this melancholy lady, who loved wandering in the fields and thinking about unusual things."[5]

I feel the same way, Virginia.

I was heading toward Eastwell, the Winchilsea estate. The farther I traveled on the narrow Kent road to Boughton Lees—Westwell, Goat Lees, Boughton Aluph, Kemps Corner—toward Wye, the more peace and contentment flowed within me. I imagined Anne being driven home by carriage to Eastwell, after visiting her dear friends, Lord and Lady Thanet, in nearby Hothfield, where I had practiced my driving.

One curve unfolded into another. Approaching an English cottage at the curve of a road bordered by Hawthorne hedgerows—another perfect stand-in-time moment, an indescribable feeling of belonging there. But I didn't, and the ache of it made my throat hurt. I *had* to have lived here in a previous life. The pull was too strong. It held on to me too magically.

Under a stunning, ominous sky, I pulled up to Eastwell. There were several vehicles in the car park, beyond arched gates but a distance from the gray stone and turreted manor. The charming ivy-covered country house was magnificent. I walked from my car up to the estate in refreshing wind. I passed through the outer cobbled courtyard, walking by neatly stacked rows of firewood. Inside, I found oak-paneled walls with leaded windows and a fire burning full in the large stone fireplace that scented the inviting space. Only one of the deep leather armchairs and love seats was occupied. I sat. No one bothered me, even though, clearly, I was not dressed for the wedding reception taking place.

The vast manor house was gorgeous, and the gardens were spectacular. Though not the initial seventeenth-century home, the garden walls were original. Up until that time I had failed to sense Mary's presence, but here in the gardens Anne's gentle presence was everywhere. No wonder she was content to leave the court after James and Mary were deposed. What a fruitful place. I walked around to the back of the estate. The wedding party was being photographed on the terrace steps. I snuck a few photos.

The clouds grew more threatening. I roamed the manor, keeping away from the bridal party—except in the loo—until the rain passed. Convivial generations of ladies primped in front of Victorian mirrors. I washed my hands, making a joke about something to do with their conversation. As usual, after hearing me, they asked if I was American. They were curious about me, but no one questioned my presence. Since I looked artsy, I think the employees and guests assumed I was one of the wedding photographers. I had been discreet but busy with the 35mm Nikon that hung from my neck.

Again, I sank into a deep-seated leather chair by the fireplace and observed. The reception was on the east side of the manor. The dining hall was straightaway, still empty, but formal tables were set with stunning crystal, beyond more stunning leaded glass. A man sat across from me, mournfully.

Perhaps he was a recently widowed member of the groom's family, or maybe he was a man stood up by his mistress. This would be a perfect place for a romantic rendezvous. I imagined returning with Tony. They would go nuts for his southern accent!

Back outside, I sat under a flowering tree in the east garden, avoiding intermittent drizzle, soaking in the walled garden and breathing in the colors, wondering how it would feel when I painted from home, using photos I took. When I cried at the end of Lord Attenborough's PBS series on treasure houses of Britain, when the camera panned the staircase on the last episode, had it been Eastwell? Was this where I had lived a previous life?[6] What fitting happenstance that would be. Kismet.

I could have stayed there for days, but the storm was imminent. Regretfully, I said my imaginary goodbyes to dear Anne and continued on. I wish I had thought to look for her burial site when I was there to pay my deep respect.

It was time to head east to the Straight of Dover. I took the M20—of course I missed it a few times and circled a few roundabouts! I giggled. Six years before, after my Oxford tutorial with Peter, the same thing had happened in Wales. I was traveling with a fellow Bread Loaf colleague, also studying in Oxford for the summer. Poor Patricia held on as I grazed many a left-sided hedgerow on the passenger side.

When I descended into Dover, the cliffs took my breath away.

They *are* white. Dazzling.

From the car, I took a few photos of the cliffs and the mammoth port but had to focus on my descent and then the signs directing me farther north, up the coast to Deal. I would definitely return to Dover and cross over to France. I wanted to experience the sun and the sea on the channel. I wanted to conjure Mary's feelings as she escaped by boat to endure a then twenty-four-hour journey to Calais, France, in winter darkness with the infant heir to the throne.

Approaching the coastal town of Deal, I broke the side-view mirror of the rental car, causing my stomach to lurch. It took some time, but I made my peace with it.

The inn was proving very hard to find. I slowed to ask for directions twice—good thing it stayed light so late in the summer. Did more than a few turns on a roundabout or two. It took me a while to find the St. Crispin Inn, off a side road, but it was worth it.

My room was authentically enchanting, up a narrow staircase, above the pub where I ordered my Pimm's and lemonade and then a delicious filet of trout. Afterward, I got cozy in my room; I enjoyed a gentle rain with windows wide open. I looked forward to a new adventure tomorrow. *Does it get any better than this?*

First thing next morning, I retraced my steps back to the Dover P&O Ferry Docks and soon boarded *The Spirit of France*. The enormous ferry to Calais was entertaining. The sun was shining, but storm clouds were on their way from the east, just as predicted. Two scally-capped Irish blokes joined my table on deck. They could have been out of a Frank McCourt novel, one a quiet listener, the other with the gift of profane gab, but what a storyteller.

"Jesus, you're a different sort of chick, you are," he said when I told him I had no phone for the trip, just wanted to enjoy my "present."

Behind sunglasses, he looked at me.

Quickly surrounded by four empty Beck's beer bottles, he laughed. "Jesus, your husband is probably having the time of his life, out with the gents every night, having a pint."

I sassed back good-naturedly, "I hope so."

He shared his homegrown philosophy more raucously with each longneck.

"It's all about the chicken. Some people always get the chicken. Some people only get the feathers. But feathers aren't so terrible. Jesus, you can always make a fuckin' pillow."

Calais wasn't much, but it was fun to "be in France." The port was depressing. Though it was mainland Europe's closest geographical point to the United Kingdom, I sensed the town wanted nothing to do with British tourism either. Not a T-shirt or key chain to be found, although I located a few postcards.

After the luxury of her royal life in Britain, Mary-in-exile must have been apprehensive and depressed in the bleak port town. I walked and took a few photos. Then I ate lunch in a charming restaurant back garden. I pitifully tried to order my Bloody Mary in French. I had always read French better than I had spoken it. Before walking back to the port, I bought Tony a souvenir pack of French cigarettes. Once again, I lucked out with the rain, which didn't begin until boarding.

The channel was a different beast on the return trip, churning green-gray waves mixing with steady, hard rain against a ceiling-to-floor picture window. No one was out on deck for this ride. This was more how Mary would have experienced the crossing.

I imagined. But I stayed inside the cabin!

The Kent sky was sunny again the next morning at the St. Crispin Inn. I planned on exploring all day by car. In the mahogany-paneled dining room, adjacent to the bar area, I waited for my eggs and sausage, sipping on coffee from a sterling carafe left on the table. On my way out, I "borrowed" one of many small, comfy throw pillows from the banquette where I had eaten the night before. I needed a cushion for my bruised backside. I was still a little nervous about driving the narrow roads, but I gulped and took off. I stopped in picturesque Sandwich for a few hours and roamed the quaint village, which contained wonderful small shops and friendly people. In an antique store, I found the perfect teacup for my collection and a tiny umbrella at a thrift shop, my fourth of the trip. I needed it a few hours later when I was caught in a brief shower. Dodge that rain!

Next, I drove the back roads and ended up in Canterbury and took an obligatory roam through the touristy cathedral town. I had a quick outdoor lunch at a Pret A Manger, my default eatery, then window-shopped. Back at the car, I looked at the map for a while, deciding my next move. Definitely north, toward the sea. I experienced more tears of joy. *If I lived here, would I still feel this way?*

I headed north toward the Saxon Shore, winding curve right, winding curve left, and past a primary school. Mothers and nannies collected their uniformed charges at afternoon dismissal. Was I even on a public road? I passed a small RV (called Caravan) park, complete with deserted wooden snack bar and video arcade. I knew the sea was close.

Then, there were the Roman towers at Reculver.

Roman ruins at Reculver, Herne Bay, Kent
CREDIT: Peter Watson, 2009, CC BY-SA 2.0 UK
(https://creativecommons.org/licenses/by-sa/2.0/uk/deed.en),
via Wikimedia Commons

Reculver was another magical find, a cliffside Roman ruin and cliff walk.[7] I walked down to the rocky shore in a reflective mood, contentment and bittersweet combining. Had Anne Finch ever walked this shore? Had she returned by carriage to Eastwell, her skirt hem stiff from seawater?

A young woman appeared, and though hundreds of feet separated us, the spell was broken. I hiked back to the precarious iron stair and ascended, holding on to the rail. No more falls, please. I strolled through vegetation in the low sandy dunes. Sedge, marram, and couch grass struggled to poke through the loose sand. Clusters of sea holly and flowering sea spurge reveled in the breeze. I met the footpath along the cliff and hiked for a while, snapping photos of dogs being walked by their masters—more often masters being walked by their dogs—romping in the blackthorn scrub and crowberry, enjoying the sun and wind.

Once again, I *hated* to leave. I was at peace. When I found a bench perched atop the bluff, I sat and stalled the inevitable. Sadly, the coastline was eroding at about three feet per year. *If I am ever lucky enough to return, will all of this be gone?*

Returning to my car, I roamed the back roads, looping around the port town of Ramsgate before heading back to A256 and the inn. I had a light dinner, read, and fell sleep.

On my last morning in Kent, after breakfast, coffee, dressing, and settling my bill, I got into my rental for one last auto-adventure. I had about three hours before the car was due in Ashford. My first stop was St. Margaret's Bay. It had to be the place Peter had raved about—a cliff-side enclave overlooking the British Channel. *Could I live here? Yes!* I crossed the main road for a roam-about, the last part in a fairly steady rain. It was glorious, but it was time to leave the back roads. I entered the motorway to Ashford, to return the rental car and hop a train to Hatfield, near St. Albans, just north of London. There, I would spend the night and visit Hatfield House—one of Britain's twelve Treasure Houses.[8] Anne Finch and her husband, Heneage, lived there for a short time after James II and Mary exiled to France. The subject of Finch's poem "A Nocturnal Reverie" was the mistress of Hatfield, Ann Tufton Cecil, Anne's cherished Lady Salisbury.

I joked with the car-rental attendant that the side-view mirror should be called "American mirror-glass" because I was sure I was not the first Yankee to misjudge the left side of the road. The cracked mirror cost only £27.50. He knew immediately. I laughed. I paid and hailed a friendly taxi driver, who took me the short distance to the Ashford rail station. Though the rain had stopped, I wasn't up to dodging.

On the train to London/St. Pancreas, I chatted with a friendly Brit rendezvousing with college mates, as all my train companions seemed to be doing when train traveling to London. They were going to do a historic pub crawl. We talked about security and American politics. Brits seem to enjoy chatting with an American. Saying hello invited conversation; they immediately detected my accent.

Somehow in talking about the beauty of Kent, the gent inspired me to find that wild hair[9] and journey to Edinburgh for a night. James and Mary lived there off and on, at Holyrood Palace, where Charles II thought they'd be safer, due to James's intense, unflinching Catholicism. Queen Elizabeth II stayed there at least once a year, every summer. Just days before, I didn't think my injured lower back would take a five-hour train ride, but it was so much better, and I had my *borrowed* pillow placed just so to relieve the pressure. Tony often teased me about my former propensity to steal sunglasses from Walmart. I can now add pillow theft to my rap sheet. I meant to mail it back. Honest.

I was too close to Scotland. I had to go for it. I don't know the chap's name, but I thought of him all day and giggled to myself because we had laughed at how often I dodged the ever-present rain—so often, when I needed to be outside, it would disappear. He said whatever writing I ended up with should be titled *Rain Dodging*.

Chapter Twenty-Six:

Hatfield to Holyrood

———·❦·———

ONCE I CHECKED IN TO THE HOTEL IN HATFIELD and found the bus stop to St. Alban's for a late-Saturday-afternoon walkabout, the sky had cleared. I reached St. Alban's and walked toward City Centre. The outside street markets were closing up, but there were groups of people still roaming. I found myself in the intimate apple orchard of St. Alban's Abbey. I looked at my watch to see if it was close to Evensong. *Could be.* I walked around the cathedral, which was enormous. Peeking into a door, I heard a lovely—aren't they all—British accent echo through a completely empty nave.

Carefully and quietly, I opened the door, which squeaked, picked up a brochure, and wandered in. Tentatively, I walked forward, thinking the voice I heard might be a priest rehearsing. The nave, I later read in the brochure, was one of the longest in Europe. I continued creeping forward, past a partial wall, a fourteenth-century nave screen, and discovered Saturday Evensong was in progress. It had been the actual sermon I'd heard, echoing via speakers. An usher with oily, balding hair and a clipped mustache, wearing a mustard-yellow suit jacket, invited me to sit where I wouldn't interrupt the ongoing service. He reminded me of the Man in the Yellow Suit in *Tuck Everlasting*.[1] I could just see the choir-master and one male adult chorister to my left, but ahead of me in the North Transept was a breathtaking stained glass masterpiece, the Round Rose window, unveiled by Princess Diana in 1989.

The haunting Evensong choir brought me to tears. There had been so many quiet moments of wonder, of discovery, of just-right. And there I was, almost at the end of this blessed adventure, just as I had been at Westminster Cathedral weeks ago for Evensong, as if bookends to a journey of a lifetime, a journey of literary and historical discovery, a journey of geographical incredulity, and a gifted journey of respite from the worry for my sweet Tony. I contemplated how our "holes" had brought us together. Had that even been healthy?

"Holes are what you make of them," a therapist had reas-sured me. "We often follow the pattern of what the familiar is. It's what we are drawn to."

By now I understood I had gravitated toward chaos in my life because it was the "pattern of the familiar." For the very first time, I wondered if that was what had brought my folks together—their holes. I had always accepted the story that it had been my mother's short stature attracting my five-foot-four father. But yikes, what damage they had done with *their* holes.

I said my prayers for Tony and my prayers of gratitude for this incredible fellowship. I followed the procession through the South Transept, sincerely thanking one of the priests before exiting. If I had walked farther, past the Presbytery and High Altar, I would have seen the tomb of Humphrey, Duke of Gloucester,[2] namesake of the Oxford reading room where I would end my research later in the week.

I climbed a city hill before realizing it was Holywell Hill, where "La belle Jennings" grew up with her sister Sarah, later

Sarah Churchill, Duchess of Marlborough. This breathtaking view would have been the same. Uncanny. I stood there for a while as folks bustled by on the quaint city street, again reminded how compared to this, American antiquity is a mere 250 years old. I bussed back to the hotel in Hatfield, splurged with a glass of Prosecco at dinner, completely enveloped in my travel cocoon.

I was feeling a bit palace-weary the next morning, as I walked through George's Gate from the charming Hatfield train station.

I was early; the house opened at noon on Sunday. So I enjoyed strolling in the old Stable Yard turned upscale boutique and airy restaurant courtyard. Locals enjoyed Sunday brunch against a backdrop of local farmers selling their wares under white canopies. A duo in the corner played Beatles' songs. Somehow just right. *Again, how do I keep doing this?*

I meandered through the expansive gardens—the West Garden and Sundial Garden. I relished a trek into the woods, where whimsical tableaus were set into the landscape. One flip-flop bogged down in mud. *Oh shit, I can't go through the manor house with a muddy foot.* I did my best to wipe it off. I circled back via Old Palace Garden, ready to enter the house with the first group of early tourists. My flip-flop was dry.

Hatfield is a residence. It has been the home of the Earl of Salisbury and his family for over four hundred years. Henry VIII confiscated Hatfield Palace from its original owner. Henry sure was good at that. It became a residence for his children, Mary, Elizabeth, and Edward, each by a different mother.[3] Here, Elizabeth I and Edward grew up and schooled together, happily.[4]

The clerk at the Stable Yard gift shop was a sophisticated, elderly man who volunteered one Sunday a month, relishing the chance to share anecdotes with tourists. His nickname was Scotch, and he spoke proudly of the influence of the current Lady Salisbury on Hatfield House, down to the objects d'art selected for the shops. I finished my bit of browsing and strolled over to the cash register. On cue, he inquired as to my origins.

"Nashville. Tennessee."

As usual, my response solicited smiles and personal stories of Music City, USA.

Aging and elegant, Scotch chirped, "Oh, that's wonderful. My grandmother, who as you can imagine was quite old, had *everything* money could buy."

He continued, his Scottish accent irresistible. "We asked her, 'Ma'am, if you could have anything in the world for your impending birthday, what would it be?'"

"I want to go to the Grand Ole Opry," she echoed back.

"And so we sent her there."

"And did she enjoy her visit?" I laughed.

"Oh, my goodness, yes," he exclaimed, handing me my small package.

I pushed it into my over-the-hip backpack, giggling.

"Thank you so much. You have made my day."

I wish I had shared his lady's connection to my book.

I was still giggling as I reappeared into the sunny Stable Yard, where the duo was singing "Ticket to Ride"—how appropriate—as visitors nibbled on Sunday brunch and sipped mimosas. No need today for my charity-shop umbrella. Browsing at a honey stand, I conversed with a Swedish couple. That is what I loved. Cultures sharing stories and conversations bookmarked with mutual respect, making associations on a different level than the academic links that filled my summer. I was enveloped in a magic shell of grateful solitude, intense focus, and moments of passionate connection. Throughout my journey, I stumbled upon small, intimate neighborhoods that protected their landmarks, loved them, and felt pride in their histories.

Inside Hatfield House? Perfection. No wonder it appears in so many films, including *Lara Croft: Tomb Raider* and Johnny Depp's version of *Charlie and the Chocolate Factory*. My favorite rooms had to be King James's drawing room, still the principal reception room, and the library, holding over ten thousand volumes dating from the sixteenth century to the present.[5] Both rooms were intimate despite their size, rooms to feel right at home. Modern family photos blended among famous masterpieces, priceless tapestries, and marble carvings.

King James drawing room, Hatfield House, Hertfordshire
CREDIT: Reproduced with permission of the
Marquess of Salisbury, Hatfield House.

I recognized the mirror enfilade layout of the rooms. The green hues at Hatfield House matched some of the other palace rooms I had toured . . . a perfectly muted but rich color. Malachite. Celedon. Visceral. My heart sighed. Reason fell into place. An artist's palette in orgasm. Exquisite.

I had a lovely chat with another elegant, elderly docent in the Armory, again happy to share his information.

"This room was built as an open loggia in the Italian Renaissance style. Windows were added in the mid-nineteenth century. There had been no interior passage on the ground floor to connect the two wings."

The white-haired volunteer continued, "Quite inconvenient, wouldn't you agree?"

I wanted to reply that the room would have been heaven had it remained open, but I have yet to visit Britain in the winter, so I only nodded. I considered strolling down the long front walk to find the Elizabeth I accession oak tree, but I had a train to catch.

I hurried back to the hotel to collect my bag and returned as quickly as I could to Hatfield Station, switching trains in Stevenage.

"Hitching Arlesey, Biggleswade, St. Neots, for Peterborough. Grantham, Dorchester, York, Newcastle, Berwick upon Tweed," chimed the intercom, all the way to Edinburgh. The land grew more mystical as the train traveled north along the North Sea coast.

Edinburgh, the capital of Scotland, is on the Firth of Forth, a deep inlet gouged into the East Coast. The city is dramatically located on a series of volcanic hills.

My taxi dropped me off in front of my B and B, under the shadow of Edinburgh Castle and the Castle Rock. The Georgian row house was the former home of Kenneth Grahame, author of *The Wind in the Willows*.[6]

At twilight, in search of dinner, I walked the narrow cobblestoned Rose Street. By now, I understood how to order properly in a pub. I decided on fish and chips, watched football on the pub telly, and walked back to my room as darkness descended.

Since I hadn't researched this leg, I deduced my best use of time would be to buy a bus pass and tour my way to Holyrood Palace. The next morning, I walked to Waverley Bridge and bought my tour ticket. Everything felt very natural. I wasn't a tourist, not quite a national, but past the tourist stage.

I had figured out how to figure out what I needed, pretty seamlessly. Mistakes I made were usually hilarious. With my limited Spanish, I directed an anxious Hispanic woman to the correct bus and informed her of the fare. On the upper deck, open to the drizzle, I pulled out a hat and my umbrella.

Sometimes you dodge, sometimes you don't.

Fortunately, again as at Windsor Castle, I had missed the queen's annual visit by a week; had I not, the Palace of Holyroodhouse, which sits at the base of the famous extinct volcano Arthur's Seat, would have been closed to the public. Its lovely setting against a mountain background, its stone walls and large, high rooms built around a ninety-four-foot-square central courtyard, must have reminded Mary of the Palazzo Ducal in Modena.

During her extended stay in 1681, Mary was still recovering from the grief of her last miscarriage.[7] The new state apartments were light and lofty, lavishly adorned with carving, plasterwork, marble masterpieces, and magnificent tapestries. The apartments were modern compared with the Tudor inconveniences of St. James.

Now, I think of Queen Elizabeth II's hearse waiting, with the backdrop of Arthur's Seat behind. I am thankful I have memories of being there.

Though Mary and James spent considerable time at Holyrood, for me, it was James's grandmother, the tempestuous Mary Queen of Scots, whose ghost lingers. Her chambers in the northeast corner tower had been returned to their original sixteenth-century state, her bedchamber incredibly small at the top of a narrow stone spiral staircase, her tiny supper room in a turret just off the bedchamber. At the bottom of the staircase, the outer chamber was now devoted to a display of Stuart and Jacobite relics. For me, the trinkets encased in glass created an intimacy. To see hair clips and fans, ear bobs and cameos, that royal women had actually worn made them seem more real. James II and Mary of Modena took up residence twice.[8]

I wrapped up my time in the contemplative Abbey nave that remained, adjoining the palace. Desolate and neglected, open to the sky, its origins go back to the twelfth century. Hard to believe that Charles I's Scottish coronation was held here four hundred years ago. I tried to visualize its former timber roof trusses and stone vaults. When I was ready, I walked over to the bus stop, behind the outlandish, incongruent, postmodern Scottish Parliament building. I jumped back on a tour bus proceeding up the Royal Mile in Old Town. Writer Daniel Defoe called it "perhaps the longest, largest, and finest street, not in Britain only but in the world."[9] On the previous tour bus, I had scoped out the quaint street and wanted to wander there to shop for my own trinkets and grab a bite. By now it was raining hard—so much for rain dodging—and the flagstone, as in Oxford, was as slippery as hell. *Can you say "paranoia," boys and girls?* I ducked into The Royal Mile Gallery, selling old prints of Scotland, maps, and classic Victorian prints of old paintings. I purchased a small print, *The Baker*. Back at my B and B, I picked up my bag and taxied back to Edinburgh station, where I grudgingly paid thirty pence to pee before getting back on the train to Oxford. *Isn't frugality a Scottish stereotype?* I was glad I made the trip. Always, as with Cambridge, I would have wondered.

Chapter Twenty-Seven:

Goodbye

MY LAST FULL DAY IN OXFORD. I WAS ON MY way to wrap up the final hours of research in the Duke Humfrey's Reading Room. I did not want to leave. I was sick that my time in the library had been sliced to one day because of a banana peel, pun intended, but as during my convalescence, I tried to put it behind me. I took my time getting to the library. Walking back and forth between Cornmarket and Broad Streets, I listened to street musicians, savoring my last morning along the pedestrian promenade and making last-minute purchases.

I stopped in the Radcliffe Camera locker room to store my belongings one final time. Still very sore, I inserted a coin in the lock and treated myself to the antiquated elevator instead of the boundless wooden stairs I normally climbed. Inside the Reading Room before leaving for Kent and beyond, I had completed request cards for four books focusing on origins of salon culture, where I was sure my connection to Mary and her literary court lay. It was where my quest had been heading before I took my terrible tumble.

The magnificent Duke Humfrey's Reading Room was named after Humphrey of Lancaster, first Duke of Gloucester.[1] It took thirty years to build. If you are a Deborah Harkness—*All Souls Trilogy*—fan, her heroine, Dr. Diana Bishop, conducted her research here. It was also the Hogwarts library in the Harry Potter films. The books in the very oldest section are in oak bookcases that protrude from the walls on both sides, with rows of readers' desks crammed between. The reading room ceilings are incredibly gorgeous panels, each painted with the coat of arms of the university. I had been looking forward to spending a week in this charmed section of the Bodleian. It was hard to grasp that these glorious rooms were designed in the fifteenth century.

A tour was underway in the main hall. One last time, I felt gratitude for permission to research today in the oldest reading room at Oxford. The librarian's enormous carved wooden circulation desk alone was worthy of oohs and aahs. Sitting at a reader's carrel in one of the narrow rows, a steady delightful breeze carried in from an open casement window. *Please, young man behind me, don't close it!* I settled into my wooden straight-back chair—back be damned—and worked all day, my focus on the origins of salon culture.

The salon, an important place for the exchange of ideas, developed in sixteenth-century Italy. Between 1540 and 1560, women writers were numerous enough to be considered a significant group for the first time in Italian literary history. The word "salon" first appeared in France in 1664—when Mary of Modena was six years old—from the Italian word *sala*, the large reception hall of Italian mansions. Salon culture flourished in France throughout the seventeenth and eighteenth centuries, emigrating from Italy.

Cultural historians have studied salons in depth. Historian Dena Goodman claimed salons were at "the very heart of the philosophic community" and went as far as declaring that salons were integral to the process of Enlightenment. Joan Landes, professor of early modern history and women's studies, wrote that the salon was an offshoot of the traditional court. Others compromised by declaring that the public and private spheres overlapped in the salons. No matter what angle, the role of women within them was *paramount*. The essential role women played as *salonnières*—mistresses of ceremony—received more serious study only at the end of the twentieth century, with the emergence of feminist theory. Even then, though, feminist studies in the 1970s concentrated on individual stories rather than historical origins.

The salon differed from the court. It mixed different social ranks and orders. In the seventeenth and eighteenth centuries, continued Landes, "Salon[s] encouraged socializing between the sexes and brought nobles and the middle class together. Salons helped facilitate the breaking down of social barriers."[2] Here, women could be powerful influences. In eighteenth-century England, writer and salonnière Elizabeth Montagu (1718–1800) held salons where the expression "bluestockings" originated. The original bluestockings (*les bas-bleus*), meaning "intellectual women," gathered for the next three hundred years. They were the center of the life in the salon and carried an important role as regulators, selecting their guests and deciding about the subjects of their meetings—social, literary, or political. They also had the role as mediator by directing discussions. The salon was an informal university for women. They were able to exchange ideas, receive and give criticism, read their own works, and hear the works and ideas of other intellectuals. Still, William Hazlitt, now considered one of the prominent critics and essayists of the English language, reportedly said, "The bluestocking is the most odious character in society . . . she sinks wherever she is placed, like the yolk of an egg, to the bottom, and carries the filth with her."[3]

The women-led salon was also the primary means for women to enter the commercial-print world of sixteenth-century Italy. One such very important circle—and connected to Mary of Modena—was created on Ischia [Is' kee ə], a volcanic island known for its thermal waters located a short seventeen miles southwest of Naples, Italy. One of the most important developments in the origins of salon occurred on Ischia and was integral to my quest.

Ischia was a utopia for women receiving dispatches from husbands fighting in war zones, while remaining safe from peril themselves. They were unrestricted by male dominance. There, in 1509, mistress of Ischia Castle, Constanza d'Avalos, established a poetry salon. She was joined by her niece, poet Vittoria Colonna, a member of the House of Este, Mary of Modena's noble family. Vittoria Colonna was Michelangelo's muse. Her book, *Rime*, published in 1538, was the first by a woman under her own name.

Also working with them in establishing the salon was Maria d'Aragona, who grew up in the castle with Vittoria. Their sisters also joined the literary circle. Because these women lived their adult lives virtually as single, they experienced complete artistic freedom. Many of the more important Italian salons of the day were led by these women or were offshoots of one of their salons. Their influence as female patrons in the salon circle was felt throughout Italy from Naples to Milan. Salon culture spread quickly through Europe.

Through Vittoria's travels to and residence in Naples, the salon culture spread there first and later up the length of Italy to Ferrara, just forty-five miles from Modena, where Vittoria launched a "moveable salon" while visiting Duke Ercole II d'Este. It was common for aristocrats to travel through Europe, including the Colonna-d'Aragona women.

Dazzling circles formed in the smaller courts, stimulated by the presence of beautiful and educated patronesses, one such being Isabella d'Este, 1474–1539. Both Isabella and Vittoria were sixth-generation House of Este—Maria Beatrice of Modena was seventh-generation. By the seventeenth century, in Rome, Princess of Colonna, the daring Marie Mancini—sister of sensational Hortense Mancini *and* also Mary of Modena's cousin—was a major salon hostess and a published author of memoir.

In fact, salon culture could be considered the precursor of modern publishing as a method of moving culture forward. With the rise of the publishing industry, the importance of the women-led salons *increased* in Italy. They served as focal points for social interaction and intellectual friendships between poets and editors. Many ambitious women used the salon to pursue a form of higher education. Although not connected to the state, the salons were steeped in church and state politics, provoking a pope or two.

Undoubtedly, under the tutelage of her strong mother Laura Martinozzi, one of the seven famed Mazarinettes,[4] Mary of Modena grew up in an atmosphere of intellectual freedom for women.

However, she did not have the power to choose her own court. Not even a queen had that kind of power. Many women, including former lovers of her husband, were thrust upon her as political prizes awarded to families by the king. I maintain she continued to sustain intellectual freedom for women in her husband's court. With James having grown up in exile in France, he was familiar with salon culture, and as a result was more open to intellectual women and the arts than his British counterparts. Carole Barash wrote that Queen Henrietta Maria, wife of Charles I, and the mother of Charles II and James II, introduced the *précieuses* tradition to the English court.[5] Barash claims that the Stuart court returned from exile in France with French literary practices[6] and that James II, short as his reign was, was crucial for English women developing a sense of themselves as public writers. Salon culture is the link. I am very comfortable with this progression of feminist history and its connection to Mary's court.

An unexpected delight. The joy of research on my last day. *Breathe.*

HOW IDEALIZED AND NAIVE WERE MY INITIAL assumptions. That Mary had artists and writers in her coterie was not of her making. But Mary of Modena encouraged the women in her court to pursue intellectual and artistic interests, and she encouraged patronage among the women in her court. Mary of Modena's support of the literary and artistic in court, through participation and patronage, allowed the women in her court a world of theater and art, an idyllic world of female friendship, and a model in which women were central.

It is important to me that I pass on knowledge of the early vestiges of European feminism to teach younger generations of women our illustrious histories. Women's studies go further back than Betty Friedan and Gloria Steinem's second-wave feminism of the 1960s and 1970s or the suffragettes of the early twentieth century.

I am satisfied knowing that in my roundabout way I came up with a viable conclusion.

Quite a last day of study.

I packed up my laptop, notes, and pencils. I signed out, feeling the same nostalgia as from my morning walk. I said farewell to the librarian on duty, admired the ornate mahogany circulation desk one more time, and walked to the antiquated back elevator.

The elevator doors started to close when an elderly lady appeared. Without my glasses, I found the open button to allow the woman in. I had never seen her before. I saw senior scholars rarely, female scholars even less in the Bodleian libraries.

Ah, the irony.

Graceful with her ebony cane, the older woman entered. Softly, the elevator door closed. Something about her was quite lovely. Smiling gently, I could not take my eyes off of her. Comfortably elegant, the woman was dressed in soft, loose layers of muted grays and creams, with a touch of citrine. Snow-white hair in a loose bun caught with a sterling clip. Artisan sterling earrings framed a still-exquisite jawline. Although I was curious, something compelled me not to invite conversation in the slow-moving elevator. Something otherworldly. We exited. I followed behind her to the centuries-old stone stairway that would take us down to courtyard level. A young male student stopped to let her access first.

She lightly replied, "No, no, please go on. I am rather slow and would only keep you waiting."

That could be me. A few decades on.

THE SNOW-WHITE BUN VANISHED FROM VIEW. I stopped in the Radcliffe Camera gift shop and perused until, behind a glass case, I found a ring, sterling and gold, with a soft water pearl amid Miltonian scrolling, an intricate leaf pattern taken from the endpapers within a copy of *Milton, Early Poems, 1896.*

John Milton. *Paradise Lost. Ahhh.*

Reading it had been a literary experience. After our wedding ceremony, Tony and I strolled back to our bungalow from the river's edge where my dear colleague, an Episcopal priest, had performed our ceremony. In the tiny kitchen, Tony and I shared a private toast before reuniting with our guests. I read verses from Milton's epic poem, in Book IV, where Adam and Eve express delight in their union.

I hoped the ring would serve as a talisman, to remind me to write every day.

Walking along Oxford's historical Catte Street, the narrow picturesque path from the Bod to the Queen's Lane bus stop on High Street, I could not erase the genteel, ethereal woman from my mind. My enchanted time at the Bodleian was ending. The day had been surreal—saying goodbye, breathing in sense-of-place to recall forever. All day, I felt mirrored in a time warp. I had an uncanny, though calm, feeling. That genteel lady *was* me—in twenty, say twenty-five years. Not exactly a doppelganger, but . . . as I had shared with young Tobey, six weeks before, while we waited side by side on a rickety bench at the Heathrow bus station, thirty years before, heavily pregnant, I watched Lord Attenborough reveal a glimpse of a possible previous life.

Magically, I ended my stay gifted with a glimpse into my future, a sense that not only would I be back, but I would still be sharp—and researching my ass off.

Appendix I

———⁕———

Attendants not previously mentioned in the court of Mary of Modena as the Duchess of York and as Queen.[1]

A **lady-in-waiting**, historically a noblewoman, was looked upon as a confidante and personal assistant attending a royal woman or a high-ranking noblewoman. Whether receiving compensation or not for her services, a lady-in-waiting was considered more secretary, courtier, and companion to her mistress than a servant. Ranked between the lady of the bedchamber and the woman of the bedchamber, at the time of Mary of Modena, a lady-in-waiting's duties included assisting the queen at dressing, waiting on her when she ate in private, guarding access to her in her bedchamber and closet, and providing companionship. She participated in the queen's pastimes, for instance, dancing, music, reading, and embroidery. The lady-in-waiting took care of the queen's wardrobe, guarded her jewels, and accompanied her when she traveled without the king. A lady-in-waiting could not get married without the queen's permission. They served for several years and did not retire. If a lady was unable to carry out her duties due to ill health, she still kept her title.

Mary of Modena brought four close friends with her from Italy, and two became ladies-in-waiting. Confidante Contessa

Vittoria Davia Montecuccoli was an Italian noblewoman, a daughter of a marquis. She was eighteen years old when she accompanied Mary on her escape from England to France. For Vittoria's loyalty, she was awarded the titles of Countess of Almond and Peer of Scotland. The truest friends, Mary and Vittoria called each other cousin. Until her death, she remained with Mary.

Countessa Lucretia Pretonari Vezzani was an old childhood friend who was also with Mary when she escaped to France. Contessa Eleonora Molza and Contessa Torricsi also came with Mary from Italy. Old childhood friend Pellegrina Turini, who had served Mary since her birth, became a woman of the bedchamber.

Women of the bedchamber, in Mary's time, attended the royal women and helped them bathe, get dressed, get undressed, and so forth. The bedchamber women came in before the queen's prayers, which was before her majesty was dressed. The queen was often required to change her clothes during the day. Women of the bedchamber helped her. The bedchamber-woman also pulled on the queen's gloves when she could not do it herself. When the queen dined in public, the bedchamber-woman brought the chocolate. They were placed in rank below the ladies-in-waiting.

Susannah Armin, Lady Bellasyse, from Yorkshire in northern England, was a woman of the bedchamber until she married Sir Henry Bellasyse, Knight of the Bath and close friend to James. She was widowed young in 1667 and became one of James's lovers; he procured rank of baroness for her. Even though she had formerly been one of James's mistresses, she was a consistent correspondent with Mary once in exile.

Frances, Countess of Bantry and Duchess of Tyrconnel, known as La Belle Jennings, was one of the most celebrated beauties at the court of Charles II. Her first appearance there at age fifteen caused a sensation. Frances rejected James when he was duke. She was almost alone among her competitors in maintaining a reputation of chastity. In his memoirs, Count de Gramont compares her with Aurora, the goddess of spring. "Miss Jennings adorned with all the blooming treasures of youth, had the fairest and brightest complexion more dazzlingly than had ever yet been seen. Her tresses were of a most beauteous flaxen."[2] From French Ambassador Courtin: "Her tresses were a perfect blond. She is small but has a fine figure, a splendid complexion, quick brilliant eyes, and the finest and whitest skin I have ever seen."[3] She became a maid of honor to Mary when she was Duchess of York and became lady of the bedchamber once Mary was queen. Frances was with the exiled court of James and Mary at St. Germain. She died as a result of falling out of bed and is buried in a vault in St. Patrick's Cathedral in Dublin. Her younger sister was Sarah Churchill, the famous Duchess of Marlborough.

Maid of honor, in the time of Mary of Modena, had to be the granddaughter of a peer, if not nearer in blood; the office could not be held by anyone below that rank without special provision. She had to be a good conversationalist, because she met foreigners at court and dealt with private foreign correspondence.

Lady Sophia Stewart Bulkeley was the sister of Frances Theresa Stuart, Duchess of Richmond. Sophia's marriage to Henry Bulkeley, Master of the Household to King Charles II and King James II, placed her about the court, and she was appointed maid of honor to Queen Mary of Modena, and then lady of the bedchamber. She followed James and Mary into exile.

Lady Anne Digby Spencer, Countess of Sunderland, wife of Robert Spencer, second Earl of Sunderland, Althorp,

Northhamptonshire, was one of the Hampton Court Beauties. She was at the birth of Edward, along with Susannah Belasyse, one of only two women in attendance.

Groom of the stole was a powerful individual who had the right to attend the monarch at all times and to regulate access to her private quarters, including the bedchamber.

Penelope O'Brien, Countess of Peterborough, was groom of the stole. She was present while the queen delivered the Prince of Wales. Her niece, Carey Mourdaunt (née Fraser) was a maid of honor to Mary of Modena and one of the Hampton Court Beauties painted by Sir Godfrey Kneller. O'Brien's father was a first Baronet and physician to Charles II.

Lady Mary Mordaunt, Duchess of Norfolk, daughter of Penelope O'Brien.

Elizabeth Bromley, woman of the bedchamber.

Mrs. Powis (Powis Castle, Wales) was governess to Mary's children. She was an ugly, bustling woman with a heart of gold, Catholic, and completely loyal friend to Mary, "a most pious lady and in the opinion of all, well fitted for so great an employment."[4]

Mrs. Margaret Dawson was also in Anne Hyde's court as dresser.

Lady Harrison, "mother of the maids."

Lady Jones, chamber keeper.

Appendix II

Stuart Family Tree 1567–1714[1]

The Succession to the Crown Act 2013 changed succession laws. The right of male primogeniture no longer applies.

(1566–1625) **JAMES I** (VI of Scotland)

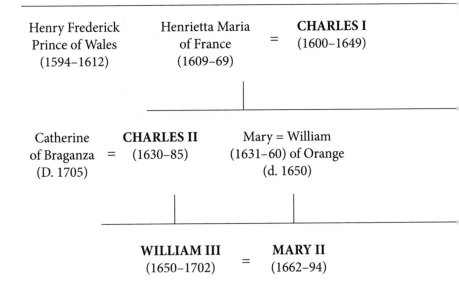

Henry Frederick Prince of Wales (1594–1612)

Henrietta Maria of France (1609–69) = **CHARLES I** (1600–1649)

Catherine of Braganza (D. 1705) = **CHARLES II** (1630–85)

Mary = William (1631–60) of Orange (d. 1650)

WILLIAM III (1650–1702) = **MARY II** (1662–94)

Begin House of Hanover = **GEORGE I** = Sophia Dorothhea of Celle (1666–1726)

=   Anne of Denmark (d.1619)

Frederick V = Elizabeth
Elector Palatine
(d. 1632)

(1) Anne Hyde   **JAMES II**   (2) Mary of
(d. 1671)   =   (1633–1701)   =   Modena
(d. 1718)

George of   **ANNE**   **End of**
Denmark   =   (1664–1714)   **Stuart**
(d. 1708)   **House**

James Francis Edward   Sobieska
= Maria Clementina   (d. 1735)
'The Old Pretender'
(1688–1766)

Charles Edward
'The Young Pretender'
(1720–88)

Appendix III

**Mistresses and (Natural) Offspring of
Charles II and James II**[1]

Charles II
    wife: Catherine deBraganza, no offspring
    mistresses and offspring:
    Lucy Walter
        1. James Crofts, Duke of Monmouth
    Elizabeth Killigre
        1. Charlotte FitzRoy
    Catherine Pegge
        1. Charles Fitzcharles, Earl of Plymouth
        2. Catherine Fitzcharles
    Catherine Sedley, no offspring
    Barbara Villiers
        1. Anne Palmer Fitzroy
        2. Charles Fitzroy, Duke of Southampton, second
           Duke of Cleveland
        3. Henry Fitzroy
        4. Charlotte Fitzroy
        5. George Fitzroy, Earl of Euston, Duke of Grafton,
           Earl/Duke of Northumberland
        6. Barbara Fitzroy

Nell Gwynne
1. Charles Beauclerk, Duke of St. Albans
2. James, Lord Beauclerk
Louise Renée de Keroualle
1. Charles Lennox, Duke of Richmond,
  Duke of Lennox
Hortense Mazarin, no offspring
Frances Stewart, no offspring
Moll Davis
1. Lady Mary Tudor

James II

first wife: Anne Hyde
1. Mary II of England
2. Anne of Great Britain
second wife: Mary Beatrice of Modena
1. James, Prince of Wales
2. Louisa Maria Teresa
mistresses and offspring:
Margaret Brooke, no offspring
Catherine Sedley
1.Catherine Darnley
Susannah Armine, Lady Bellasys, no offspring
Arabella Churchill
1. Henrietta Fitzjames
2. James Fitzjames, Duke of Berwick
3. Henry Fitzjames, Duke of Abermar
Sophia Stewart Bulkeley, no offspring

Appendix IV

Child Sexual Abuse Statistics and Referrals[1]

CHILD SEXUAL ABUSE IS ANY SEXUAL ACTIVITY between adults and minors or between two minors when one forces it on the other. This includes sexual touching and non-touching acts like exhibitionism, exposure to pornography, photography of a child for sexual gratification, solicitation of a child for prostitution, voyeurism, and communication in a sexual way by phone, by internet, or face-to-face. Untreated child sexual abuse scars children and destroys families. It is a major public health problem and a crime punishable by law that must be reported.

About one in every four girls and one in every thirteen boys in the United States experience sexual abuse at some time in their childhood. Eighty-two percent of all victims are female. Females sixteen to nineteen years old are four times more likely than the general population to be victims of rape, attempted rape, or sexual assault. The vast majority of sexual abuse is committed by someone that the child or their family knows. The long-term emotional and physical damage after sexual abuse can be devastating to the child.

When sexual abuse has occurred, a child develops many distressing feelings, thoughts, and behaviors. The child

266

may become withdrawn and mistrustful of adults, become depressed, intentionally harm themselves, and/or become suicidal. Children who experience sexual abuse and other adverse childhood experiences (ACEs), such as physical abuse or neglect, have a higher chance of developing depression, post-traumatic stress disorder, drug addiction, and suicidal behaviors later in life.

Child victims of long periods of sexual abuse often develop low self-esteem, a feeling of worthlessness, and an abnormal view of sex. Victims are four times more likely to develop symptoms of drug abuse, four times more likely to experience PTSD as adults, and about three times more likely to experience a major depressive episode as adults. They even have a higher chance of developing physical conditions such as heart disease later in life.[2]

No child is prepared to cope with repeated pain and fear of sexual abuse. To complicate matters, a child who knows and cares for the abuser becomes trapped between affection or loyalty for the person and the fear, pain, and betrayal that goes along with the sexual abuse. Some children who have been sexually abused display sexualized behaviors that are not appropriate for their age and may try to pressure siblings or peers into sexual behavior. Some sexually abused children become child abusers themselves as adults.

There will be over 500,000 babies born in the United States this year that will be sexually abused before they turn eighteen. Forty-five percent of victims do not tell anyone for at least five years, and, of course, some never disclose.

As one child expressed it, "Abuse is like a boomerang. If you don't deal with it, it can come back to hurt you." On the other hand, children who have the support of an understanding caregiver and effective treatment can recover without long-term effects.[3]

I am impressed with the resources offered by RAINN (Rape, Abuse & Incest National Network). Here is the link: https://www.rainn.org/statistics/children-and-teens.

More resources:
24-hour National Sexual Assault Hotline: 800-656-4673

National Domestic Violence Hotline: 800-799-7233

Childhelp National Child Abuse Hotline: (call/text) 800-4-A-CHILD; 800-422-4453

American Psychological Association: https://www.apa.org/topics/trauma/memories

National Center for Missing & Exploited Children: https://www.missingkids.org/gethelpnow/cybertipline

Suicide & Crisis Lifeline: 988

Notes

------ ·⟨⟩· ------

Chapter One: Getting There

1. With over thirteen million printed items, it is the second-largest library in Britain after the British Library. It can be seen in the opening scenes of *The Golden Compass*, *Brideshead Revisited*, and *The Madness of King George* and in the first two *Harry Potter* films, in which the Divinity School doubles as the Hogwarts hospital wing and the Duke Humfrey's Library as the Hogwarts library.

2. I had fun coming up with titles for my research papers:
   "Eroticized Nationalism: The Seduction Game"
   "Flags to Flatware: An Argument for a Global Approach to Citizenship . . ."
   "Balance—Point: Marriage as Dance in . . . *To the Lighthouse*"
   "She Writes in White Ink: Virginia Woolf's Need for Marriage and Writing . . ."
   "Last Laugh: The Riddle of Kafka's 'The Metamorphosis'"
   "Nothing as It Seems: [in] Shakespeare's Title, 'Much Ado About Nothing'"

3. Decades ago, there was a mesmerizing PBS series narrated by Lord Attenborough called something like *Treasure Houses of Britain*. In the last installment, when Lord Attenborough was summing up, the camera panned ancestral oil portraits

hanging along a carved grand staircase. The shot rested on a landing before descending a gracious stairway. By the time the moving camera reached the main floor, I was sobbing. It overcame me with an overpowering sense that, there, I had lived a previous life. Occasionally, unsuccessfully, I search online for that miniseries, trying to discover which manor house had caused my epiphany. I maintain that anything is possible.

Chapter Two: Meet Mary

1. Notable Lincoln College alumni include Theodor Seuss Geisel (Dr. Seuss) and journalist Rachel Maddow. Years after the success of his Cold War spy novels, novelist and Lincoln graduate John le Carré revealed that his fictional spy, George Smiley, was partly modeled on former Lincoln rector Vivian H. H. Green, priest, author, teacher, and historian. (Green was the only Lincoln Fellow to vote against accepting women to the college.)
2. Epic account of the fall of mankind from Heaven, by John Milton, 1608–1674, reputably the most gifted writer of his time. *Paradise Lost* is a masterpiece.
3. See Appendix II for the Stuart family tree.
4. Carolyn Lougee Chappell, *Le Paradis des Femmes: Women, Salons, and Social Stratification in Seventeenth-Century France* (Princeton, New Jersey: Princeton University Press, 1976), 14.

Chapter Three: She Was a Bitch but the Room Was Lovely

1. *The Toilet of Venus* by Spanish seventeenth-century artist Diego Velázquez. In 1914, in London's National Gallery, Canadian suffragette Mary Richardson attacked the painting with a meat cleaver, the knife markings slicing across

Venus's back and hip. Richardson received a six-month jail sentence as punishment.

2. *Union Prayer Book*, new rev. ed. (New York: Central Conference of American Rabbis, 1940).

Chapter Four: The Bod

1. Famed architect Christopher Wren, then professor of astronomy at Oxford, designed the Sheldonian Theatre, built between 1664 and 1669. It is named after Gilbert Sheldon, then Archbishop of Canterbury. He financed nearly the entire £14,470—£2,355,329 today, over two and a half million USD—himself, in an age where a craftsman's wage was between £3 and £6 per year.

Chapter Five: All in the Family

1. Born between 1636 and 1649: Anne-Marie, Laura, Laure-Victoire, Olympe, Marie, Hortense, and Marianne.

2. Maria Mancini and Hortense Mancini, *Memoirs*, ed. and trans. Sarah Nelson (Chicago: University of Chicago Press, 2008).

3. "The travelers halted two days before the ascent of the dreaded Mont-Cenis, at the French-Italian border. The carriages were taken to pieces: the ladies were carried on chairs, the rest of the company rode or walked. They were able to take to wheels again at Malverne, as a new road had recently been made . . . Their progress was slow, between 20–30 miles a day." —Carola Oman

4. Mary made the ten-hour channel crossing on the *Catherine* royal yacht. Cruel irony, for Mary's main rival was her husband's mistress, Catherine Sedley, Countess of Dorchester.

5. Brett Dolman, *Beauty, Sex, and Power: A Story of Debauchery and Decadent Art at the Late Stuart Court, 1660–1714* (London: Historic Royal Palaces, 2012), 43.

6. Mary, once a widow, confessed to an audience of nuns at the convent of Chaillot that she had "not at first loved her husband." She had cried every time she saw him.

7. The crown reverted to James I (Catholic) when Elizabeth I (Protestant) died childless. Next, James I's eldest son, Charles I (Catholic), was executed, marking the beginning of the (Protestant) Protectorate, led by Puritan statesman Oliver Cromwell. Charles II was "quietly" Catholic.

8. Charles and James grew up in France with their cousin, Louis XIV.

9. Out of wedlock.

10. George Savile, *A Character of King Charles the Second: And Political, Moral and Miscellaneous Thoughts and Reflections* (London: James Esdall, 1750), 17.

11. See Appendix III for a list of mistresses and their offspring.

Chapter Six: Special Collections and a Bearded Maître d'

1. From "Birches" by Robert Frost, first published in 1915 in the *Atlantic Monthly*, along with *The Road Not Taken*.

Chapter Seven: Commencements

1. Given to Middlebury graduates each year during commencement, the canes are made of Vermont ash with brass tips and birch knobs. They are modeled after the cane that Gamaliel Painter carried around, one of Middlebury's founders, a Revolutionary War veteran and judge who helped found the college in 1800.

2. Before being granted access to the library, new readers are required to agree to a formal declaration. Those not attached to the university are still required to recite the declaration orally prior to admission: "I hereby undertake

not to remove from the Library, nor to mark, deface, or injure in any way, any volume, document or other object belonging to it or in its custody; not to bring into the Library, or kindle therein, any fire or flame, and not to smoke in the Library; and I promise to obey all rules of the Library."

Chapter Eight: Ochre and Burnt Orange

1. Elisabeth Kübler-Ross, *On Death and Dying: What the Dying Have to Teach Doctors, Nurses, Clergy and Their Own Families* (New York: Scribner, 1997).

Chapter Ten: Never Anger a Stalwart Stallion

1. High Table is the dining room ritual at Oxford and Cambridge for special evenings of fine china and crystal, candlelight and conversation. The master, fellows, and distinguished guests, dressing formally or in their academic robes, dine at an elevated "high table," while at the same time, students eat at long refectory tables, perpendicular to the raised dais.
2. *The Perils of Pauline* was a 1914 American melodrama film serial, shown in weekly installments. Often remembered as an example of the "damsel in distress," today many analyses maintain that Pauline was more resourceful and less helpless than the classic stereotype.

Chapter Eleven: Wasn't Much fer Stickin' Around but He Sure Could Make Me Laugh

1. It is now a comedy club.

Chapter Twelve: Training

1. Kris Kristofferson, introduction to *The 30th Anniversary Concert Celebration*, Columbia Records, recorded October 16, 1992.
2. Bullen, Annie. *Pitkin City Guides: Bath* (Hampstead, England: Pitkin Publishing, 2005).
3. Christopher Morris, ed., *The Illustrated Journeys of Celia Fiennes c.1682–c.1712* (Exeter, England: Webb and Bower, 1982).
4. Prince Harry, Duke of Sussex, interview by Oprah Winfrey, *Oprah with Meghan and Harry: A CBS Primetime Special*, March 7, 2021.
5. British researchers have used high-tech archaeological sensing techniques, including optically stimulated luminescence, to reveal hundreds of new features hidden beneath the dirt in lands surrounding Stonehenge, including seventeen previously unknown circular monuments. Far from a solitary structure, Stonehenge appears to have been just one part of a much larger landscape of shrines. Dalya Alberge, "New Tests Show Neolithic Pits Near Stonehenge Were Human-Made," *Guardian* (UK edition), November 23, 2023, https://www.theguardian.com/science/2021/nov/23/new-tests-show-neolithic-pits-near-stonehenge-were-humanmade.
6. The Blue Stockings Society was an informal women's social and educational movement in England founded in the early 1750s as a literary discussion group. Both men and women were invited to attend, including those who were not rich enough to dress properly for the occasion and appeared in everyday blue worsted stockings. The term "bluestocking" came to refer to the informal quality of the gatherings and the emphasis on conversation rather than on fashion.

Chapter Thirteen: Queenie Parties

1. Chappell, *Le Paradis des Femmes*, 14.
2. Mancini and Mancini, *Memoirs*.
3. Barbara K. Lewalski, *Writing Women in Jacobean England* (Cambridge, MA: Harvard University Press, 1993), 1–2.
4. Carol Barash, *English Women's Poetry, 1649–1714: Politics, Community, and Linguistic Authority* (Oxford: Oxford University Press, 1996), 23.
5. "As far back as the mid-15 century, the vulgar maxim about *children* being best *seen and not heard* was previously of *maids* not *children*." Medora Gorden Byron [Modern Antique, pseud.], *The Spinster's Journal*, vol. 1 (London: A. K. Newman, 1816).

Chapter Fourteen: Pretty Maids All in a Row

1. Aphra Behn, "Sir Patient Fancy: A Comedy as It Is Acted at the Dukes Theatre" (London: E. Flesher for Richard Tonson, 1678), https://digital.library.upenn.edu/women/behn/fancy/fancy.html.
2. Women would circulate their poetry through selected networks of "social authorship," in which participants were often identified by pen names.
3. Upon his deathbed, Charles implored to James, "Don't let poor Nelly starve."
4. The Duke of Monmouth.
5. A pastoral poem draws on the tradition of the ancient Greek poets. It explores the fantasy of withdrawing from modern life to live in an idyllic rural setting, living a rich and fulfilled life. It seeks to present a bucolic backdrop as not only preferable to urban life but the ideal place for humans to exist. Pastoral literature can be traced back to Greece, circa the third century

BC. James Green, "Pastoral Poetry: Arcadia Through the Ages," The Society of Classical Poets (website), April 29, 2018, https://classicalpoets.org/2018/04/29 /essay-pastoral-poetry-arcadia-through-the-ages/#.

6. Aphra Behn, *A Pindarick Poem on the Happy Coronation of his Most Sacred Majesty James II and His Illustrious Consort Queen Mary* (London: J. Playford for Henry Playford, 1685).

7. Martin Haile, *Queen Mary of Modena, Her Life and Letters* (London: J. M. Dent, 1905), 46.

8. Margaret, Duchess of Newcastle, *The Life of William Cavendish, Duke of Newcastle, to Which Is Added the True Relation of My Birth, Breeding and Life*, ed. C. H. Firth (London: Routledge, 1674).

9. Margaret, Duchess of Newcastle, *Orations of Divers Sorts, Accomodated to Divers Places, Written by the Thrice Noble, Illustrious, and Excellent Princess, the Lady Marchioness of Newcastle* (London, 1662).

10. Toward the end of Cavendish's short lifetime, Mary of Modena's court as Duchess of York was developing, and famed diarist Samuel Pepys noted that court women, such as Frances Teresa Stuart and good old troublemaker Hortense Mancini, were wearing male riding costumes as daywear. The androgynous effect was both intentional and noticed.

11. Reminiscent of Maya Angelou's poem "Caged Bird." Listen here: https://www.poetryoutloud.org/poem/caged -bird/.

12. Kathleen Jones, A Glorious Fame: The Life of Margaret Cavendish, Duchess of Newcastle, 1623–1673 (London: Bloomsbury, 1990).

13. Agnes Strickland, *Lives of the Queens of England, from the Norman Conquest; with Anecdotes of Their Courts*, vol. 5 (Philadelphia: Lea and Blanchard, 1847).

14. He was so influential during the Restoration that the era came to be known in literary circles as the Age of Dryden. Dryden dedicated his libretto, *State of Innocence*, based on and a tribute to John Milton's *Paradise Lost*, to Mary of Modena.

15. See Appendix I for other attendants, *not literary*, in Mary's court.

16. John Heneage Jesse, *Memoirs of the Court of England During the Stuarts, Including the Protectorate*, vol. 6 (Boston: Francis A. Niccolls, 1840), 254, 256.

Chapter Fifteen: Loving London

1. An early eighteenth-century English men's club in London with strong political and literary associations. The club's name came from innkeeper Christopher Catling's famous mutton pies—Kit-Cats. The club played a central role in the Glorious Revolution of 1688 that deposed James II.

2. Mary Hopkirk, *Queen Over the Water* (London: John Murray, 1953).

3. See Appendix III for a list of natural children of both Charles II and James II.

4. It was only in the late nineteenth century that Catholics were allowed to worship freely again in the UK and the Catholic Church was officially reestablished in Britain. Building began on Westminster Cathedral, the mother church of England, in 1895, and it took eight years to build.

5. David Ross, "Westminster Cathedral," Britain Express (website), accessed March 12, 2023, https://www.britain express.com/attractions.htm?attraction=1478.

6. Commonly referred to as The Courtauld, it is a college of the University London, specializing in art history and conservation. The Courtauld is among the most prestigious specialist colleges for the study of art history in

the world. The art collection is known for its French Impressionist and Postimpressionist paintings, housed in the Courtauld Gallery.

7. The present five-story stair is a replica of what was there until the original suffered significant damage in I Blitz during World War II. It was rebuilt in the early 1950s using original plans, which had been kept safe in architect Sir John Soane's House in Lincoln's Inn Fields, the largest public square in England. It was initially known as the Navy Stair but renamed the Nelson Stair, in honor of the heroic vice admiral Horatio Nelson, 1758–1805, one of the greatest naval commanders in history.

8. Wages for women at court were two hundred pounds per year, plus room and board. When they left court, they received a pension for life, and the crown paid their dowry if they married. (Barash, *English Women's Poetry*, 152).

9. The word "banquet" had a different meaning back then, not a feast at all. After the main courses in the Dining Hall, celebrants would walk over to this separate palace building, to walk off some of the meal's heaviness. There, servants offered guests a banquet of exotic desserts before the entertainment—lavish masques—began.

10. Rubens was paid £3,000, equal to £848,432 in 2022.

11. Princess Diana's coffin was kept for a few days at the Chapel Royal in the Palace before being taken to Kensington Palace on the eve of her funeral at Westminster Abbey in 1997. It was also the London residence of Princesses Beatrice and Eugenie before their marriages. The immediate palace complex includes the former home of Charles III and his sons, William and Harry. From 2008 onward, the Princes William and Harry's staff moved into their own offices in St. James's Palace. The staff also began serving Catherine, Princess of Wales, upon her marriage to Prince William in 2011. Of course, all that has changed now for Prince Harry.

12. Royal births were public affairs, humiliatingly enough. But there were accusations of a smuggled imposter baby into Mary of Modena's birth chamber as a replacement for another stillborn child, precipitating William of Orange's takeover, called the "Glorious Revolution."

Chapter Sixteen: Popcorn, Parkinson's, and Party Girls

1. On January 8, 1918, President Wilson set down his Fourteen Points as a blueprint for world peace to be used for peace negotiations after World War I, based on reports generated from 150 political and social scientists. Most of Wilson's Fourteen Points were nixed by the leaders of England and France. Wilson discovered that England, France, and Italy were mainly interested in regaining what they had lost and gaining more by punishing Germany. However, Wilson's capstone point called for a world organization, later known as the League of Nations, that would provide some system of collective security. The United States never joined. Prophetically, Wilson suggested that without American participation in the league, there would be another world war within a generation.

Chapter Seventeen: Palaces and Politics

1. Camilla mentioned her great-grandmother's affair with King Edward VII to Prince Charles when they first met at a polo match: "My great-grandmother was the mistress of your great-great-grandfather. I feel we have something in common." Alice Frederica "Freddie" Edmonstone Keppel was the favorite mistress of King Edward VII. They met when he was fifty-six and she was twenty-nine

and stayed together for twelve years, through his coronation as King Edward VII until his death in 1910. ("Olivia Hosken, "Who Is Alice Keppel? Camilla's Ancestor Was Mistress to King Edward VII," *Town and Country*, November 24, 2020, https://www.townand-countrymag.com/ leisure/arts-andculture/a34659540/ alice-keppel-camilla-ancestor-mistress/.)

2. Haile, *Queen Mary of Modena*, 19.

3. Mary lived sixty years.

4. Haile, *Queen Mary of Modena*, 51.

5. Ibid., 130.

6. A canopy of gold cloth held over Mary's head was carried by sixteen barons of the Five Ports, and her purple velvet train, bordered with gold lace and lined with ermine and white silk, was twenty feet long. The dress was white-and-silver-embroidered brocade. Every seam was covered in diamonds. She had three new crowns, one encrusted with so many stones that no gold was visible. Clearly, the religious consequences of this monarchy wasn't the only thing weighing Mary down.

7. Verrio (c. 1636–1707) was responsible for introducing Baroque mural painting into England. He served the Crown over a thirty-year period. Celia Fiennes called Verrio "the best hand in England." It took him twelve years to complete the Windsor murals.

8. Grinling Gibbons, the Michaelangelo of Wood, was the most celebrated British woodcarver of the seventeenth century. Gibbons emigrated to London from Rotterdam and quickly attracted attention. He was given his first royal commission by Charles II to produce decorative carving for Windsor Castle. His subsequent decorative work at Windsor Castle took six years and set the seal of royal approval on the ornate style. It established his fame. Evelyn wrote in 1671, "[I] saw him about such a work, as

for the curiosity of handling, drawing and studious exactness, I never in my life had seene before in all my travels." Gibbons was only nineteen years old when he emigrated to England. Artists and craftsmen were in high demand following the Great Fire of 1666, only one year earlier.

9. Including a chest of silver filigree containing ten filigree fruit dishes as a "push present," and the same year a splendid diamond-and-pearl pendant for no particular reason.

10. Also in the court of James II's first wife, Anne Hyde, as dresser.

11. Percy M. Thorton, *The Stuart Dynasty* (London, 1891), 179.

12. The Most Noble Order of the Garter is an order of chivalry, one of the most senior orders of knighthood, founded in the fourteenth century. On the annual iconic Garter Day procession, the royal monarch and the knights process in grand velvet robes, insignia, and plumed hats. It is one of the most traditional ceremonies in the monarch's calendar.

13. Samuel Pepys, diary entry dated February 26, 1665, from The Diary of Samuel Pepys: Daily Entries from the 17th Century London Diary (website), https://www.pepysdiary .com/diary/1666/02/26.

14. In a Baroque palace, access down an enfilade suite of staterooms was determined by the rank of the visitor. The first rooms were more public, making way to the bedroom. Protocol dictated that servants escorted visitors down the enfilade to the farthest room their status allowed. If the visitor was of equal or higher access, the host would meet his guest before taking him back to the bedroom. At parting, the same ritual would be observed.

15. Oman, Carola. *Mary of Modena* (London: Hodder and Stoughton, 1962).

16. The construction of St. George's Chapel was begun in 1475 by Edward IV and completed by Henry VIII in 1528 in high-medieval Gothic style. It can accommodate approximately eight hundred people for services.

Chapter Nineteen: Bermondsey or Bust

1. Dolman, *Beauty, Sex, and Power*.
2. Haile, *Queen Mary of Modena*.
3. Pepys, Samual, *The Diary of Samuel Pepys: Daily Entries from the 17th Century London Diary* (New York: Modern Library, 2001).
4. All information about dress comes from Ian Mortimer, *The Time Traveler's Guide to Restoration England: A Handbook for Visitors to the Seventeenth Century: 1660–1700* (London: Vintage, 2017).
5. Clare Armstrong Bridgman Jerrold, *The Fair Ladies of Hampton Court* (Boston: Little Brown, 1911), 18, 20.
6. Sarah Nelson, introduction to *Memoirs*, by Maria Mancini and Hortense Mancini, ed. and trans. Sarah Nelson (Chicago: University of Chicago Press, 2008), xxvi.
7. For instance, he had all of his female servants' front teeth knocked out to prevent them from attracting male attention. He forbade his wife to keep company with other men, made midnight searches for hidden lovers, insisted she spend a quarter of her day at prayer, and forced her to leave Paris and move with him to the country.
8. Hortense Mancini's list of lovers included Anne, Countess of Sussex, one of Charles II's illegitimate daughters, who was obsessed with Hortense. Can't you just picture Mary bemoaning Hortense's presence!

Chapter Twenty-Two: Final Days

1. Any more than this remains private.
2. Ephebophilia is primary sexual interest in mid-to-late adolescents, generally ages fifteen to nineteen.

Chapter Twenty-Three:
Cambridge

1. Sandra Dean Sullivan, "Representations of Mary of Modena, Duchess, Queen Consort and Exile: Images and Texts" (PhD thesis, University College London, 2008), https://discovery.ucl.ac.uk/id/eprint/1349620/1/487129_VOL1.pdfb8i.

Chapter Twenty-Five:
Kent or Bust

1. Published in 1713. http://www.poetryfoundation.org/poem /180927.
2. The transfer of power without any bloodshed from Catholic James II to his Protestant daughter, Mary, from his first marriage, and her Dutch husband, William of Orange.
3. Read the full poem here: https://www.poetryfoundation .org/poems/50564/the-introduction.
4. Carol Barash, "The Political Origins of Anne Finch's Poetry," *Huntington Library Quarterly* 54, no. 4 (Fall 1991): 327–328.
5. Virginia Woolf, *A Room of One's Own* (London: Hogarth Press, 1929).
6. In chapter one, I mention watching a PBS series with Lord Attenborough, and when the camera panned ancestral oil portraits hanging along a grand staircase, "It overcame me with an overpowering sense that, there, I had lived a

previous life." The shot rested on the landing. "By the time the moving camera reached the main floor, I was sobbing."

7. During the first and second centuries, a Roman settlement grew up at Reculver, most likely around a harbor. In the early third century, a fort was built, but by the fifth century the Romans had abandoned their defense of Britain, and the fort at Reculver fell into disuse. The earliest monastic church on the site, founded in the seventh century, survives, and the twelfth-century church towers stand out on the skyline for miles around, acting as a navigation marker for shipping. However, coastal erosion has brought the edge of the beach to the towers, and much of the site has been lost to the sea.

8. The Queen Elizabeth Oak on the grounds of the estate is said to be the location where Queen Elizabeth I was told she was queen, following her sister Mary's death.

9. The southern idiom "to have a wild hair" dates to the 1950s and means you're itching to do something, literally referencing itchy stray hairs under the collar after a haircut.

Chapter Twenty-Six: Hatfield to Holyrood

1. Natalie Babbitt, *Tuck Everlasting* (New York: Farrar, Straus and Giroux,1975).

2. Humphrey, Duke of Gloucester, 1390–1447, was the youngest son of Henry IV of Shakespeare fame. Humphrey received a scholar's education but fought in his brother Henry V's French campaigns successfully in part to his knowledge of warfare, gained from his studies. During the legendary Battle of Agincourt, Humphrey was wounded. As he fell, Henry V stood over him, protecting him from a French assault. King Henry VI arrested Humphrey on a charge of treason. He died after three days of imprisonment, aged fifty-six, some suspecting poison. Duke

Humphrey was a patron of Oxford, donating more than 280 manuscripts to the university, considered a very generous donation: the university at the time only had twenty books. Prior to Gutenberg's invention of the movable type press, circa 1450, books were hand-copied and only for the very wealthy. Humphrey is buried at St. Albans Abbey, Hertfordshire, a half-hour train ride north from London. ("Humphrey Duke of Gloucester," English Monarchs—Kings and Queens (website), accessed March 12, 2023, https://www.englishmonarchs.co.uk/plantagenet_55.html.)

3. Catherine of Aragon, Anne Boleyn, and Jane Seymour, respectively.

4. During her much older half-sister Mary's reign, Elizabeth was a virtual prisoner there. But it was also here, supposedly reading the Bible under a giant oak tree, that Elizabeth I heard the news of her accession: her sister, Mary Tudor—Bloody Mary—was dead. How conflicted she must have felt but also how victorious.

5. Famously, James II, when still Duke of York, requested a stay at Hatfield en route to Scotland. The third earl expressed his regrets, explaining that he would not be home. The Duke of York still arrived with his entourage, including Mary. The manor house was empty of everything, including provisions. James's servants found firewood and a barrel of beer in the cellar. The duke left eight shillings as payment for both.

6. See chapter one, opening quotation.

7. Between 1675 and 1682, Mary gave birth to five children, none of whom survived, the blame popularly assigned to James's affliction with venereal disease in the 1660s.

8. In 1679 and again in 1681–82.

9. "Where to Stay in Historic Edinburgh," WIMDU (website), accessed March 12, 2013, https://www.wimdu.com/blog/where-to-stay-in-historic-edinburgh.

Chapter Twenty-Seven: Goodbye

1. Amanda Vickery, "Not Just a Pretty Face," *Guardian* (UK edition), March 7, 2008, https://www.theguardian.com /books/2008/mar/08/art.
2. Joan B. Landes, *Women and the Public Sphere in the Age of the French Revolution* (Ithaca, NY: Cornell University Press, 1988), 21.
3. Elizabeth Eger, Bluestockings: *Women of Reason from Enlightenment to Romanticism* (London: Palgrave Macmillan, 2010), 206.
4. The "Mazarinettes" were the nieces of the very influential Cardinal Jules Mazarin, chief minister of France for both Louis XIII and Louis XIV. The cardinal was also an important patron of the arts, introducing Italian opera on a grand scale to Paris and assembling a famed art collection, much of which is in the Louvre today. Mazarin also founded the first true public library in France, the Bibliothèque Mazarine.
5. Barash, *English Women's Poetry*, 32.
6. Barash, *English Women's Poetry*, 33.

Appendix I

1. Oman, Carola. R. O. Bucholz, ed., *Office-Holders in Modern Britain: Volume 11 (Revised), Court Officers, 1660–1837* (London: British History Online, 2006). 26.
2. Count de Gramont, *Memoirs of the Court of Charles II by Count de Gramont* (New York: Collier & Son, 1910), 254–55.
3. Count de Gramont, *Memoirs of the Court*, 257.
4. Haile, *Queen Mary of Modena*.

Appendix III

1. "Descendants of James II of England," Familypedia (website), accessed March 12, 2023, https://familypedia. fandom.com/wiki/Descendants_of_James_II_of_England.

Appendix IV

1. Darkness to Light, "Child Sexual Abuse Statistics: The Magnitude of the Problem," updated December 22, 2015, https://www.d2l.org/wp-content/uploads/2017/01 /Statistics_1_Magnitude.pdf.
2. Rape and Incest National Network, "Children and Teens: Statistics," accessed April 13, 2023, https://www.rainn.org /statistics/children-and-teens.
3. The National Child Traumatic Stress Network, "What Is Child Trauma? Trauma Types; Sexual Abuse; Effects," accessed March 12, 2023, https://www.nctsn.org/what-is -child-trauma/trauma-types/sexual-abuse/effects.

Bibliography

———⚜———

Astell, Mary. *A Serious Proposal to the Ladies for the Advancement of Their True and Greatest Interest. Part I. By a Lover of Her Sex.* 4th ed. London: J. R. for R. Wilkin at the King's Head in St. Paul's Church-Yard, 1701.

Barash, Carol. *English Women's Poetry, 1649–1714: Politics, Community, and Linguistic Authority.* Oxford: Oxford University Press, 1996.

Barclay, Andrew. "The Impact of King James II on the Departments of the Royal Household." PhD thesis, University of Cambridge, 1994. Classmark: PhD.18523.

Barclay, Andrew. "Mary Beatrice of Modena: The Second Bless'd of Woman-Kind?" In *Queenship in Britain 1660–1837: Royal Patronage, Court Culture and Dynastic Politics,* edited by Clarissa Campbell-Orr, 74–93. Manchester: Manchester University Press, 2002.

"Bath." *Pitkin City Guides.* Andover, England: Pitkin Publishing, 2011.

Braithwaite, Richard. *The English Gentlewoman.* London: Alsop & T. Tavvcet, 1631.

Bucholz, R. O., ed. *Office-Holders in Modern Britain: Volume 11* (Revised), Court Officers, 1660–1837 (London: British History Online, 2006).

Chappell, Carolyn Lougee. *Le Paradis des Femmes: Women, Salons, and Social Stratification in Seventeenth-Century France*. Princeton, New Jersey: Princeton University Press, 1976.

Clarke, Deborah. *The Palace of Holyroodhouse*. London: Royal Collection Enterprises, 2012.

Clegg, Melanie. "The Wild and Very Amazing Life of Hortense Mancini." *Madame Guillotine* (blog). May 29, 2010. https://madameguillotine.co.uk/2010/05/29 /the-wild-and-very-amazing-life-of-hortense-mancini.

Clegg, Melanie. "The Wild, The Beautiful and The Damned at Hampton Court." *Madame Guillotine* (blog). April 5, 2012. https://www.madameguillotine.co.uk/2012/04/05 /the-wild-the-beautiful-and-the-damned-at-hampton -court/.

Dolman, Brett. *Beauty, Sex, and Power: A Story of Debauchery and Decadent Art at the Late Stuart Court, 1660–1714*. London: Historic Royal Palaces, 2012.

Dorman, Margaret, Sebastian Edwards, Alexandra Kim, Joanna Marschner, Deirdre Murphy, Lee Prosser, David Souden, and Lucy Worsley. *Discover Kensington Palace*. Surrey: Historic Royal Palaces, 2012.

Eger, Elizabeth. *Bluestockings: Women of Reason from Enlightenment to Romanticism*. London: Palgrave Macmillan, 2012.

Fraser, Antonia. *The Weaker Vessel*. New York: Alfred A. Knopf, 1984.

Gale Contextual Encyclopedia of World Literature. "Margaret Cavendish." October 16, 2020. https://www.encyclopedia .com.

Godwin, Susan Jacqueline. *Anne Finch, Countess of Winchilsea and her Nocturnal Reverie: A Quest for Calm in the Gardens of Eastwell*. Oxford: Oxford University, Lincoln College, 2006.

Harkness, Deboarah. *A Discovery of Witches: A Novel*. New York: Penguin Books, 2011.

Haile, Martin. *Queen Mary of Modena, Her Life and Letters*. London: J.M. Dent, 1905.

Hatfield House. Ipswich, UK: Greenshoots Print, 2011.

Hawkins, Gerald. *Stonehenge Decoded*. Garden City, NY: Doubleday, 1965.

Historic England. "The Cross Bath." Historic England, 2020. Retrieved November 9, 2020. https://historicengland .org.uk/listing/the-list/list-entry/1394182.

Hopkirk, Mary. *Queen Over the Water*. London: John Murray, 1953.

Jerrold, Clare Armstrong Bridgman. *The Fair Ladies of Hampton Court*. Boston: Little Brown (digitized from); Forgotten Books, 1911.

Jesse, John Heneage. *Memoirs of the Court of England During the Stuarts, Including the Protectorate*. Vol. 6. Boston: Francis A. Niccolls, 1840.

Landes, Joan B. *Women and the Public Sphere in the Age of the French Revolution*. Ithaca, NY: Cornell University Press, 1988.

Lewalski, Barbara K. *Writing Women in Jacobean England*. Cambridge, MA: Harvard University Press, 1993.

Lewis, Diane Scott. "Aphra Behn: Audacious Playwright and Spy for King Charles II." English Historical Fiction Authors. October 16, 2013. www.https://englishhistory authors.com/2013/10/Aphra-behn-audacious-playwright -and-spy.html.

Mancini, Maria, and Hortense Mancini. *Memoirs*. Edited and translated by Sarah Nelson. Chicago: University of Chicago Press, 2008.

Marsden, Jonathan. *Windsor Castle*. London: Royal Collection Enterprises, 2012.

Maynard, Chuck, ed. *Alexander Pope: An Essay on Man*. London: Methuen, 1982.

McGovern, Barbara. *Anne Finch and Her Poetry: A Critical Biography.* Athens: University of Georgia Press, 1992.

Micheline Green Guide, ed. *Great Britain.* Watford, England: Micheline Travel Publications, 2006.

Morris, Christopher, ed. *The Illustrated Journeys of Celia Fiennes c.1682–c.1712.* Exeter, England: Webb and Bower, 1982.

Mortimer, Ian. *The Time Traveler's Guide to Restoration England: A Handbook for Visitors to the Seventeenth Century, 1660–1700.* London: Vintage, 2017.

The National Child Traumatic Stress Network. "What Is Child Trauma? Trauma Types; Sexual Abuse; Effects." Retrieved July 2022. https://www.nctsn.org/what -is-child-trauma/trauma-types/sexual-abuse/effects.

Ockerbloom, Mary Mark, ed. "Anne Finch, Countess of Winchilsea (1661–1720)." A Celebration of Women Writers. Retrieved July 2006. http://digital.library.upenn .edu/women/finch/finch-anne.html.

Oman, Carola. *Mary of Modena,* 1962. London: Hodder & Stoughton; First Edition, 1962.

Orr, Clarissa Campbell, ed. *Queenship in Britain 1660– 1837: Royal Patronage, Court Culture and Dynastic Politics.* Manchester: Manchester University Press, 2002.

Reynolds, Myra. *The Learned Lady in England 1650–1760.* Boston: Houghton Mifflin, 1920.

Robin, Diana. *Publishing Women: Salons, the Presses, and the Counter-Reformation in Sixteenth-Century Italy. Women in Culture and Society Series.* Chicago: University of Chicago Press, 2007.

Smith, Hilda. *Reason's Disciples: Seventeenth-Century English Feminists.* Urbana: University of Illinois Press, 1982.

Stevenson, Jane, and Peter Morrison, eds. *Early Modern Women Poets (1520–1700): An Anthology.* New York: Oxford University Press, 2001.

Strickland, Agnes. *Lives of the Queens of England; From the Norman Conquest; with Anecdotes of Their Courts.* Vol. IX. Philadelphia: Blanchard and Lea, 1.

Sullivan, Sandra Dean. "Representations of Mary of Modena, Duchess, Queen Consort and Exile: Images and Texts." PhD thesis, University College London, 2008. https:// discovery.ucl.ac.uk/id/eprint/1349620/1/487129_VOL1. pdfb8i

Thurley, Simon. *Hampton Court Palace.* London: Historic Royal Palaces,1996.

Williams, Abigail, and Kate O'Connor. "Who Is Aphra Behn?" Retrieved June 29, 2014. www.https://writersinspire.org /who-aphra-behn.

Acknowledgments

———⌒⌒⌒———

MY HUSBAND, TONY, ENCOURAGES MY TRAVELS and writing. *Always*. Recently I asked, "How are you so understanding of my need to explore?" He replied gently, "It was who you were when we met." Complete support.

Thank you to my dynamic, fearless daughter, Jesse-Justin Cuevas Stambaugh, who somewhere along the way became "my parent." Lovingly.

Thank you to my constant Cleveland friend, Dr. Cynthia Griggins, for being a beta reader with invaluable suggestions: Carhenge forever!

The seeds for *Rain Dodging* germinated years ago, during my Oxford tutorial. Professor Peter McCullough, first my professor, then steadfast friend: From the beginning, you supported me. I am grateful.

To my "Teachers as Writers" cohorts Shellie Michael, also a beta reader, Jennifer Weinblatt, and Cathy Parsons for your decades of sharing and encouragement.

Copy and developmental editor Lorraine Fico-White, I am indebted to you for your *invaluable* work. "I liked you from the get-go." (Sorry, probably a cliché.)

To my cherished Women in Publishing colleagues, owner Alexa Bigwarfe, collaborators and friends Pat Black-Gould, Leslie Ahmadi, Corinne Anderson, Edye Lane, Nancy

Bissonnette Bordine, Christina Dankert, Antoinette Martin, Michelle Oucharek-Deo, Nancy Cavillones, and Toby Dorr, who designed my website, encouraging input!

For your *patience* and expertise, thank you to Brooke Warner, Shannon Green (citings are a bitch), Julie Metz, Barrett Briske, Crystal Patriarche, Leilani Fitzpatrick, and Tabitha Bailey from She Writes Press and SparkPoint Studio—no words, ironically.

Wayne Halper, my attorney (and former USN parent), how you humored me!

Speaking of USN, thank you to my University School of Nashville family for twenty remarkable years together: Connie Fink, John Kleiner, Tobey Balzer, Katie Sandidge, Freya Sachs, Kate Pritchard, Helen Tarleton, Anna Claire McKay, and Jeff Greenfield.

Finally, thank you to the Shayne/Meador family, whose Helen Meador Travel Fellowship made my adventure possible.

Please visit my website at
www.susanjgodwin.com.

About the Author

SUSAN J. GODWIN is a fervent educator, writer, and free-lance artist whose world has always been steeped in books, from *Harold and the Purple Crayon*—she couldn't resist drawing on her bedroom wall, no matter how many reprimands—to her first job as a library book mender in her Shaker Heights High School basement to teaching English at the prestigious University School of Nashville. A former Oxford scholar, Godwin has received writing awards from the University of Michigan, Middle Tennessee State University, and Bread Loaf School of English. Though writing is her true passion, she is also a visual artist working primarily in oils and pastels. Her home is outside of Nashville, in Dickson, TN, on the banks of a winding Tennessee river, in a hayloft renovated by her sweet, sexy husband, Tony—with help from their rotty, Roady!

Author photo © Leila Grossman, Grannis Photography

SELECTED TITLES FROM SHE WRITES PRESS

She Writes Press is an independent publishing company founded to serve women writers everywhere. Visit us at www.shewritespress.com.

The Field House: A Writer's Life Lost and Found on an Island in Maine by Robin Clifford Wood. $16.95, 978-1-64742-045-1. When Robin Clifford Wood stepped onto the sagging floorboards of Rachel Field's long-neglected home on the rugged shores of an island in Maine fifty years after Field's death and began dredging up the brilliant but largely forgotten writer's history, the journey took her farther than she ever dreamed possible.

Four Faces of Femininity: Heroic Women Throughout History by Barbara McNally. $24.95, 978-1-63152-884-2. Through the stories of forty-three remarkable women, McNally explores the many ways in which women have changed the course of history—and demonstrates how crucial it is that women from every background be provided with role models that inspire.

Dearest Ones at Home: Clara Taylor's Letters from Russia, 1917-1919 edited by Katrina Maloney and Patricia Maloney. $18.95, 978-1-63152-931-3. Clara Taylor's detailed, delightful letters documenting her two years in Russia teaching factory girls self-sufficiency skills—right in the middle of World War I.

The Trail to Tincup: Love Stories at Life's End by Joyce Lynnette Hocker. $16.95, 978-1-63152-341-0. Can grief result in a deeper and richer life? To answer this question, psychologist Joyce Hocker dives deeply into four family deaths within a span of two years and finds, to her surprise, that dealing with family artifacts after these deaths, especially written records, connects her back in history to ancestors, providing perspective and relief.

Singing Out Loud: A Memoir of an Ex-Mardi Gras Queen by Marilee Eaves. $16.95, 978-1-63152-666-4. Marilee Eaves has struggled her whole life to fit into her lineage—the long line of kings and queens of the secret elitist Mardi Gras societies that rule New Orleans—but when, as a student at Wellesley, she's hospitalized at McLean psychiatric hospital, she begins her journey to break free and stand on her own two feet.